# AFTER UTOPIA

# AFTER UTOPIA

## Modernity, Socialism, and the Postcolony

Aditya Nigam

Viva Books

New Delhi | Mumbai | Chennai | Kolkata | Bangalore | Hyderabad | Kochi | Guwahati

First Published 2010

Viva Books Private Limited

4737/23, Ansari Road, Daryaganj, New Delhi 110 002
Tel. 42242200, 23258325, 23283121, Email: vivadelhi@vivagroupindia.net

76, Service Industries, Shirvane, Sector 1, Nerul, Navi Mumbai 400 706
Tel. 27721273, 27721274, Email: vivamumbai@vivagroupindia.net

Jamals Fazal Chambers, 26 Greams Road, Chennai 600 006
Tel. 28294241, 28290304, Email: vivachennai@vivagroupindia.net

B-103, Jindal Towers, 21/1A/3 Darga Road, Kolkata 700 017
Tel. 22816713, Email: vivakolkata@vivagroupindia.net

7, GF, Sovereign Park Aptts., 56-58, K. R. Road, Basavanagudi, Bangalore 560 004
Tel. 26607409, Email: vivabangalore@vivagroupindia.net

101-102, Moghal Marc Apartments, 3-4-637 to 641, Narayanguda, Hyderabad 500 029
Tel. 27564481, Email: vivahyderabad@vivagroupindia.net

First Floor, Beevi Towers, SRM Road, Kaloor, Kochi 682 018
Tel. 0484-2403055, 2403056, Email: vivakochi@vivagroupindia.net

232, GNB Road, Beside UCO Bank, Silpukhuri, Guwahati 781 003
Tel. 0361-2666386, Email: vivaguwahati@vivagroupindia.net

*www.vivagroupindia.com*

ISBN: 978-81-309-1024-6

Published by Vinod Vasishtha for Viva Books Private Limited
4737/23 Ansari Road, Daryaganj, New Delhi 110 002

Printed & bound by Sanat Printers, Kundli 131028

# CONTENTS

# PREFACE

This book was initially conceived as a book on marxism, way back in the early 1990s. After eighteen years in the communist movement, ten of them as a full-time political functionary, like many others I was faced with an unexpected situation at the turn of the decade. The collapse of socialism posed serious questions that needed serious thinking. Almost side by side, cataclysmic political developments inside India started throwing up new questions. The rise of the Hindu Right on the one hand and the struggle around the Mandal Commission on the other were rapidly transforming the terrain of politics.

I realized in those eventful years that all those who swore by 'revolution' had been reduced to role of helpless spectators. They had virtually nothing to say either about the collapse of socialism or about the momentous battles then being fought in the depths of Indian society. Marxists had little to say, either about the rise of the Hindu Right or the great battle for equality fought by the Dalits and the backward castes. But that was not all. Later developments were to reveal that they did not have anything of significance to say even about the new face of late twentieth century capitalism. Questions of the impending ecological crisis and the serious challenge they posed to their notions of Progress, industrialization and development, too seemed to have made no impression on the Left.

It was in that context that the idea of this book took shape—primarily as an exercise in self-clarification. Events, however, have moved very, very rapidly since, forcing me to keep revising and rewriting bits that were already written over the years. In fact, the entire book had to be re-conceptualized at least four or five times. At one time, I decided to abandon the project altogether, mainly because I realized that a book on marxism no longer made sense. I realized that if at all, it had to be a book on radical politics rather than on marxism, which has now taken over the banner of social conservatism, at least in India. It is worth underlining though, that if marxism cannot be the only reference point in the project of reinventing the Left, it must nonetheless be one of the important reference points.

It is of course true that official marxism does not exhaust the entire range of marxist ideas and politics in India and I have had the benefit of a continuous and stimulating exchange with a range of friends who stand by that larger tradition. We have worked together, exchanged ideas and fought and through all this I learned that there was a larger universe of marxists who were keen to rethink. I have been fortunate to have had the opportunity of working with some such people in the Delhi Janwadi Adhikar Manch that was formed in Delhi in late 1996, at the initiative of some naxalite groups. Among these, I must specially mention P K Shahi of AIFTU, who has been fighting a major battle among the naxalite groups, arguing for an autonomous workers' movement. I have also benefited from an ongoing exchange and debate with friends associated with the Communist League of India (Marxist-Leninist), especially Subhash Gatade and Ravi Sinha and have had the opportunity of debating some important issues in their journal *Sandhan*. The presence in my political world of the young and dynamic friends of the Progressive Students' Union (PSU)—Naveen, Lokesh, Rakesh, Bhagwati, Naresh and others has also been important. A discussion organized by Arvind Ghosh and friends in Nagpur, around John Holloway's *Change the World Without Taking Power*, similarly introduced me to another set of friends with whom parts of this book may be seen to be in dialogue. Friends like Chandra Bhan Prasad, always ready to feed and provoke, have forced me over the years to see the world very differently.

However, with the beginning of the new millennium things seemed to move with even greater rapidity, transforming the everyday experience of time and space for millions of Indians. There was something ineluctably new here that defied the old language. The new experience was captured very innovatively by friends and colleagues in the Sarai Programme at CSDS, Delhi, which was beginning to make available to many of us an entirely new language. We have had our own quarrels but the intellectual debt that I incurred even through the occasionally heated arguments remains. In those heady days, I was also introduced through Sarai and its work on "Intellectual Property" to a whole new world of scholarship and to new theorists at the Alternative Law Forum, Bangalore. Intense ongoing engagements, fruitful and frustrating at the same time, with friends like Shuddhabrata Sengupta, Jeebesh Bagchi, Ravi Sundaram, Lawrence Liang and others, continued. Then there are other colleagues at the CSDS with whom I had the benefit of continued discussions and whose moral-intellectual support I could always count upon though many of them might have found my continued investment in something called 'marxism' a trifle quaint: Ashis Nandy, D L Sheth, Ravi Vasudevan, Rajeev Bhargava, Awadhendra Sharan, Sarada Balagopalan, Ravikant, Abhay Dubey.

I also remain indebted to many of my old and some new friends with whom we began an interesting, collective, virtual journey—Kafila (www.kafila.org). Then there is the larger universe of friends and comrades (kafila and non-kafila), with whom I have always been in conversation, and whose support and encouragement has always been there: Mukul Sharma, Charu Gupta, Apoorvanand, Sohail Hashmi, Javeed Alam, Sumit Sarkar, Tanika Sarkar, Ranjani Mazumdar, Mahmood Farooqui, Danish Husain, Shivam Vij, Ishwar Singh Dost, Shahid Amin, Avinash Jha, Sudhir Chandra, Geetanjalishree, Harsh Sethi, Monobina Gupta, Kaushik Ghosh, Gautam Bhan, Aarti Sethi, Aman Sethi, Sunalini Kumar, Ujjwal Kumar Singh. Some of them have read the manuscript—in part or fully—and have given comments that have been a great help.

Different parts of this book were presented in academic seminars or political forums and discussed with a larger audience. Comments from these discussions have greatly helped in giving the arguments their final shape. The initial ideas that went into Chapter 2 were first presented at a late night meeting organized by the PSU in Jawaharlal Nehru University (JNU). Later, a somewhat more elaborate form of the argument was presented in the Youth Forum of the India Social Forum in October 2006. Subsequent versions elaborated in the wake of the developments in Nandigram were presented at seminars on Globalization, organized by the Department of Political Science, Calcutta University (January 2007), in Sarai-CSDS (April 2007), the Conference on Asian Modernization Experience organized by the Asian Literature Institute of the Chinese Academy of Social Sciences Beijing (October 2007) and the Joshi Adhikari Institute of Social Sciences (February 2008). Discussions in all these places helped immensely in improving the argument. One version of it was published in the *Economic and Political Weekly* (24 March 2007).

Chapter 3 was originally presented in a workshop in Delhi (August 2005) as part of an ongoing collective intellectual exchange on the idea of the 'postnational'. The discussions in this workshop and the comments of my colleagues on the Postnational Collective, namely, Malathi de Alwis, Mary John, MSS Pandian, Nivedita Menon, Pradeep Jeganathan, S. Akbar Zaidi and Satish Deshpande have shaped the argument to a large extent. A version of this article was subsequently presented at a seminar at the International Center of Advanced Studies (ICAS), New York University (March 2006). I am grateful to the participants of the seminar and to Timothy Mitchell in particular, for the very valuable comments that I received there.

Parts of chapter 6 were written while on a fellowship at the Shelby Cullom Davis Center for Historical Studies, Princeton University, and presented at the Fellows' Seminar in April 2006. I thank my colleagues at the Davis Center for their comments, especially Gyan Prakash, Igal Halfin, Jennifer Wenzel and Jacqueline Stewart.

Chapter 7 was initially presented at the seminar on 'Reconstructing Democratic Concerns in Modern India' organized by Lokniti, CSDS and I am especially grateful to Peter de Souza and Rajaram Tolpadi for pushing me to write.

I also thank the editors at Viva Books for taking the trouble to put the book together. I am indebted to Bhola Nath Varma who commissioned this manuscript and in a way forced me to complete it in time.

I am also grateful to all my other colleagues at the CSDS, Delhi where I work. The entire staff of the CSDS has always been ready to support and but for them, this work could not have been done. My special thanks to Himanshu Bhattacharya, KAQA Hilal, Sujit da, Vikas, Sachin, Kunwar Singh, Jabar Singh, Harsh, Ramesh and all others.

Finally, as always, Nivedita has read painstakingly through different drafts and not just offered comments but also edited the manuscript in a way that has certainly made it more readable. Many of the ideas here too, have of course been first discussed as hunches with her. My ever grateful thanks to her. And to Anirban who has also read parts of the first draft and whose keen interest in ideas and politics made it a pleasure to discuss some of these ideas with him.

# INTRODUCTION
## Theory, 'Authenticity', Politics

This book initially started out as a book on marxism, more specifically on the theory and practice of marxism in the postcolony. There is, of course, no way of talking of marxism only in relation to the colony or postcolony, given the specific history of marxism's birth and given that as a doctrine and as a theory, it came to India (and indeed to other postcolonies) mediated by Western, metropolitan communists or directly through the Communist International.

The 'crisis of marxism' was experienced in these parts largely as a consequence of the collapse of actually existing socialism, and had a different resonance from the 'crisis of marxism' in the West. In the West this crisis has been experienced repeatedly, almost from the time of the birth of marxism, with the emergence of mass social-democratic parties and their highly bureaucratized apparatuses on the one hand and peaceful capitalist expansion on the other. It is a testimony to the vastly different contexts and the transformations that marxism underwent here that as a doctrine or as ideology, it experienced no serious crisis—and thus produced no serious critiques—till the penultimate decades of the twentieth century. There was probably only one exception, that of M N Roy. Roy's move away from marxism led to some interesting theorization about political forms, especially the party-form and the centralized state. His reflections on what he called radical-democracy in his 'middle period' constitute, in my opinion, an important resource for thinking about alternative political forms which I discuss in detail in Chapter 7.

This work is written with the conviction that our present cries out for a reinvention of the great dream, of a world beyond capitalism and a world without borders that marxism once dreamt of. It is written with the conviction that the only way in which the world today can be saved from an impending all-round disaster, brought on by the ravages of capital and Empire, is by once again foregrounding questions of class and property relations in our political and intellectual agenda and by reclaiming the earth from capitalism. But it is also written with the deep awareness of the post-utopian world that we inhabit. We are all illegitimate offsprings of Utopia—the Utopia of High-Modernism and its most vigorous advocate, 'Marxist-Leninist' socialism. Institutional marxism remains the father-in-denial for us, for the 'monstrosities' that it produced; on the other hand, the very emergence of a post-utopian radical imagination is predicated on a *parricide* of sorts—the elimination of the Party-Father-Leader as the fount of all meaning, from its imaginative horizon.

The struggle against corporate globalization is undoubtedly a crucial question today but as I will argue in this book, this struggle is being conducted in extremely complex circumstances, underlining the need to evolve multifarious and varied responses to the new situation. The responses to globalization cannot be of just one kind—for globalization itself is not just one single thing.

Ours is a world in the throes of rapid transformation. The transformation is truly unprecedented in its scope—telescoping notions of time and space in ways that has probably never happened before. Possibly the only precedent that we might have had in history of such rapid, large-scale global changes is the one we associate with the onset of modernity and capitalism, when old structures were torn asunder: when 'all that is solid melt(s) into air and all that is holy was (is) profaned', to put it in the evocative words of Marx and Engels. Such times of wrenching transformation are usually accompanied by large-scale dislocations and are known to initiate extremely complex and contradictory processes. There was certainly much to celebrate in the demise of the old world and the advent of the new, but as Marx realized as he began to work on his magnum opus, *Capital*, the celebratory tone of the *Communist Manifesto* had to be qualified. The 'so-called primitive accumulation' that he discussed in the last section of the first volume of *Capital*, that is, the historical process of the separation of the immediate producer from 'his' means of production, now appeared to him as involving 'robbery and murder'. The dispossession of the traditional communities was not something that he could celebrate in the manner of the *Communist Manifesto* any more. Here, in what is often presented as his most 'scientific' text, Marx speaks with unexpected passion and anger at the dispossession of traditional communities. We also know how the engagement with the question of the Russian peasant communes and their relationship to the supposed inevitability of capitalism as the bearer of historical progress, threw him into an ever more troubled re-examination of his 'scientific' theories (Chapter 2 deals with this at greater length). A deep ambivalence, in other words, begins to mark his quest. Something of that ambivalence must mark our response to what has come to be known as 'globalization' in the present conjuncture. This seems to be elementary. Yet, it has eluded much of our contemporary discourse which seeks a single, unproblematic answer to the question of globalization. Most often it tends to simply bypass the complicated questions that present themselves before us in the contemporary world.

The bundle of phenomena that come together in this catch-all term called 'globalization' have their own discrete histories. There is a history of technology and the outbreak of the 'communications revolution'. There is a history of what we might call the 'late bourgeois revolutions', namely, the collapse of actually existing socialism, the embarkation of the remainder (China, Vietnam) on to the high road of capitalism and privatization (although still conducted under the sign of 'marxism' and 'socialism'), and the rolling back of the post-war social contract embodied in the welfare state. Coeval with these is the explosion of discourses of particularistic identities that I have elsewhere called the 'insurrection of little selves', which has a separate history, linked to that of the crisis of the emancipatory discourses inaugurated by modernity (Nigam 2006). Closely linked to these is the history of the postcolonial condition that makes its dramatic appearance in the period of this crisis. To a large extent, the emergence of xenophobic nationalisms worldwide or the resurgence of radical political Islam of our times is rooted in that history. These different histories do not follow a single logic and cannot be reduced to the outcome of the inevitable, internal movement of the capitalist system. Nor can they be reduced to some grand conspiracy of capital, as if it were a single and undifferentiated whole. These diverse and discrete histories come together in extremely complex ways and impact upon each other producing the contemporary conjuncture. This coming together must be seen as entirely contingent and historical—produced by a series of 'encounters'—in the sense of the late Althusser.

Nevertheless, it is interesting to see in this conjuncture, the play between the 'development of productive forces' (telecommunications technology, etc.) and 'social relations' (understood broadly). One of the forces articulated in this conjuncture called globalization—one that has assumed a dominant presence—is that of new technology, reconfiguring in its wake, many of the existing social relations (not *only* of production). However, when Marx wrote the famous 1859 *Preface* (to *A Contribution to the Critique of Political Economy*) he was of course so overpowered by the dominant ideology of Progress that he could only see the 'conflict' between the productive forces and the social relations of production as resolving in *one particular way*: 'the social relations of production turn into fetters for the further development of the productive forces; then begins the epoch of social revolution'. What we see happening before our eyes is something very different, suggesting that possibly this 'resolution' can take very different forms, including the reinforcement of dominant structures of power and accelerating the dispossession of the already marginalized. It suggests that there may not be a single and necessary 'resolution' to any 'social contradiction'; that eventually the question of technology is also meshed with the logic of power and therefore subject to the contingency intrinsic to it. Thus, the late bourgeois revolutions could actually take place 'after'—or within—the 'socialist'/state-socialist world, just as 'socialism' itself could actually emerge only in societies that were not-yet capitalist. In fact, at one level, the collapse of these systems can itself be read as a consequence of this play: the inability of the old command structure to absorb or deal with rapid changes in technology and its molecular diffusion. We are witnessing the after-effects of that appalling failure today.

## Left Wing Conservatism and the Party-Form

A spectre is haunting communism worldwide: the spectre of capital; the spectre of its own entrapment in the great 'emancipatory' dreamworld of capital. From Communist Party-ruled People's Republic of China to the Workers' Party-governed Brazil; from the South Africa ruled by the Tripartite Alliance,[1] to the Communist Party-led Vietnam—not to forget our very own CPI(M)-ruled West Bengal—it is really the same story. Unless one believes that they have all 'become bourgeois' or are 'revisionist'—which of course, begs the question—this state of affairs cannot but be seen as a predicament common to a certain kind of politics. Till some time ago, the problem, so we were told, was 'reformism': because 'revolutionaries' inevitably sold out to the bourgeoisie. However, 'real revolutionaries' were always confident that once *they* managed to 'make revolution' and take over state power, things would be fine. Unfortunately, it is precisely in societies where communists or Leftists of different kinds hold virtually untrammelled power, that the abjectness of this surrender to capital is most visible.

For some time after the collapse of the Soviet Union, we were also told that it was the lure of capitalism and consumption that 'bought over' the populations of these otherwise socialist societies and thus led to the collapse of socialism.[2] So it is clear now that it was the spectre of capital that has haunted socialism all through—sometimes *as capitalism* and sometimes *through its 'fifth column'*—the so-called 'revisionists' and 'reformists' of different shades.

This experience of twentieth century socialism and marxism poses significant theoretical questions that are relevant for all kinds of newer movements and struggles. The question therefore needs to be posed more starkly. What we see of twentieth century radicalism and marxism today, in the form of its complete abjection before capital, should also be connected to another factor: in most parts of the world, but especially in India, *this* 'marxism' embodies the most conservative social and political values on questions such as caste, gender, sexuality, ecology and nuclear power. This conservatism is only too well-known by now, experienced repeatedly by movements that have come up in the past few decades and can actually be tracked issue by issue—both in the practice of these parties and also in the public pronouncements of their leaders.

It is interesting that while marxist intellectuals in the West have, however hesitantly and haltingly, made serious efforts to theoretically take on board issues of race, gender, sexuality and ecology, in India the pride of marxist radicalism rests on how stridently it opposes anything new. One has to recognize though, that even in the West, it is *the intellectuals* rather than the conventional parties of the Left who have made the effort to deal with these issues theoretically. The distinction is of critical importance and must be confronted head-on. For parties have their own reasons and explanations for maintaining this distinction.[3] The apparatus and the *apparatchiki* always feel the need to insulate the 'ranks' from the polluting influence of the intellectuals; only thus can the fidelity to the 'party line' be maintained. Antonio Gramsci once wrote of party bureaucracies that they are 'the most dangerously hidebound and conservative force' which are often responsible for the parties becoming irrelevant. French parties, he observed, 'are all mummified and anachronistic—historico-political documents of the various phases of past French history, whose outdated terminology they continue to repeat' (Gramsci 1971: 211). He thus talks of occasions when parties become detached from the social groups or classes they once represented—the social group/s in question no longer being willing to trust 'the organization in its present form, with the present personnel' (Gramsci 1971: 210).

Surely, a part of this transformation of marxist parties must have something to do with this bureaucratic apparatus, but it must also be seen as a product of what Etienne Balibar calls the 'party-form' itself (Balibar 1994: 152-3)—especially with the form of the vanguard party and its rigidly bureaucratic structure. In an interesting exploration of the relationship between the intellectuals and the apparatus, Balibar points out that 'in the period of social democracy' Marx and Engels were 'in charge' of the 'party's theoretical direction', while the task of deciding the political direction 'was in the hands of "organic intellectuals" of the party apparatus with whom they found themselves in a constantly ambivalent relation of conflict and mutual use . . . .' The conflict, even then, was apparent enough, Balibar suggests, but in the twentieth century, 'the authentic "theoreticians" . . . were to end up keeping silent, being excluded, or dying, while the names of the 'great' leaders were to be engraved "in the hearts" of the militants' (Balibar 1994: 154-5). An irreversible split, in other words, between 'theory' and 'practice' had already been instituted.

We will need to return to the question of the relationship of the 'intellectual' to the apparatus. For it encapsulates a whole series of other questions and has a salience in contexts outside of marxism, in other political traditions. For the present, let me stay with the experience of the party-form.

It is instructive in this context to look briefly at some of the new formations that have emerged around the world. Boris Kagarlitsky has, not very long ago, surveyed a whole range of political initiatives across the world that he groups under the rubric, 'Third Left' or 'Third Socialism' (Kagarlitsky 2000). In these formations, which he also refers to as 'new wave' Left formations in different parts of the world, he includes a wide range of experimental forms, ranging from the more well-known ones like the Zapatista movement in the Chiapas region in Mexico and the PT in Brazil, to the less discussed initiatives like the Party of Democratic Socialism (PDS) in Germany, the Party of Communist Refoundation (PRC) in Italy, the Party of Freedom and Solidarity (PFS) in Turkey, the Socialist Party of Labour in the Philippines and other initiatives in different parts of the ex-soviet world. Most of these new wave formations, according to him, are formed through a process of regrouping of various different currents of the Left and *often include others currents like feminists and environmentalists.*

Of these new groups, the Italian *Rifondazione Communista* (Party of Communist Refoundation or PRC, its Italian acronym) is perhaps the most clearly aligned to the old tradition and still prefers to retain the label of 'communist' in its name. It is, according to Kagarlitsky, 'a unique coalition of diverse currents', which include 'nostalgic communists, united around Armando Cossutta; Eurocommunists who remain true to the ideas of Enrico Berlinguer . . . ; supporters of his intra-party critic Pietro Ingrao; Trotskyists from the former *Democrazia Proletaria* party; and neo-marxists from the *Il* Manifesto group' (Kagarlitsky: 116). These different groups are 'united mainly by hostility to the conciliationist policies of the 'official' Left—a reincarnation of the Italian CP, now known as the Party of the Democratic Left. The PRC has emerged as an important force in the traditional areas of communist influence and is a 'broad union of reformist, alternative and revolutionary currents' (Kagarlitsky: 116). The German Party of Democratic Socialism, on the other hand, emerged when in 1989, an extraordinary congress of the former ruling Socialist Unity Party (of East Germany) itself decided to transform it into the PDS. It was described as 'a modern, pluralist left party combining social-democratic, socialist, communist, anti-fascist and pacifist traditions.' *This transformation was preceded by a veritable revolt within the party, demanding a complete overhaul and reorientation.* This was a part of the overall 'mass outburst of democratic energy' in the erstwhile East Germany that was felt even in the workplaces (Kagarlitsky: 118). The PDS has seen an ongoing internal conflict between the erstwhile *apparatchiks* (some of whom continue to be in the new party) and the 'grassroots democratic Leftists'. Wolfram Adolphi, an intellectual close to the party, speaks of the 'realism' that has become crucial to the political existence of the PDS, given that it paradoxically combines 'the experience of eastern communist reformism and of the extra-parliamentary opposition of the 1960s and 1970s in the West Germany' (Kagarlitsky: 125).

In Turkey, the Party of Freedom and Solidarity (PFS) emerged in the late 1990s. Its precursor was the Unified Socialist Party (BSP), formed by the coming together of ten revolutionary groups in 1995. According to Kagarlitsky, Ufak Uras, a leader of the PFS, describes the party as 'pluralist' and 'transparent', *a distinctive coalition of the revolutionary Left, of socialists, of rank and file social democrats, of feminists, of greens, of anti-militarists, of anarchists* (Kagarlitsky: 137). With 30,000 members in 1997, Uras sees the task of the party as that of 'refounding the Left'.

The PT in Brazil, of course, is the most widely discussed of these new wave parties of the Left. Described as a 'heterodox "mass-based and socialist" party that has grown steadily in influence from a single mayoral victory in 1982 to the elections in the later 1990s that brought 187 PT mayors to power', the PT, in a way represents a unique case (Baiocchi ed., 2003: 1). It is unique in the first place because, unlike the other parties mentioned by Kagarlitsky, the PT had practically no connection with the dominant traditions of the Old Left. From the beginning it sought a democratic road to socialism and disavowed any connection with the Soviet Union. But it is also unique in another, more significant way. The PT was a party spawned by the militant new labour movement in the outskirts of Sao Paulo, unlike the usual trajectory in which parties build up their own union bases.[4] As Emir Sader puts it, following the collapse of socialism, '(a)n entire topography of the Left was obliterated' and '[f]rom its ruins—in Chiapas or Porto Alegre, Seattle, Genoa, Barcelona and elsewhere—have grown the groups and networks that are questioning neo-liberal globalization. They point towards an entirely new ideological, political and geographical design' (Sader 2002: 87). It is in this rather different design that PT is located. The PT functions in extremely novel ways, following its own course in the uncharted waters of the post-soviet world. Its experiments in participatory democracy, particularly its fascinating success with participatory budgeting, are now too well known to bear repeating (Baiocchi 2003; Abers 2001). The truly interesting thing is that it has managed to evolve a different organizational form where different political tendencies of the Left, from erstwhile Maoists and Trotskyites to liberation theologists and anarchists function within the same organization.[5] It is with this kind of a structure that it has been successfully running municipal governments for many years now. It is this that has made possible a Left opposition to Lula to remain and function within the party.

Kagarlitsky draws on the idea of a 'Third Left' proposed by Finnish economist Jan Otto Andersson and Spanish sociologist Jaime Pastor, both of whom seem to have arrived at the idea independently and mean quite different, though not incompatible things by this term. Andersson proposed this idea during the mid-1990s, during a debate on the programme of the Finnish Left Union. According to Kagarlitsky, he refers to the bourgeois republican movement, which instituted the ideas of liberty, citizenship and democracy as the 'First Left' and working-class socialism of the social-democratic and communist parties as the 'Second Left'. As distinct from these, Andersson suggests that the 'Third Left' must combine the values of radical democracy, human rights and socialism (Kagarlitsky: 98). In Andersson's view, the 'Third Left' necessarily builds on earlier traditions even as it transcends them. He sees the New Left of the 1960s, followed by the environmental and feminist movements of the 1970s as its precursors (ibid.: 98). Pastor sees the Third Left as a primarily anti-capitalist movement which must be 'ready to renew both the content and the forms of political action, *beginning with the political party form itself*' (ibid.: 99). Kagarlitsky concludes his observations by noting that 'municipal politics is becoming the main strategic area of work' for these new formations. Unlike the social democratic and communist movements of the past, the new generation of Left parties see 'municipal socialism' as a laboratory of change (ibid.: 140).

Even a cursory look at these different formations will reveal that, as a matter of fact, the very form of the political party is being recast: *the political party itself emerges here as a coalition, built from below*. This is a crucial change in the radical political practice of the last few decades. And yet, the overpowering hold exercised by the old idea of a party organized around a single ideology is so strong that even someone like Kagarlitsky, who welcomes these new developments, remains captive to it. He considers this 'eclecticism of the pluralist Left' to be a 'necessary evil'—something that has the limited purpose of helping it overcome its own sectarian traditions. He therefore still longs for the emergence of a new '*more organic ideology* [that] will be formed in the process of struggle' (Kagarlitsky: 140). What if these new party structures were not simply the intermediate form on the way to the emergence of another party structure woven around a single totalizing ideology? What if these new forms demand they be taken seriously in their own right as new formations commensurate with the challenges of the new era?

My point here is that we need to dispense with the idea of the permanence of parties and organizations, which can fulfill *the* radical agenda *for all time to come*. As experience itself shows, the forms—of organization and of struggle—are in themselves historically constituted in practice. This is a point that Rosa Luxemburg had the occasion to make in her polemic with Kautsky, when she asserted that organization was not a static phenomenon but a process; that workers evolve organizational forms most appropriate to the struggle (cited in Gombin 1978: 94). And like there are no transhistorical organizational forms, there are likewise, no transhistorical forms of struggle. If most of the parties discussed above by Kagarlitsky have had to take the work of municipal government seriously, it is also a reflection of the need to change gear and move into a different mode that is propelling most of these parties. In fact, it is a point worth thinking about seriously that even from within the most reformist parties, there have emerged sections that are still animated by the desire for change.

Most significantly from the point of view of my argument above, Kagarlitsky suggests, despite his longing for an organic ideology, that there might be a connection between new forms and the struggle against political opportunism. Thus, he suggests that *such openness and looseness might often act as a guarantee against opportunism, since no leadership can take the loyalty of the membership base for granted.*

It can easily be seen that when a party goes into government—and very often this may be of critical importance, as the experience of the CPI(M) in India shows—the existence of different tendencies with their own relative autonomy can ensure that there is at least a healthy public debate and opposition on matters of policy. Similarly, the relative independence of mass organizations and trade unions from the party can act as an important check and can help in a proper negotiation of the interests of the social groups concerned. In this sense, the case of the COSATU in South Africa is interesting as it emerged as an independent partner of the Tripartite Alliance that rules the country in the post-apartheid period. It certainly provided much greater space for the negotiations in the interest of workers than if it had been represented through the SACP or the ANC. As opposed to this, we have the instance of the West Bengal government where the CPI(M) being in government made its trade union and other organizations mere appendages of the government.

In the Indian context, the idea of permanence of communist parties and their internal bureaucratic structures is so deeply entrenched that a suggestion of this kind is likely to be met with horror. Here the idea of the party's permanence is fortified by the formal acceptance by most party-leftists of the Stalinist metaphysics of 'the party of the working class'. The claim is that the communist party has a transhistorical existence and is bound in some fictive *necessary relationship* with the 'working class', which is itself seen as a singular metaphysical entity with little connection with the actually existing working class. From this proposition emanates their other claim that there can be one and only one party of the working class. Such metaphysics has long been part of Stalinist catechism through which Indian communists came to learn their marxism.

The above view, long abandoned by most informed marxists, continues to live and animates the inner lives of communist parties in

India and therefore needs to be contested. It is this view that informs their relationship to other democratic and radical forces in the country. Such a view of the party-class relationship is predicated upon an essentialization of both the 'working class' and the communist party. For, if we are to allow for the fact that the working class is never a fully formed entity, but is continuously being made and unmade in the course of historical changes, then there is clearly no way in which its interests can be defined in an *a priori* fashion. At the most, we can think of a historically contingent relationship between the working class and the communist party/ies. That is to say, their claim to 'represent' the working class can at best be seen as an act of conscious alignment or affiliation with the class. But in that case, this is not something that is special to a communist party. It can be argued that there could be many different ways of aligning with the working class, which need not be mediated by the doctrinal injunctions of 'marxism-leninism'. At any given point of time there could be many different parties, trade unions, social movements that thus identify themselves with the working class—as indeed has always been the case.

What then *is* the 'working class'? Can we assume that it comes into existence, always-already fully formed, with interests that are transparent to the naked eye, as it were? The actually existing working class is always in the process of being formed and re-formed. Its interests too are constantly in the process of changing. Any insistence on some *a priori* notion of working class interest actually ends up trying to freeze it in a particular historical form. If it is true that the working class is itself in a state of being formed and re-formed, it is a process that requires a concrete historical examination and forms of organization and struggle commensurate with its present. And once we are able to dislocate the question of working class interests from the posited metaphysical relationship with the 'science of marxism-leninism', then it is truly open to debate as to what course serves its interests best at any given point of time. As an instance, let us turn to the question of the reconstitution of the working class in the context of the rapid transformation of global capitalism in the past few decades. We now know that in the first place, the old Fordist assembly line production processes have rapidly given way to post-Fordist forms of industrial organization, which have led to the virtual decimation of the old kind factory-based working class. Outsourcing of production has meant greater flexibility for capital and greater insecurity for the workers. The small sweatshops that now produce for the big giant corporations have become virtually impossible to police in terms of the labour practices that they adopt. In the second place, the shift since the 1990s, towards greater informatization and marketing has altered the very character of the working class, and the move away from production has produced the need for a different kind of workforce. It is rapidly transforming the very mode of existence of the labouring population. How do all these developments actually reconstitute the working class? This is a question that has yet to be studied in greater depth, at least in the Indian context. However, at least one thing is clear: the old factory-based working class is rapidly going out of existence. The old workers are either pushed once more into a kind of informal economy outside the pale of all legality, or a new work force is emerging that is involved in new areas like call centres and the new service economy. All this is rapidly altering the conditions and with it, workplace organizing is also becoming almost impossible.[6]

The new working class that is coming into existence calls for entirely different forms of organizing and mobilizing. Today, in the age of global production, where corporations have shifted the production sites from the industrialized countries to the Third World, leading to massive increase in unemployment in the West and heightened exploitation in the peripheries, struggles against corporations cannot but acquire a global form. With the emergence of global networks of production, where actual production may be outsourced to sweatshops in low-wage, low-environment-regulation areas, the struggle cannot simply be conducted at the corporation level. The workers producing Nike shoes, for instance, are often not Nike employees. The struggle then must shift to entirely different, primarily political levels. In this new scenario, the struggle entails counternetworks across the globe, not only of workers' unions but also of organizations that track, document and campaign on issues of labour and environmental standards. It must also tie up with consumer movements that insist on fair labour practies.

These new forms must also take into account the logic of the information economy and indeed also of the possibilities opened up by it. Much more sustained reflection is required then on how, with the drastic restructuring of the working class, old forms of organization and resistance can continue. Can parties that came into existence in the mould of the Bolshevik party have any relevance for the contemporary world? Can the relationship between the two remain unchanged? Once we dispense with the fiction of the CP's claims to represent 'the working class', we might be in a much better position to discuss them as simply one of the many radical groupings in society and in fact representing just one of the many possible forms of working class and popular politics.

## Subjectivity and Politics

One of the key questions that marxism failed to deal with, thanks to its faith in the productivist/economic reductionist paradigm, is the problem of how subjectivities are constituted. It lived with the happy illusion that with the logic of production playing itself out, the problem of 'consciousness' would automatically resolve itself. 'Social being determines consciousness' Marx had claimed in the *Theses on Feuerbach*. It was understood by generations of marxists schooled in official marxism as a straightforward unmediated relationship between 'being' and 'consciousness'. If you are a worker, you must be revolutionary—if not now then later, once the veil of 'false consciousness' is torn away. Georg Lukacs, among others, saw the need to introduce 'mediation' between the two. 'The danger to which the proletariat has been exposed since its appearance on the historical stage', he argued, 'was that it might remain imprisoned in its immediacy together with the bourgeoisie' (Lukacs 1971: 196). His solution however is not convincing, for he 'resolves' the problem by simply invoking a metaphysical 'logic of the totality': 'Thought' and 'existence,' says Lukacs, neither 'correspond' to nor 'reflect' each other; rather, what is reflected in the 'real consciousness' of the proletariat is 'the new positive reality arising out of the dialectical contradictions of capitalism,'—and this is the 'inevitable consequence of the process in its totality'(Lukacs: 204).

Lenin's deployment of Kautsky's idea that 'socialist consciousness' can only be brought to the working class from without, actually militates against any notion of a straightforward relation between being and consciousness, for it assumes another level—that of the conceptual/theoretical or the representational. In both Kautsky and Lenin, this made some place for a certain autonomy of the intellectual domain of ideas, though unlike Kautsky, Lenin was never really comfortable with this implication of the 'role of intellectuals'. Even though Lenin reproduced the relevant passage verbatim from Kautsky in *What Is To Be Done* (thus elevating this idea to a canonical one), he actually substantially transformed its meaning (Lenin 1973: 47-8). Kautsky, it should be remembered, was at pains to underline that 'socialism and the class struggle arise side by side and not one out of the other; each arises out of different conditions' and that 'modern socialist consciousness can arise only on the basis of profound scientific knowledge'. What is more, to him, 'the vehicle of this science was not the proletariat but the *bourgeois intelligentsia*' (emphasis original).

The crucial difference between Lenin and Kautsky was this: for Kautsky, the domain of intellectual production and the domain of production and class struggle were two different domains, and the intelligentsia (in this case, Marx and Engels) was therefore critical in the production of socialist theory and its introduction into working class struggles. The site of this production was also the site of production of other forms of modern knowledge (e.g. 'economic science'). To Lenin, on the other hand, to the extent that he was interested in this question at all, the site of the theory's production was the revolutionary apparatus.[7] His interest was largely in the 'transmission' problem for he was engaged in a life and death battle against the 'Economists' who in his understanding 'worshipped spontaneity'—and spontaneity was something that he deeply abhorred. He therefore emphasized the profoundly vanguardist idea that left to itself the working class could at best only produce 'trade union consciousness'—'socialist consciousness' had to be injected from outside. Barely six years later, Lenin accepted the contextual nature of this formulation in so many words, when he said that '*What Is to Be Done* is a controversial correction of Economist distortions and it would be wrong to regard the pamphlet in any other light.' He was candid enough to accept that it was necessary to place 'exaggerated' emphasis on this aspect in order to foreground the idea of a party of professional revolutionaries and that 'at the time of the Second Congress', he had no intention of elevating his formulations on spontaneity and consciousness 'to the programmatic level, constituting special principles.'[8] It seems then that to Lenin, this formulation was more of an expedient, something whose theoretical implications he was unwilling to confront.

In Althusser's rendering in the 1960s, this idea of the importation of theory from outside was linked to a whole new and rigorous conceptualization of the idea of Theoretical Practice—Theory constituting an independent practice, existing in a separate domain, with its own rhythms and punctuations. He therefore criticized all those marxists like Georg Lukacs and Karl Korsch who placed theory 'in an expressive relationship with the proletariat', that is, saw marxism as an *expression* of 'true proletarian consciousness'. However, it is Kautsky's position that we must really address, for that is where the question of the autonomy of the intellectual domain is squarely posed, and where 'theory' is certainly related to 'practice' in some fashion (arises 'side by side') but not reduced to a mere 'expression' of class struggle or production relations.

It is important, in my view, to reflect upon this question a bit more. For, it has implications that go far beyond the immediate theory and practice of marxism. The more specifically esoteric aspects (e.g. 'true proletarian consciousness') apart, this debate has a lot of resonance with some fairly widely accepted ideas about the whole enterprise of theorizing and knowledge production and its relationship with 'practice', especially in India. Cutting across political traditions, from gandhians and lohiaites to marxists of different hues, there is a rhetoric of intellectual populism that thrives on a de-legitimation of the intellectual domain as something 'inauthentic'—an 'ivory tower', cut off from 'reality' so to speak. It is quite common in India to find even politically engaged academics asserting that actually 'real political theory' is produced by 'the people' or by 'activists'—even produced in slums. Different traditions might have different reasons for making these assertions. Marxists will argue somewhat in the vein outlined above, while gandhians or socialists would prefer to make their case in the name of an authentic indigenous tradition and in opposition to 'Western derived theory/knowledge'. Even in the latter case though, eventually, this logic of the primacy of 'practice' underwrites the manifest discourse of indigeneity.

This is not a simple problem, however. Behind this question lurk larger philosophical issues related to the 'subject' and the business of 'knowledge production'. At one level, the Heideggerian and post-structuralist critique of the idea of an autonomous, self-determining subject (in relation to whom the external world is the 'object' of knowledge and representation), a critique I find persuasive, alerts us to the problems inherent in this division between the subject and object. The idea of 'theoretical practice' can also be very easily read as an uncritical endorsement of this division. The actual philosophical issues involved are much more complex than is possible to deal with here. However, it seems to me that this critique of the philosophy of the subject, namely, of *knowledge and thought as representation*, must point towards a more complex understanding of both 'the subject' (as *constituted* rather than autonomous, after Althusser and Foucault) and representation (as always-already *constitutive*, after Derrida) rather than lead to a search for a pure space outside representation. As Derrida would say, all critiques of representation involve a 'naïveté of representation'; as though representation 'follows a first presence and restores a final presence'. And so one does not really ask how much of presence and how much of representation there is within presence, in the first place (Derrida 1976: 296). Thus 'in criticizing representation as the loss of presence, in expecting a reappropriation from it . . . one situates oneself within the self-evidence of the distinction between presentation and representation . . . ' (Derrida 1976: 296). For Derrida, the move from 'graphic writing' to 'phonetic writing', which constituted 'a total revolution in the structure of representation', was to permanently put a question mark over this idea of presence (ibid.: 299).

I am more persuaded by this argument and its implications than those that attempt to find a pure space outside representation (and subject). And to extend this logic of Derrida's argument to our specific discussion above, I would suggest that an argument or knowledge does not become more 'authentic' (that is, unmediated, true, etc.) simply because it comes 'from the people' or 'from the slums'. Thought—even in its non-theoretical or non-academic forms—is never unmediated 'Truth', based on some apparent transparence of meaning. All 'presence' says Derrida, is meaning deferred, delayed. Writing retroactively becomes the model, the paradigmatic form, of 'representation'—opening up between the 'representer' (the signifier) and the 'represented' (the referent) a wide chasm of the play of meaning (the signified).

What this means is that all knowledge, irrespective of the site and mode of its production, calls for a deconstructive exercise, 'meaning making' being a critical activity here. Meaning is not simply there; it needs to be unravelled by identifying and interrogating its assumptions. A certain scepticism, therefore, about the claims of all knowledge is called for. I think it is important nevertheless to maintain that the work of 'knowledge production' goes on in different sites including everyday practical (i.e. 'non-theoretical') production and theorizing, as a specific practice with its own demands, proceeds by actively engaging with these different sites. We might, in fact, more productively see knowledge produced in these different sites, each as 'expressions of a world' and in some form affecting and transforming the other.[9] However, like every other social practice, theorizing must be seen as having its own specificity and cannot simply be collapsed into some generic thing called 'practice'.

It is interesting that Althusser returns to this question repeatedly. In a 1978 essay, 'Marx in His Limits', he revises his earlier understanding that provided an exclusive place to theory and theoretical practice. Here he argues against the idea of the autonomy of the intellectual domain, and attempts to 'rescue' Lenin from Kautsky's 'idealist deviations'. In this essay he tries to argue (against his own position of the 1960s) that marxism arose *as an internal product of the labour movement* and was not injected from outside. He does this by showing how Marx's and Engels' theorizations arose out of their deep involvement with the workers' movement. And here he is not very convincing, for 'involvement' or alignment is still not 'being inside'. Consequently, this difficulty remains with Althusser, even though this particular intervention can be understood as a step towards grasping the multiplicity of sites of the production of knowledge.

Finally, it is in a letter written to Argentinian philosopher and communist militant Mauricio Malamud, in 1984, when he is also in a sense, finally free of the constraints of party membership that Althusser makes some of his most critical observations on this matter. 'For a long time', he says, 'we celebrated the "*fusion*" of the workers' movement and marxist theory as a historic event, repeating Engels' and Lenin's formulas after Marx's, without considering the fact that this "fusion" had either not been realized at all, or had just barely been realized, and that, *where it seemed to have, it had been realized rather badly.*' He goes on to remark that *the workers' movement actually takes its own course, anchored in its own fighting traditions* and its own spontaneity. Its closeness or otherwise to marxist theory depends on a number of other factors that includes questions of conjuncture and specific traditions of that working class. He is candid now that marxist theory was 'produced "in the heads of bourgeois intellectuals" (Marx) who had rallied to the cause of the workers' movement and social revolution. *Thus it was produced at a distance from the workers' movement*' (Althusser 2006: 212).

It is this recognition that leads Althusser to undertake a further self-criticism: 'As for the workers' movement, we really did not pay any attention to it (can you imagine . . . ?), confident as we were that the "fusion" had been realized, and that we really could consider the CPs to be *the authentic representatives* of the revolutionary revolt of the workers . . . ' (ibid.: 213, emphasis added).

This longish meditation on the problem of 'theory and practice' was necessary to underline how within marxism, the supposed identity of the workers' movement and marxist theory has been difficult to sustain. The larger philosophical question apart, the point is that the apparatus saw to it that the relation was irredeemably ruptured, as Balibar has suggested. Equally important here, is Althusser's point that not only was the link with *marxist theory* broken, the apparatus was unable even to reflect the aspirations of the *workers' movement*—detached from both 'theory' and 'practice'.

This question of the relationship between the apparatus and marxist theory, however, constitutes only one aspect of the problem. The categories of 'experience' and 'representation' in all their complexity are still completely absent from this discourse. How do people experience their 'being'? What does it mean to them? Is 'experience' itself a category unmediated by representation—the way an agent 'sees' her world and her place in it? Do all people undergoing a similar or even identical experience, understand it in the same way? What happens when people in their millions are simply torn from their relatively secure worlds and hurled into the insecure and volatile capitalist labour markets—especially when there is not even the possibility that they will be absorbed in the labour market? What are the languages close-at-hand that they find, in order to wield them for their purposes? We know that there are no pre-given ways in which people respond to crises in their lives; that there are certain political/cultural universes within which their responses are shaped. How these may lead to different kinds of political expressions—ranging from the supposedly revolutionary to the most reactionary—are serious questions for today. We have seen in our experience how often the politics of caste, religion and linguistic and other identities structures and is structured by 'class'. I discuss these issues at greater length in Chapter 1. Nonetheless, we can usefully remind ourselves how much of marxist and marxist-influenced writing on the Gujarat carnages of 2002, sought to present the fact of closure of Ahmedabad's textile mills and the resultant unemployment (of about one lakh workers) as an explanation of the workers' involvement in the massacres. Needless to say, such explanations simply fail to ask the question as to why workers should have necessarily acted on occasions such as these, as Hindus rather than as workers.

## Ideology and Interpellation

One of the most difficult questions for any radical political practice then, is raised by the persistence of these ways of thinking and construing 'the self' and 'the world' (which are but the same thing). Marxist scholars of various hues have taken these kinds of instances of supposedly 'backward masses', to explore the question of 'reification' and 'false consciousness' in order to arrive at a more satisfactory understanding of popular subjectivity. Generations of marxists have tried at least since the advent of nazism, to also understand the 'structures of consciousness' of the 'popular masses' without much success. Some theorists like Wilhelm Reich and Erich Fromm did propose some suggestive possibilities for further exploration in terms of the sexual politics of 'repression' but none of them seem satisfactory enough—if only because of their unidimensionality. One of the reasons such efforts appear incapable of addressing the issues involved squarely, in my opinion, is because they invariably tend to pose their question in terms of a perceived 'backwardness of the masses', who are somehow resistant to the call of Reason.

Something of a departure was registered in this regard by Louis Althusser, who took the notion of 'ideology' away from notions of truth and falsehood (and therefore of 'false consciousness' and 'backwardness') and situated it in the very domain of theory and knowledge. Even though vitiated to an extent because of his radical counterposition of 'ideology' and 'science', his intervention marked something of an important break from earlier theorizations. Ideology always exists in the vicinity of 'science' (read 'theory'): it occupies it, haunts it and lies in wait for it (Althusser 1969: 170)—unless a constant struggle in theory is carried out to free it from this ever-threatening overlay. 'Science' in Althusser's view, we may recall, lives by paying attention to 'the points where it is theoretically fragile'. It depends for 'its life' on what it does not know, rather than on what it knows (Althusser and Balibar 1977: 30). Ideology, on the other hand, 'imposes obviousnesses as obviousnesses, *which we cannot fail to recognize* . . . .' (Althusser 1996: 129).

It was the great merit of the Althusserian notion of ideology that it was able to see ideology as the mode by which theories and ideas *assume a mass political character*. This point is also emphasized by Gramsci who sees philosophy, religion and common sense as existing in a common field. Thus he claims: 'Every philosophical current leaves behind a sedimentation of "common sense": this is the document of its historical effectiveness' (Gramsci 1971: 326). Common sense, Gramsci suggests, is the 'folklore of philosophy', enriched by philosophical ideas that have entered ordinary life. In Althusser's spin on this relationship, common sense is not at all so benign. It is the very stuff of ideology that relentlessly reduces every new question and every new idea to the 'already known' and the familiar, so that individuals continue to participate in the rituals of subjectivity/subjection. 'Everything was/is already known to marxism' or 'everything is already there in the scriptures' are therefore, ideological responses. So are responses that seek to relentlessly transform every threatening question into an obvious answer.

Take for instance recent critiques of modernity and its homogenizing project. One standard ideological response has been of the kind that asserts: 'But modernity was never one, it has always had different trajectories.' It will be noticed that such an assertion is not false. It is certainly true that modernity has had many trajectories. However by asserting this and incorporating elements of the critique into the very 'definition' of modernity, such a response effectively closes the possibility of asking a new question that was beginning to be asked and which could have posed a challenge to some of our dearly held certainties. It is worth keeping in mind though that in this rendering, the project of modernity is simply conflated with 'actually existing modernities'. That is what makes it an ideological move.

Or, to take another example: in the context of the collapse of socialism, the most widespread common response among various Left groups and their affiliated intellectuals in India was that 'socialism collapsed because it was backward socialism, because it was being built in societies where capitalism had not fully bloomed'. This response seeks to find an answer only in the scriptures. Once upon a time, its proponents had found it possible to acclaim Lenin's boldness and greatness in foreseeing the possibility of revolution in the 'weakest link' in the imperialist chain. The victories of the revolution in 'backward' societies of the Third World through most of the twentieth century were seen as a vindication of Lenin's revolutionary genius. Following the collapse of Soviet bloc socialism, the easiest solution at hand was to silently bury this Leninist innovation by resuscitating an old, long abandoned idea, *already* 'available' in the texts. How could socialism be built, it now began to be asked, without passing through capitalism or exhausting its potential? This 'explanation' of the collapse has acquired something of a common sense status in a whole range of marxist parties and intellectuals in India. Indeed, it sits well with a fairly widespread Western marxist disdain for Third World marxism, long seen by it as corrupted by 'peasant consciousness'.

In both the instances above, the effect is the same: the replacing of an incipient question with an answer that was apparently *already there*. That is why, says Althusser, 'unlike a science, an ideology is both theoretically closed and politically supple and adaptable'. It bends to the interests of the times but without any apparent movement. 'It moves, but with an immobile motion which maintains it *where it is*' (Althusser and Balibar 1977: 142). It is not difficult to see that this mode of reasoning shares at least two crucial traits with beliefs such as say, that Hinduism is intrinsically tolerant, or that all Muslims are potential terrorists: first, such beliefs neither require nor brook any argumentation and/or substantiation. They circle around their known and familiar territories. Second, they are all infinitely malleable and 'politically supple' beliefs which do not require us to confront any new question. And they abound in both good marxists as well as in the good old Hindu worker of the Ahmedabad textile mills. Ideology thus performs a 'practical' rather than a 'theoretical' or 'knowledge' function, insofar as it helps navigate the lanes and by lanes of everyday existence where the chance encounter with the unknown is often unnerving. From 'ideology' to 'stereotype' is actually a small step that calls for much closer examination than is possible here.

Ideology hails or interpellates concrete individuals as subjects, says Althusser (Althusser 1996: 131), such that the individual learns to see her world and her self through everyday rituals of recognition. We need to understand interpellation as the becoming-subject of an individual—by responding to the 'call', by recognizing that it is she who is being hailed. However, here we need to amend Althusser's understanding in some crucial respects. Ideology exists as material practice, in apparatuses but unfortunately, to Althusser, all apparatuses (family, church, party) are eventually reducible to 'state apparatuses'. The 'State' is the Subject (with the big S) as it were, which calls out. In his classic illustration therefore, it is not entirely coincidental that it is a *policeman* who 'hails': 'Hey you', in response to which the fictive person turns around. The actual process of hailing and interpellation are however much more complex and arise through a range of different kinds of apparatuses: the advertisement machine and its billboard calls out to you to become consumer in a particular way and you respond; you go and buy, get a credit card, go on a holiday. Likewise, the mobilizational machine calls on the Ahmedabad textile worker to act as Hindu (the other machine of class mobilization is absent here) and he responds.

In the Althusserian rendering of ideology, individuals are always-already constituted as subjects—in both senses, as freely choosing agents and as well as in their subjection to the State. Even before an individual takes birth, as it were, s/he is interpellated as subject through the elaborate set of practices that prepare for and await her arrival. Yet the difficulty in this account is that the overarching presence of the State does not really help us account for the contrary calls that the individual is always responding to, which introduces a constitutive instability into the very concept of the subject. What if what we see here is not 'the subject' but the 'subject-effect'—the individual who resides always at the junction of numerous discursive universes. In a sense, this is what provides for the possibility of political action: the subject-position of 'woman' for instance destabilizing the subject-position Muslim or Hindu or the subject-position of 'Dalit' posing a challenge before both class and Hindu subject-positions. What is missing in this Althusserian account of interpellation, then, is an adequate understanding of discourse and meaning making. It is necessary, therefore, to complicate the Althusserian notion of ideology by considering some of these aspects as well and moving away from a state-centred account.

We might more productively study the way ideology functions, if we look at how it functions, say within marxism itself: *marxism as ideology* in its concrete existence in the 'party'. Let me take a certain episode from our recent history to illustrate and examine the processes of ideology and its production of truth-effects, so central to the idea of the subject and to the 'rituals of recognition'.

## Marxism as Ideology: The Nandigram Episode

As I discuss in Chapter 5, the year 2007 was a year of unprecedented significance for Left politics and thinking in India. This has to do, fundamentally, with the eruption of a significant peasant unrest in the Singur and Nandigram areas of West Bengal, a state ruled for thirty unbroken years by the CPI(M)-led Left Front. Nandigram saw a peasants' struggle over impending land acquisitions by the government, for the purpose of handing over the acquired land to corporations for developing Special Economic Zones.

Earlier, the peasants in Singur had resisted strongly when their land was acquired by the government through a combination of force and fraud and handed over to a corporation. Coming in its wake, Nandigram became an insurrectionary event that also rapidly galvanized the students and youth, as well as the larger intellectual community in the state, in support of the struggle. The reverberations of Nandigram were immediately felt in other states of India as well.

More significantly, for the first time, perhaps in decades, there was a direct split between the CPI(M)-led party Left and vast sectors of the non-party Left, including some of the naxalite groups.[10] In the final stages of this struggle, when the CPI(M) finally moved in armed cadre to 'liberate' Nandigram, leading to widespread opposition from the non-mainstream Left, a strange message from across the Atlantic made its way into the Indian press, more specifically to the pro-CPI(M) *The Hindu*. It was signed by many luminaries on the Left in the USA and elsewhere, including Noam Chomsky, Tariq Ali, Susan George, Howard Zinn and others. While it apparently steered clear of taking a stand either fully in support of the CPI(M) or against it, it did offer some unsolicited advice to the non-

CPI(M) Left. The burden of that advice was that 'it would be impetuous to split the Left' in the face of the threat posed by US imperialism, which had already destroyed Iraq and was preparing to destroy Iran.[11] In a manner of speaking, this statement invoked the imagery of a world divided in two camps and made an impassioned plea for 'preservation of Left unity'. The statement naturally unleashed a major controversy and elicited a strong reaction from different quarters in India leading eventually to withdrawal of her endorsement by Susan George. Some of the other signatories too felt compelled to modify their stance somewhat and issue a second statement.

Several aspects of this first statement are relevant for our discussion. First, let us quickly run through the sequence of events. In the course of the Nandigram movement, 'a supporter of the struggle' approached Noam Chomsky by email, in order to elicit his opinion. Chomsky replied at length, expressing concern at the developments but refraining from making an explicit statement on certain other matters. The part about Chomsky expressing concern was apparently extracted from his message and circulated widely as evidence of his support for the struggle. This 'statement' was also used in placards in demonstrations in Kolkata. Now, this was a complete misrepresentation of Chomsky's position and while he was contemplating how to rectify it, a possibility presented itself of issuing a joint statement.[12] For Chomsky, it was a good opportunity to get out of what had become an embarrassing situation. The joint statement was then issued, signed among others by a CPI(M) affiliated intellectual based in the US. Let us merely note here the series of practices like an activist 'eliciting the support' of a world-renowned Left intellectual, Chomsky's guarded response, the activist's reading of this statement as indirect support for the struggle, its selective use in placards in demonstrations, a signature campaign that follows—all these are precisely those practical ideological rituals through which individuals are 'called upon' to act in some particular way, 'of their own free will'. And yet, it is really doubtful who exactly is a 'free agent' here. Let us take a closer look.

The email exchange between Chomsky and the anonymous supporter of the Nandigram movement provides a trigger to the entire series of developments. We are told that the anonymous supporter misinterpreted Chomsky's statement. It is entirely possible though, that it was a case of *misreading* rather than misinterpretation, even if the result was the same. As a Left intellectual of international standing, Chomsky's opinion would have been important for both the ruling CPI(M) and the movement. His text—the email message—therefore entered a highly volatile terrain where no innocent reading was possible and was read by the recipient as a statement that, among other things, supported his/her struggle. Chomsky has visited West Bengal in the past and has been hosted by the CPI(M)-led government.[13] He has had relations with CPI(M) intellectuals like Prabhat Patnaik and he therefore 'recognizes' the CPI(M) as a Left force. Now he suddenly finds himself in an embarrassing situation, pitted against what he believes is the Left in India. In all probability, he does not know any of the characters on the other side. In the meanwhile, the CPI(M) circuits have worked overtime to bring home to him the 'fact' that the mainstay of the movement is a ragtag combination of some far Left groups, a rightwing party (Trinamool Congress) and a communal Islamist party (Jamiat-ul-ulema-e-Hind).[14] He then wants to retract. It is at this point that a possibility miraculously materializes of issuing a joint statement through which the record can be set straight. The statement is issued. This now becomes another call 'to friends in West Bengal'. The voice that hails now speaks clearly, in full assumption of its global responsibility: don't be impetuous; don't split the Left; beware, imperialism is at the gates.

However, contrary to his and the other signatories' expectations, the statement misses its target. It elicits widespread and fairly negative reactions—both in West Bengal and in the rest of India, except with the CPI(M) daily in West Bengal, which publishes it prominently. The reasons for this reaction are worth outlining briefly. First, while purporting to be a neutral statement, it repeats verbatim the CPI(M) claim that 'the government has assured that there will be no chemical hub in Nandigram' and implies that the movement should take this seriously. This was hardly likely to be received calmly in West Bengal and other parts of India, for there are very strong reasons why such 'assurances' from the CPI(M) do not mean anything any more in West Bengal and will not be taken seriously. Second, the statement virtually suggested that it was the 'opposition' that was 'splitting the Left' in the face of imperialist destruction of Iraq and an impending war against Iran. Thus the signatories to the Chomsky letter were naively presenting—yet again—a CPI(M) fairy tale. There is no unified Left in India and even the attempts at united anti-war demonstrations, following the war on Afghanistan, had been taken over by the CPI(M) and all others had successfully been forced out of the protest movements. The impetuosity, if any, was on the side of the CPI(M)—or so the people on the other side might have felt.

Why then did the signatories choose to endorse the CPI(M) version on both these questions? What made it possible? Especially considering that most signatories do not share the Stalinist worldview and politics of the CPI(M)? How then do we understand this act of signing the statement? The point is that these intellectuals were expected to act in a certain way and they did. They were 'hailed', literally, and they responded in recognition.

But it is equally important that they chose to respond to one call and not to another. As far as Chomsky at least is concerned, he was doubly 'hailed'. And why precisely did they recognize the call? In the first place, this position provided the comfort of *staying with the already known*. The CPI(M), despite its formal Stalinist ideology, has been known to the signatories in a number of ways: through friends like the internationally renowned economist Prabhat Patnaik; through the fact that it represents a rare instance of a communist government that has democratically won elections and been returned to power for three decades; as the initiator of the highly publicized People's Plan in Kerala and so on. The other side, on the contrary was completely unknown. In the second place, the call had all the code words that they are accustomed to responding to—another function of ideology. Thus there was the demon of imperialism—especially the US—and the war, the destruction, and proper names like Iraq and Iran, and there was the well recognized call of united resistance.

So, even if most of these scholars, in their capacity as scholars, would seriously challenge assertions that seek to subordinate all struggles to 'the struggle against US imperialism' (the 'principal contradiction'), as political actors they react differently. Many of the signatories would even give priority to anti-race or gender-based struggles within the US, were these to ever come in conflict with the 'principal contradiction.'

On the other side, not only were all these codes missing, there was the narrative about a 'reactionary gang-up of opportunist forces'. It is important to underline two points here. First, that each time a call goes out from either side, it does so within an already existing field where we 'know' that 'we are all Leftists' and know what the conduct proper to a Leftist should be. It is this that allows a specific call to be addressed and for the call to find its addressee. Second, that even within this already defined field, what we can have, at any point, is a subject-effect that is always unstable, for the simple reason that there is always a multiplicity of calls that the individual must respond to.

Let me now turn to another text produced in the course of this drama—an article that followed this controversy, written by Prabhat Patnaik, entitled 'The Left and its "Intellectual" Detractors'.[15] I wish to analyse Patnaik's article at some length because it is not the statement of a party *apparatchik* but that of an intellectual who is himself perceived to be something of a dissident in the party, especially with respect to the issue at hand.[16] It is clear from its mode of address that this text is part of an 'inner discourse', spoken and understood only by the faithful.[17] It is a text that is meant supposedly for internal consumption but which has 'accidentally' found its way into the public domain, mainly through blogs and email lists. Its manifest addressees (with whom Patnaik often establishes direct contact through the use of terms like 'the Left' or 'the Party') are obviously the party 'rank and file.' There was clearly some deliberation behind this 'releasing' of the text into a domain for which it was not *apparently* meant, to which we should return in a while.[18]

Patnaik begins by posing a question to his party comrades, a question that he knows is topmost in their mind as well: 'why did so many intellectuals suddenly turn against the Party with such amazing fury on this issue?' After all, he claims, these intellectuals could easily have taken recourse to 'friendly criticism', written articles, and open letters, rather than express such outright hostility that even put the LF on a par with communal fascism.[19] Why did they breach the line of 'friendly criticism' and emerge in an oppositional role?

Patnaik begins his task of unravelling the secret of the supposed 'fury' of the intellectuals by underlining that these intellectuals were *already* 'strongly anti-organized Left, especially anti-Communist (and in particular anti-CPI-M), belonging to the erstwhile "socialist" groups, NGOs, or the ranks of naxalite sympathizers.' However, he appears to be cautioning his party ranks not to draw hasty conclusions from this fact. Something else has happened that needs to be understood. After all, he seems to tell them, for the past many years these intellectuals *had* been marching together and making common cause with 'the Left'.

This is apparently the 'reasonable' voice of the sage, advising the opponents against 'overreaction' while, at the same time, telling his party men not to rush to quick 'explanations' based on their 'anti-Left' character. He does this while simultaneously 'conceding' that these intellectuals are every demonic thing that you imagine them to be. But surely there is some deliberation involved in this addressing of the party ranks in full public view, where those who are being attacked are being made to listen to the tone and tenor of an inner-party speech. The voice conceals the most crucial fact—that many of these intellectuals (like Sumit Sarkar, to name one) are neither 'strongly anti-organized Left' nor 'anti-communist'; that they were fellow-travellers till the other day. In so doing, it accomplishes two purposes in one stroke: on the one hand, the most important issue to be explained (why our own supporters are turning against us?) is simply elided. They are presented as *having always been anti-communist and anti-Left*. (An incipient question, notice, has been deflected into a seemingly self-evident truth—an ideological mechanism par excellence.) On the other, the sage-ideologue has, from his 'authentic' position as an internationally recognized intellectual, pronounced his fellow-beings as unworthy creatures. Who among his comrades can actually claim to know this world of intellectuals, artistes and scholars? They all naturally look up to him for light and *he obliges in the only way he can*—for *he knows that that is what is expected of him* by his audience and the apparatus. This is a ritual of the apparatus, 'whenever the Party is under attack'. The ideologue-cum-sage alone is not the Author-voice that hails; the ideologue as well as his ranks/audience are constituted in one single plane that we may call the plane of ideology. It is not simply that the ideologue is the agent, and his ranks passive recipients of 'the line'. The ideologue *knows* what s/he must do; what the ranks want her to do. Likewise, the ranks know what they must do. The compact exists in treading and rehearsing the known.

A slight digression might be in order here. What I have said above is true of even the most authoritarian dictator. Hitler himself accepts as much in his autobiography. His repeated emphasis on the spoken word is worth recalling. 'Every great movement on earth is due to great speakers and not to great writers', he says in the 'Foreword'. He returns to this theme again and again. His reasons are telling: 'An orator receives continuous guidance from his audience, enabling him to correct his lecture' (Hitler 1936: 189). Not only does the orator get a sense of whether the 'audience is following his arguments intelligently' but also whether 'his words are producing the effect he desires'. It is true that a leader leads. But s/he does not do so entirely on his or her terms. Not infrequently, says Hitler, is it 'a case of overcoming prejudices which do not come from their [the audience's] understanding but are mainly unconscious and supported by sentiment. It is a thousand times harder to overcome this barrier of instinctive repulsion, sentimental hatred and negative bias . . . .' Thus, '*nothing but an appeal to these hidden forces can succeed here*' (ibid.: 190, emphasis added). In the discussion that follows, Hitler repeatedly turns to marxist agitation and propaganda as the model from which he learnt. It is likely that he also improved it a bit in his own way but that is beside the point.

Let us return to Patnaik. Having adequately warned his party comrades about the need to stay away from hasty explanations, Patnaik then embarks upon the task of 'explaining the conduct' of his now-demonized adversaries. In this explanation, propositions do not follow from one another nor even have any relationship with each other. Nor is any empirical evidence adduced for making a point. Everything is simply stated as an assertion. This again is a mode that, Patnaik knows very well, works only in this setting of the apparatus and its rituals. This mode of argument can not be sustained in any scholarly setting, for as mentioned earlier its first precondition is that both the speaker/author and the audience must share a certain belief structure. Anyone who has gone through the selected works of Stalin, will have noticed how his speeches are interspersed with 'Laughter', 'Cheers' and 'Exclamations' from the audience, the audience often going a few steps ahead of the leader in its enthusiasm.[20] One can, in fact, hear cheers from the ringside as one reads through the Patnaik text.

Let me summarize now the substance of Patnaik's explanation: There was a time, not very long ago, when the Hindu Right was in power and its threat was widely perceived. That forced all these intellectuals to make common cause with 'us'. Lately there has been a 'perceived decline' in the strength of the communal-fascist forces. Under such circumstances, a fracturing of the anti-communal coalition was inevitable. But this still does not explain the 'venom' and the hostility. To explain it he points elsewhere. These intellectuals, he says, thrive in the atmosphere '*of destruction of politics that the phenomenon of globalization has unleashed*'. Now what is this 'destruction of politics' that globalization is said to have 'unleashed'? In his simple world and its innocent language, it merely means that people have forgotten how to distinguish 'us' from 'the enemy' (imperialism). After all, politics is about struggle between two camps. Thus Patnaik says: '*The crux of political praxis consists at any time in distinguishing between two camps*: the camp of the "people" and the camp hostile to the interests of the "people".' And if you cannot distinguish who stands where, you will only conflate things like these intellectuals are doing. So he says: '*Not to distinguish between the camps, not to distinguish between alternative constellations of political forces, but to club them together on the basis of the identical nature of their moral trespasses, is to withdraw from politics.*'

This is truly remarkable. One must distinguish between *who* is dispossessing the peasants, or perpetrating the killings and rapes. For dispossession, killings and rapes are per se, not the problem. You should be able to find out whether they are perpetrated by the 'enemy camp' or are simply a 'friendly trespass' by the people's militia! If you fail to do that, says Patnaik, you are indulging in 'messianic moralism'—a disease he ascribes to middle class intellectuals. The 'political intellectual' should be able to see that when Narendra Modi's hordes kill and rape, it is fascism but when Buddhadeb Bhattacharya's men do the same (admittedly on a smaller scale), it is just a mistake, for which an apology should do.

It can be seen then that what Patnaik means by being political and by 'politics' is what we are calling ideology—for it always-already knows in advance the configuration of camps, their political stances and their practices, such that no new knowledge of its 'moral trespasses' can ever make a dent in the ideologue's (and his followers') commitment: the 'people's camp' is by definition always correct. Let us leave the other question of course, of how it is to be determined who is in this people's camp, for that will raise a whole series of new questions that are not directly relevant here.

To conclude these observations on ideology, let us note that such faith in a self-evident 'politics' that bases itself on a kind of argument-without-substantiation mode, is characteristic of many other kinds of politics and political tendencies such as the Hindu Right. In its broad structure of argument, it is very much like the Hindutva argument about Hindu tolerance. Once posited as an intrinsic quality of 'the Hindus', this idea of tolerance itself becomes the myth that propels the reorganization of the Hindus on an aggressively militaristic and violent basis. The idea of 'Hindu tolerance' plays about the same role in Hindutva discourse that 'people's camp' plays in Patnaik's.

Hitler believed that such ideas are based on 'sentimental hatred' and an ideologue can do no better than to pander to the masses in this respect. It seems, however, that such dispositions exist in *all* mass political mobilizations and can, even in the context of a professedly rationalist ideology, assume forms similar to fascist ones, as the experience of the Cultural Revolution in China or of Pol Pot's Kampuchea clearly show. In fact, these should be understood as affects and dispositions, rather than as 'ideas', that frame the discursive universe of both the leader and the led. The figure of the ideologue or the polemicist plays a special role in sustaining these affects but is also profoundly constituted by them. This is a seriously understudied problem and needs greater investigation which is beyond the scope of our present discussion but it seems to me that at its heart lies what we might call, after Nietzsche, a politics of ressentiment.

## Theory, Location, Politics

One of the questions that we have repeatedly encountered in our discussion above is that of 'location' of the intellectual and by implication, of 'authenticity'. This question has presented itself before us in a number of different contexts starting from whether 'theory' itself is a legitimate activity and whether practice is not the sole ground of authenticity, to whether non-party Left intellectuals have the right to pronounce on any matter of public importance where it relates to the 'The Party-movement'? Who is 'Left', in other words, and who is not? The question has also come up in the context of the site/s of theory and theorization. We have discussed this issue here in relation to marxism in general and CPI(M) in particular but this is a question of wider relevance and similar questions of location and authenticity can be seen to be raised quite regularly by all kinds of movements. Over and above these, there is however, another kind of question of authenticity that is often raised, from a larger 'world-historical' perspective. This is related more generally to the question of 'Eurocentrism' of knowledge and the location and cultural-historical embeddedness of knowledge.

To be sure, we have a serious problem here in that knowledge produced in the West has been instrumental in producing a certain self-understanding in the non-West and we are only beginning to uncover all its dimensions. In a sense, a combination of Edward Said's critique of Orientalism and a range of parallel critiques in India from a gandhian or Gandhi-inspired perspective, as for instance in the works of Ashis Nandy, provided the beginnings of a highly productive exercise of interrogating Western, modern knowledge and its effects in fashioning the Self in modern India. The subsequent work of the historians of the Subaltern Studies school has further opened up the possibilities of a critical re-examination of the entire legacy of Western thought and its reception in India in the nineteenth and twentieth centuries. This critical re-examination has yielded immensely productive lines of inquiry in recent decades in a number of areas and disciplines. The theoretical heritage of marxism however, remains woefully neglected in this respect.

Generations of Western marxist writings have discussed the trajectory of marxism in the Third World as some sort of an illegitimate product of a 'backward society'—an understanding that derives from canonical versions of marxism and has been completely internalized by Indian and postcolonial marxists. There is no doubt that the marxist encounter in the postcolonial world produced monstrosities like the Pol Pot regime or the disastrous Great Proletarian Cultural Revolution in China. Yet, we could legitimately ask: were these phenomena necessarily a consequence of the *'peasant' consciousness* of the Cambodian or the Chinese people? Could it not be, on the contrary, that these monstrosities may have had something to do with the deep xenophobia spawned by the colonial encounter itself? Can we not turn around the very manner in which Western marxisms have posed the question before us? Else, how does one explain the fact that fascism and nazism arose in the most 'advanced' and 'civilized' part of the world? It would indeed be interesting to explore the common ground shared by both anti-colonial nationalisms (even if under the sign of 'marxism') and nazism, whose relationship to the defeat in the First World War and the humiliating Treaty of Versailles is well known. It is not surprising then that they are all based on the *politics of ressentiment*, a reactive politics of revenge. It is this counterproductive, indeed destructive, politics of ressentiment and revenge that drives large parts of the world that have emerged from colonialism, holding aloft the banner of numerous revanchist nationalisms.

Given that 'actually existing socialism' was primarily a 'backward socialism' an appraisal of *that* socialist experience has a double importance for us: in the first place, it helps us pose questions about the specific meaning of this experience to our 'being'. What did our encounter with marxism mean for us? Was it the same as it was for Europe? Is it correct to say, as many Western marxists would, that the marxism represented an illegitimate creed in the 'Third World', contaminated as it was by 'backward' and 'peasant' consciousness?

Can we then, really speak of the same, Universal marxism whose so many different forms can only be seen as 'corruptions' of that Universal Ideal? I will answer this question in the negative and argue that indeed there are many more marxisms than our restricted, Eurocentric frames allow us to see. In making this argument, I will also suggest that in marxism's encounter with the postcolonial world, it entered into many interesting and sometimes very productive liaisons—overflowing, as it were the confines of the apparatuses of the communist parties and the attempts by the orthodoxies to keep its purity. Hopefully some of the chapters that follow will illustrate this, even when the discussion is not explicitly about 'marxism'. Even the orthodoxies, which will otherwise appear as so many different 'churches'—each accusing the other of 'blasphemy'—will eventually turn out to be something quite unexpected. A case in point is the CPI(M) itself which, for all its serious problems, presents a significant instance of an attempt at engaging in democratic politics. The problem with a party like the CPI(M) is not, as my argument in chapters 2 and 3 will claim, its parliamentary participation but its inability to do so subversively—that is by aligning itself with the new radical forces that emerge in each specific context. More interesting is the case of many of the naxalite groups and how they often strike somewhat unconventional paths. I discuss some of these in Chapter 5.

Indian marxism has often been accused of being a mere copy of Western or stalinist versions; of being an attempt to blindly implant Western theory on Indian soil. Mostly these critiques have come from Socialist and Gandhian quarters but as my discussion on M N Roy in Chapter 7 will try to suggest, even in his case, despite his highly European/Western theoretical proclivities, there are unexpected moments. I have also argued elsewhere that even during his marxist days with the Comintern, Roy was arguing for the setting up of Workers' and Peasants' Parties in India, along with other Indian communists. In the event, this was what led to the strange affair of his 'expulsion' from the Comintern.

There is a whole cultural history of Indian marxism waiting to be written which calls for a separate study. Some beginnings have been made in this respect with regard to Kerala (Menon 1994) and Bengal (Dasgupta 2005). There are other stories that need to be excavated as well. These stories tell us of the diversity of practices, beliefs and politics that got articulated under the sign of 'marxism' in India and how different it, therefore, is from its 'original' Western edition. M N Roy for instance, talks of his experience with the *mohajir* youth of early twentieth century India, who became the founders of Indian communism—moving straight from their Islamic beliefs to communism. The story of the enunciation of the charged and controversial thesis of Hindi *jati* (Hindi nationality), via the marxism of Ram Bilas Sharma or the stories of the fascinating movement between marxism and Buddhism in the life and work of D D Kosambi and Rahul Sankrityayan, reveal yet other dimensions of 'marxism' in India. The formation of the Progressive Writers Movement, in the wake of the publication of *Angaare*—a collection of short stories by leading Urdu writers like Sajjad Zaheer, Ahmad Ali, Rashid Jahan and Mahmud uz Zafar constitutes another story that reveals how different the beginnings and therefore, the meaning of the early marxist movement was in different parts of India.[21]

Thus as Derrida would put it, each repetition is a new creation: there is, 'between the thing itself and its simulacrum, *an opposition that holds up,*' such that 'the first time is the last time. *Altogether other*' (Derrida 1994: 10). Every attempt to copy is from the start, 'endangered' by the circumstances of that new beginning. In this lies the singularity of the event.

A recognition of this singularity opens out the possibility of a genealogical examination of marxisms in the colonies. It allows us now to look afresh at the different circumstances of these different beginnings. Marxism as a Universal theory is a 'text' with the missing addressee. The 'original' addressee was assumed to be there in the working class of the 'advanced capitalist' West. It was not a discourse that addressed itself to the peasants and nationalist elites of the colonized world. And yet, as it floats into the postcolonial world the relationship gets strangely reversed. The nationalists and *mohajirs* of the early 1920s *seek it out*—marxism becomes the addressee. It was sought out by radical elites who had their own designs and plans. Thus when the *mohajir* youth or the early nationalist youth reached out to marxism, of which they had little knowledge, they were not merely adapting themselves to marxism; they would as much adapt marxism to their needs. This marxism was not Western marxism but one which spoke in the voice of Leninism—and later maoism.

In China's context, Jiwei Ci suggests 'marxism . . . proved to be China's tortuous road to capitalism, introducing the spirit of world-mastery into Communist China' (Jiwei Ci 1994: 16). He suggests that in its quest for a new/modern self-identity, China adopted marxism that gave it both weapon to critique tradition and blind Westernization (ibid.: 38). Jiwei Ci's statement could be extended to the communist movement in India as well and I have argued elsewhere that such was indeed the case.[22] The problem really is that in the postcolonial world, we ourselves have long learnt to live as if we are 'only' the copy—our marxism, our modernity, our democracy is always ridden with a constitutive lack. It is almost as if, actually it should all have happened differently, in the classical European way but we unfortunate, backward people have the difficult task of making do with the not-so-ideal forms of these ideas and institutions. This, at least in part, is a consequence of our being so hegemonized by categories of Western thought and knowledge that allows us to play the game only in a certain way. Today, after a few decades of postcolonial scholarship, it can in fact, be suggested that in many crucial ways, the postcolonial experience sheds light on the Western itself and needs to be theoretically grasped in its own right.

Having said that, it must be stated that it is easy to make the criticism of Eurocentrism with regard to most writings of Western marxists—and

I do believe that they *are* often Eurocentric in extremely problematic ways—but I must underline that this cannot be made into an excuse for our own lack of engagement with *our present.* Marxist ideas have had a long and complex history in the postcolonial world but marxists have by and large shied away from reflecting on these experiences. On the other hand, if Western marxists have produced their works in their own contexts, that is precisely their strength. The problem does not lie entirely with them. The problem lies, equally, with our own bestowal of the status of Universal Truth on to a specific 'provincial' knowledge—to paraphrase Dipesh Chakrabarty. It is true that this idea of the universality of Western knowledge—including marxism—has to do with the heritage of Western thought itself, its claim to speak on behalf of all humanity. But simply bemoaning Eurocentrism becomes another version of a reactive politics of ressentiment. An awareness of the Eurocentrism of that body of knowledge should impose upon us the responsibility of thinking our own present and engaging with it, drawing in ideas from all manner of sources possible.

In making a critique of Eurocentrism, it is also important not to fall into some kind of an Indian or Asian exceptionalism. It is self-defeating to make the claim that recourse to any Western idea is illegitimate simply because it originates in the West. Just as Buddhism, despite being born in India, had no difficulty spreading to other East, South-east and South Asian countries, I believe a lot of Western thought and ideas have made a home in our midst. In a profound sense, thanks to the colonial encounter, 'our history' has become inextricably meshed with 'their history'. Consequently, our knowledge and our heritage are always-already marked by the continuing presence of this encounter with colonialism, modernity and the West. Extreme xenophobia, paralleled by a search for pristine 'authentic' indigenous values and knowledge, is one way in which this recognition can manifest itself, as most anti-colonial nationalisms have sought to do. But there can be at least one more way of comprehending this recognition: we, in the postcolonial world today, have the advantage of standing at the confluence of the West and the non-West. Our horizons are therefore always likely to be infinitely open and critical. At least, that is a possibility that is available to us. We do not need to see ourselves merely as living illegitimate lives framed by Western categories. We can bring these categories of knowledge to speak to our ways of 'being in the world'—using, interrogating, and playing around with these categories. If the famous 'Death of the Author' means anything, it is this—the emergence of new subjectivities, the reader-subject/s. Bodies of knowledge (texts, categories, meaning) do not remain fixed to their origins.

The challenge today is to theorize our present—the cultural-historical sources of our contemporary self as well as the ineradicably new that constitutes this moment. We are not only products of some hermetically sealed culture; we live in the confluence of many.

Among the chapters that follow, some were written as parts of a book on marxism that this work set out to be. Much of what was written was abandoned as my own thinking on many of the questions concerned underwent rapid change. Increasingly, I was also beginning to see this as a book on radical politics in a post-utopian world, where it would be important to look at new and different kinds of emergent politics, rather than look inward and speak only to a universe of marxists. Two chapters (2 and 7) have already been published in some form earlier but it was actually in the course of writing the initial version of Chapter 2 that my entire approach underwent a dramatic shift. Two circumstances were of critical significance in this respect. First, a serious dissatisfaction with the way capitalism was generally talked about as some all powerful and sovereign entity, driven by some intrinsic internal logic, subsuming everything in its train. Such an understanding leaves no possibility of transformation short of some apocalyptic 'revolution', while experience shows the converse to be the case: nowhere, as I have noted earlier, has the 'revolution' led to the 'overthrow' of capitalism; on the other hand, whatever transformations have taken place have been effected under sign of 'reformism'. Second, a chance encounter with the writings of JK Gibson-Graham, two feminist marxist scholars who write under a single authorial sign, especially their book, *The End of capitalism (As We Knew It)*, which provided me with some of the most vital cues I was looking for. Almost at the same time, the posthumous publication of the last writings of Louis Althusser helped bring together my stray thoughts. There was of course a third circumstance that arose sometime later—the debate on the Left provoked by the struggle in Nandigram. The upshot was that in the course of writing this chapter, I had to revise major chunks of what I had written till then.

Chapter 1 is an extended discussion of some recent Western marxist writings, and their renewed search for utopia and their utter inability to think the problem of identity. In this Chapter, I also elaborate on the problem of Time as it repeatedly appears in our attempt to grapple with the contemporary. Chapter three discusses the problem of Time in the context of revolutionary politics and imagination. A word of clarification is in order here. My discussions certainly benefit from and draw upon scholarship and philosophical discussions of Time in the West but to a very large extent I deal with questions that arise in the course of my own investigations. Chapter 4, 'Empire, Nation and Minority Cultures' looks at the modes of doing politics that have become apparent in more recent times, in contexts of minority existence. It argues against prevalent common sense that unlike radical political elites, minority cultures cannot afford the luxury of the Manichean imagination of a world divided into 'two camps'—'Good' and 'Evil'. It suggests rather, that most often, we find what we might call 'the opportunism of minority cultures'—smaller cultures aligning against their proximate oppressors with what radicals might consider 'bigger enemies'. Such politics raises many important questions, both about identification of the 'enemies' at any point of time, as well as the modes and ways of dealing with power. The chapter suggests that 'resistance' may not really be the only response to power.

The crisis of political High-Modernism and the emergence of social movements and newer radical imaginations, forms the substance of Chapter 5. Chapter 6 explores a strand of Dalit politics—not only because it is Dalit but more so, because of its novelty and its attempt to articulate a politics beyond ressentiment. It is for this reason that I do not mark it out merely as a form of 'Dalit politics' (though it connects its particular form with the specific history of Dalit politics) but rather wish to underline its significance as a novel form that overturns all recognizable modes of doing politics. In the final chapter, I turn to M N Roy and his attempts at articulating a politics of radical democracy which, despite problems, contains important resources for an alternative imagination.

## NOTES

1. The Tripartite alliance consists of the African National Congress (ANC), the South African Communist Party (SACP) and the Confederation of South African Trade Unions (COSATU).

2. I am not even considering here the absurd claims of a CIA conspiracy that are still popular in Indian Left circles as pseudo-explanations of the collapse. Which is not to say that CIA does not indulge in conspiracies—but those are generally in the nature of planning and supporting coups and militarist outfits of different sorts, not engineering popular rebellions.

3. I remember, for instance, a CPI(M) party meeting in 1989, soon after the Tiannanmen Square crackdown in China, where a party leader, now General Secretary of the party, castigated the 'petty bourgeois intellectuals' (i.e. intellectual fellow travellers of the party) for their 'characteristic vacillations'—which he counter posed to the 'steadfastness of our working class comrades'. As it happens, I used to be working in the trade unions those days, among the very workers whom the leader invoked and many of us found it amusing that their (entirely legitimate) *complete unconcern* about what was going on in China was sought to be rhetorically presented by him as 'revolutionary steadfastness'. On a much larger scale, this same attitude is reflected in the way the same party has dealt with the intellectuals who have revolted against its politics of violent reprisals in Nandigram. More tellingly, the attitude of the party leadership towards its own intellectuals (i.e. party members who happen to be intellectuals) is worth registering here. In June 2007, for instance, West Bengal chief minister and Polit Bureau member of the party said in a television interview of his own party colleague and renowned economist, Prabhat Patnaik, that he had read what Patnaik had written, and 'didn't agree' with what he had said regarding the industrialization of West Bengal and developments in India, China, etc. He said he did not accept their views because, '*I feel they are a bit academic. They don't understand the real situation*' (emphasis added). See report in *The Telegraph*, 'Buddha scorns advisors', 29 June 2007, http://www.telegraphindia.com/1070629/asp/nation/story_7989814.asp, downloaded on 11 December 2007.

4. For interesting discussions of the PT, see also Rebecca Abers, 'Practicing Radical Democracy--Lessons From Brazil' http://www.orl.arch.ethz.ch/disp/pdf/147/147_5.pdf, 2001, and Emir Sader 'Beyond Civil Society—The Left After Porto Alegre', *New Left Review*, 17, Sept.-Oct. 2002, pp. 87-99.

5. In a way, it is a modified Left wing version of what the Indian National Congress, in its heyday during the nationalist struggle, used to be.

6. For some fascinating accounts of new labour in IT companies and call centres, see *Gurgaon Workers' News* at http://gurgaonworkersnews.wordpress.com

7. In a footnote, Lenin says, for example, 'this does not mean that workers have no part in creating such an ideology'. They do, but *not as workers*, 'but as socialist theoreticians, as Proudhons and Weitlings . . . ' see V.I. Lenin, *What Is To Be Done*?, Peking: Foreign Languages Press, 1973, p. 48.

8. This reassessment appears in the 'Preface' to the collection called *Twelve Years*. I have cited this from a 1978 essay by Louis Althusser who returns to this theme

once again, and was to return yet again some years later. This reference is from 'Marx in his Limits' (See Louis Althusser, *The Philosophy of Encounter: Later writings, 1978–1987*, London and New York: Verso, 2006, p. 22).

9. It is worth underlining here that this mutual transformation does not occur only through 'dialogue' but often through sheer osmosis or even clashes and conflict.

10. One should differentiate here between the non-party Left and the Naxalites, for most Naxalite groups have always been hostile to the CPI(M). The non-party Left—including intellectuals and movements—on the other hand, have generally been critically supportive of the mainstream parliamentary Left and have, therefore, often urged these parties to actually join the government whenever the situation has emerged. However, in the wake of the rise of the Hindu Right, a working relationship had emerged between all shades of the Left, including most sections of the Naxalites.

11. The statement entitled 'To Friends in West Bengal' was signed by Noam Chomsky, Tariq Ali, Howard Zinn, Susan George, Victoria Brittan, Walden Bello, Mahmood Mamdani, Akeel Bilgrami, Richard Falk, Jean Bricmont, Michael Albert, Stephen Shalom, Charles Derber and Vijay Prashad.

12. This account is from an email communication from Chomsky himself, following the eruption of the controversy. He wrote it as a clarification after he received a counterstatement signed by some non-CPI(M) Left intellectuals in India.

13. The same is also true of some others like Tariq Ali.

14. What this (presence of an Islamist party in the movement) might mean to American radicals in the 'post 11 September' world is anybody's guess. Many radicals—including many who should know better—seemed to have bought into this propaganda of 'jihadi presence' in the movement. Subsequent developments, though unfortunate, where this organization and some other Muslim outfits are said to have instigated riots in Kolkata, opposing the continued stay of Bangladeshi writer Taslima Nasreen in the city seemed to some of them to confirm their worst fears. This is not the place to go into a detailed discussion of the exact sequence of events leading to these riots but it is by now well documented that the '*Path Sanket* episode' (*Path Sanket* being the CPI(M)-run little magazine which published an 'innocuous' letter that led up to the riots), pointed to the involvement of at least some CPI(M) circles in the riots. For details, see Mohd Shafi Shamsi, 'The Magazine that Fanned Kolkata Fire', *Indian Express*, 2 December 2007, at http://www.indianexpress.com/iep/

sunday/story/245599.html. (last downloaded on 15 April 2008). The alacrity with which the CPI(M) and the Left Front government asked Taslima Nasreen to leave the city also raised doubts as to their real motives in this regard.

15. For the full text of this article, see http://www.pragoti.org/pragoti/news_detail.php?news_id=431, last downloaded on 15 April 2008.

16. Here I will not go into the substantive parts of Patnaik's claims but confine myself to the ideological dimensions of the text.

17. It was subsequently published in the CPI(M) weekly, *People's Democracy*.

18. In what can only make sense in inner-party speech, Patnaik 'concedes' that the Left Front government had 'made serious mistakes' but immediately asserts that these are not an issue any more because no less than the chief minister himself had accepted this 'in so many words'. It is, of course, a matter of interpretation as to what the chief minister has accepted, but let that pass for now. In the same vein, he goes on to say that, earlier too, the government 'had categorically assured that there would be no chemical hub' in Nandigram, but neither the 'opposition' nor the 'intellectuals' were prepared to listen. These are statements repeatedly made by official spokespersons of the CPI(M) and repeated verbatim in the letter by Chomsky et al. It is important to note here that the burden of this claim is to emphasize the supposed 'unreasonableness' of the 'opposition' and the 'intellectuals' and to suggest that their intentions are *mala fide*. Missing completely from Patnaik's text is the peasant who, on the point of losing his land, rose up in virtual revolt against the local machinery of the CPI(M). A point that is repeatedly obfuscated is that like in many other areas of West Bengal, there was practically no opposition to the CPI(M) and the Left Front in the Nandigram area before the land acquisition drama began. That is to say, CPI(M) and LF supporters, at the point of being dispossessed, turned against their own party. Overnight, they became the 'Opposition'. The appearance of such critical terms and phrases in the letter by Chomsky et al., also account for the way it was destined to be received and read. Such rendering of protests—as the handiwork of 'outside' forces—is common and can be seen from the hundreds of daily instances of social and political struggles. All 'opposition', including spontaneous protest, has to be 'caused by' the machinations of some evil force or attributed to the crass self interest of some of the players. In the Nandigram context, the protestors were initially termed 'outsiders' and were later given more concrete shape and form in the figures of Mamata Banerjee and her Trinamool Congress, the Maoists and Islamic fundamentalists.

19. The reference here is, among others, to Professor Sumit Sarkar, long fellow traveller of the CPI and CPI(M) and widely respected as a marxist of integrity. Sarkar has been one of those intellectuals on the Left who have visited both Singur and Nandigram and written about it, largely because people like him were not *a priori* pre-disposed to believe what was being said against the Left Front. Unlike Patnaik, Sarkar has also been a regular physical presence in all political protests, including street demonstrations, that have been organized by the Left--both the CPI(M) as well as non-party Left. Being more directly politically engaged (and not a Leftist merely by virtue of his baptism), Sarkar, it seems to me, has had much greater emotional investment in the Left. His anger at being let down, may have thus assumed a somewhat disproportionate dimension when he compared the happenings in Nandigram to those in Gujarat. Such comparisons, in my view are never helpful. However, that said, it is worth recognizing that there *was* an element of truth in Sarkar's assertion, to the extent that the way the state's machinery, the party apparatus and gangs of criminals colluded to carry on reprisals at the peasants and the way information was suppressed—all these were strikingly similar in both cases. It is unlikely that Sarkar himself meant anything more than this.

20. Interestingly, there are no such interspersed appearances of the audience in Lenin's speeches in his collected works.

21. The collection raised a storm among the more orthodox Muslims and was banned by the colonial government—not for its 'politics' but for its treatment of 'another politics', namely, sexuality.

22. Aditya Nigam, 'Marxism and the Postcolonial World—Footnotes to a Long March', *Economic and Political Weekly*, vol. 34, nos. 1 and 2, 9 January 1999.

# 1

# IN SEARCH OF UTOPIA

## Humanism, Identity, Radical Politics

*I was at the jail where a lot of protestors were being held and a big crowd was chanting 'This is What Democracy Looks Like!' At first it sounded kind of nice. But then I thought: Is this really what democracy looks like? Nobody here looks like me.*

—Jinee Kim, Bay Area organizer during Seattle protests

*In this new globalized context, the victories of identity politics have amounted to re-arranging the furniture while the house burned down. Yes, there are more multi-ethnic sitcoms and even more black executives—but whatever cultural enlightenment has followed has not prevented the population in the underclass from exploding or homelessness from reaching crisis-levels in many North American urban centers.*

—Naomi Klein

11 September 2001. A landmark of our contemporary history; an event that decisively transformed the way we experience the world. The immensity of the tragedy brought forth by 11 September is matched only by the spectacular grandeur of the operation. To paraphrase Walter Benjamin's evocative rendering of messianic time, this event 'blasted the postcolonial present out of the continuum of history' and took it to the heart of the 'Present'—the present of world capitalism and Empire. It was as if, suddenly the postcolonial, consigned to some remote past, had violently exploded in the present of the First World. History, one might

argue, decisively turned in another direction thereafter. It was the War that increasingly came centre stage, first against Afghanistan and then against Iraq, the generalized 'War on Terror'.

The dramatic suicide attack on the twin towers of the World Trade Center was orchestrated most probably from somewhere in West Asia, the backwaters of world capitalism. Or was it? In all probability, it was the handiwork of those who have been at the receiving end of over a century of imperialist plunder and colonization but it is not quite so clear that the attack was masterminded by any centre.

This politics has now acquired a molecular dimension—an activity that goes on in the pores of society, daily and hourly, such that no 'war machine' can ever hope to monitor all its activities. Heinous and eminently condemnable though it is, this act of violence and the discourse that produces it—the discourse of a resurgent political Islam—is among other things, also a discourse of anti-imperialism. It is a discourse that is inseparably bound by a thousand strings with the history of imperialist cannibalism in these parts of the world. These include of course, the colonization of Palestine and the creation of Israel—which now endlessly reproduces the great conflicts of the past. The Soviet intervention in Afghanistan in the late 1970s and the US-Soviet power games in the region too need to be seen as parts of the same history. Interestingly, the attack is orchestrated by a network that transcends all national location and identity and challenges US power by its sheer ubiquity—now in the US, now in Bali, now in Istanbul, now Iraq itself.

Ironically, in this story, the Huntingtonian drama of the 'clash of civilizations' is being put in place by radical Islamists in order to challenge the inequities of global power relations. It may not be possible to reduce the entire discourse of an Osama bin Laden to 'anti-imperialism' but it is equally difficult to disentangle it from the history of imperialism, colonialism and orientalism.

1 January 1994. A rebellion in southern Mexico, now well-known as the Zapatista revolt in the Chiapas mountainous region. This revolt became the harbinger of a new phase of mass struggles against global capitalism and the neo-liberal Washington Consensus. Coming barely three years after the collapse of the socialist world, this rebellion presaged a new round of radical mass upsurges through South America. It was to be followed very soon by the 18 June 1999 Anti-Capitalist Carnival on the streets of London, which gave the world the first glimpse of what was to be known as the 'Battle of Seattle' in November 1999. This battle, we now know, inaugurated a whole new range of struggles and mass demonstrations in

major capitals of the Western world, all of which have become milestones of a new long march—Seattle, Prague, Melbourne, Genoa, Quebec . . . Soon these currents merged with the World Social Forum, which itself emerged in synergy with the fascinating new experiment in popular democracy that had been underway in Brazil from the late 1980s, under the auspices of the Workers' Party.[1] 'Another World is Possible' rapidly became the banner of what has since come to be known as the counter-globalization movement. It is a movement that not only challenges the predatory capitalism of the present but also seeks to reinvent the vision of a world without borders and a future beyond capitalism. Long after the old dream of socialism turned into a nightmare and collapsed 'under the weight of its own contradictions'—a phrase that the Old Left was fond of using about the capitalist world—there began renewed attempts to chart out a different course, in a different era and in very different ways from that old vision. Without a centre, without any blueprint and without the burden of old shibboleths to carry, the new movement moves ahead in an uncertain world through an articulation of different radical practices into a new assault on global capitalism. A distinctly post-utopian initiative, one might say.

Two modes of anti-imperialism. Two modes of resistance against the power of global capital. One articulated within an explicit discourse of anti-capitalism and the other within a discourse of civilizational hurt/injury. We could, in fact, say that there are two imperialisms at work here: one that is the object of the counter-globalization movement and the other, that of bin Laden and resurgent radical Islam—and they bring forth two different kinds of resistance. Yet, one might have something to say to the other. Imperialism or 'Empire' is not merely a phenomenon of economic exploitation or political dominance; it is also undergirded by a cultural frame that appears before us in the garb of universalism—of universal values and therefore invisible *as culture*. We can hardly pretend any more to evade this question of cultural difference and its implication in power relations.

We have today, a world of decentred networks of power and counter-power, of resistances and struggles, not all of which are easy to weld into a common movement. Often these different impulses may be seen to act at cross purposes. This despite the fact that the desire for defeating Empire is often so strong that portraits of Che Guevara and Osama bin Laden can appear together on buses and walls in Bolivia.[2]

These are catastrophic times. The world after the demise of socialism and the Old Left, times of corporate plunder of the planet's resources, the world of xenophobia and sectarian violence, the world of the global symbiosis of state terrorisms and freelance terror[3]—this is the world we live in. It is a world that defies comprehension in terms of the vocabulary of the Old Left. And yet, it is a world that cries out for a new radical transformative project. With rapidly sharpening inequities and accelerated dispossession of the already marginalized on the one hand and the frightful ascendance of xenophobia, sectarian violence and intolerance across the globe, the need to reinvent a political project that can articulate a whole range of democratic aspirations can hardly be overstated in this context. It is a world that imposes on us the responsibility to *think* this catastrophic present. Mere critique of 'globalization' or of so-called 'identity politics' by regurgitating old 'truths' are not of much use here. Nor is it enough for us any longer to merely think in terms of a 'revival' of the revolutionary subjectivity of the 'working class' or of an imagined 'multitude' that would represent, in its abstract being, the 'essence' of the revolutionary dream—as is being done by many on the Left, especially after the new anti-capitalist upsurges.[4]

## A Renewed Search

The slogan, 'Another World is Possible', raised at the World Social Forum (WSF) a few years ago, became the occasion for and inaugurated a new moment in the search for a new social imaginary—of a world beyond capitalism and without borders—in a period that has been marked by widespread cynicism with regard to any project of social transformation. The collapse of the socialist project heralded, in a very real sense, the collapse of the utopian imagination itself—at least as far as challenges to global capitalism are concerned. It was not just the communist movement and the Old Left that lost its moorings with the collapse of socialism. The triumphalism in global capitalist circles that marked that moment of collapse threw all radical social critique of capitalism into disarray. The WSF and the different currents that periodically meet there, made possible a space of connection and represented the desire to forge a new radical imagination.[5]

In a sense, it was only fitting that Porto Alegre became the venue for the inauguration of this novel venture, for it was there that one of the most innovative experiments with popular democracy was initiated in recent times, under the auspices of the Workers' Party (the PT or *Partido dos Trabalhadores*). The PT, we have seen, emerged in the course of the struggle against military dictatorship in Brazil and evolved its own innovative organizational form, where different political tendencies, from liberation theologians to erstwhile Trotskyists and Maoists, coexist with independent trade unions and organizations of landless labourers, within a larger, broadly Left, political formation. It is also interesting that the PT emerged as a major political force on the scene around 1989 when the socialist world was collapsing. It, therefore, had to embark on its journey in a context where there were no blueprints to follow. It was this fact that Marco Aurelio, the International Secretary of the Workers' Party, underlined when he stated that 'The Berlin Wall did not fall on us'. He was clearing the way for a new imagination that would not be constrained by 'traditions of dead generations that weigh like a nightmare on the brains of the living'.

'Porto Alegre' came in the wake of a resurgence of popular struggles in South America and the anti-corporate and anti-capitalist protests across the Western world and bore the mark of those struggles. As mentioned earlier, the first intimations of a popular revolt against the IMF/World Bank propelled neo-liberal order came from the Zapatista uprising in the Chiapas region in Mexico in the beginning of 1994. This was followed some years later by the massive Bolivian struggles against the privatization of water and the popular rebellions in Argentina and Venezuela. Today, the entire South American continent has registered a shift to the Left, broadly speaking, as the last election results in Chile and Bolivia have shown. It was in this period that the counter-globalization movement began taking shape in the West, starting in Seattle. It was the mark of these movements that made WSF the platform it became. What is interesting about the slogan 'Another World is Possible' is that it has, like Marx said of the Paris Commune, 'no ideals to realize, no blueprints to which the world must conform'; it represents that 'real movement' that has emerged to challenge the fortresses of global capitalism.

If the practical movement on the ground is treading carefully, provisionally and in a spirit of a search and experimentation, the radical intelligentsia has started taking its own flights of messianic fantasy—attempting to reinvent Utopia, as it were. Sections of the Old Left have suddenly begun to see in these movements a possible resurrection of their Socialist Utopia. A series of volumes have also appeared in the past few years that seek to address this moment of the death of utopia though they come from a range of different positions.[6] Two of them became cults in the short period since they appeared, namely, *Empire* by Michael Hardt and Antonio Negri, and *No Logo* by Canadian journalist Naomi Klein. Hardt and Negri followed up *Empire* with its sequel *Multitude*, while John Holloway published a tract apparently theorizing from the Zapatista experience, *Change the World Without Taking Power*. Another volume, the special millennium number of the *Socialist Register* entitled *Necessary and Unnecessary Utopias*, is a collection of essays that are located in a slightly different world of the Old Marxist Left in Britain—although many of the essays in it seek to grapple with contemporary issues in quite unconventional ways.[7] If the *Socialist Register* essays can be seen as a response from the more 'realistic' and 'pragmatic' Left position, then *Empire* represents an attempt that is at once more breathtaking and prophetic in its mode. At one level, it effects a radical political-intellectual break with established ways of Left wing thinking; at another it simply seeks to re-present the notion of an apocalyptic revolutionary upsurge in a new garb. Naomi Klein's book is a first-hand reportage of the gathering storm and was written in the period when the anti-corporate struggles in the West were getting together but had not yet made their public appearance. True, London's 18 June 1999 Carnival had provided a glimpse of the shape of things to come but it wasn't quite clear to many that it was anything more than an isolated protest. At another level, Klein's book is much more than reportage as it presents a fascinating analysis of the change in corporate strategies in the nineties and the links that these could have with the emergence of these movements. Equally importantly, it represents a stance that seeks to critique what has come to be known as 'identity politics' in the last two decades, and the virtual disappearance of class/economic questions from the radical agenda. In that sense, therefore, all these works emanate from this moment of the 'Death of Utopia' and attempt to recuperate the global utopian vision.

Interestingly, all such visions, whichever tradition they may emanate from, do not seem to be able to sustain their utopian vision without reference to a universalist and metaphysical insistence on something like an 'essential human nature'. Human beings, this humanist mythology claims, *naturally desire autonomy and freedom* and will therefore rebel against injustice.

Let me just illustrate this stance with a couple of recent instances. Writing in the millennium number of the *Socialist Register (2000)*, on Utopias, Terry Eagleton for example, explicitly addresses the moment of the 'Death of Utopia'. He argues against all former Leftists who, he believes, have surrendered to pessimism, and goes on to claim that, 'If there is *one moral certainty* in all this, it is *surely* that people will rise up against the system *the moment it is rational for them to do so.*'[8] Now, Eagleton is acutely aware that such a 'rational moment' has come but rarely in the entire history of capitalism. He knows that for the most part we have only seen sporadic revolts and rebellions—sometimes undoubtedly heroic and inspiring but nevertheless, not enough to make sweeping generalizations about moral certainties. Unless one subsumes the history of anti-colonial revolutions against imperialist domination and extreme feudal oppression, into the global narrative of anti-capitalist/socialist struggles as much marxist theorization has tended to do, how does one account for this elusive rationality?[9] In any case, Eagleton will still have to explain why in his own society—the society of advanced capitalism—such a moment has never come. Since Eagleton knows this, he goes on to say that such moments 'do not of course come' since it is not rational to rebel against a system, however grave its deficiencies, as long as it still gives you something. '*Once it is not capable of this* [delivering something, that is]', he claims, 'men and women will take to the streets as surely as night follows the day.'[10] In other words, to paraphrase Eagleton, howsoever morally repugnant capitalism might be—and there is no dearth of evidence on that count—people will not rise against it as long as they get something out of it. Why then does Eagleton merely repeat the mythology of popular revolt? It does not take much effort to see that this is so because, once he gives up on the *ground of human nature*, he cannot keep his 'optimism' alive. It is this search for certainty that gives his optimism a foundation. In a companion essay, Leo Panitch and Sam Gindin also lament the fact that the recent past has seen 'too many disillusioned people on the left coming to their senses' by abandoning the goal of socialism. They have either become victims of what they call 'postmodernist pessimism' or have adopted 'social democracy's "third way"'.[11] In this essay, Panitch and Gindin attempt to transcend pessimism by making a case for utopian thought, for which they take recourse to Ernst Bloch's contention that the 'utopian intention' is the real motor force of history. What is important for our immediate purposes, however, is their claim that '*the socialist "utopian goal" is built around realizing our potential to be full human beings.*'[12] In this context their enunciation of socialist strategy and perspective is predicated upon the centrality of 'work' because, they argue, even while it 'blocks the *full development of the workers' human potential,*' it provides a 'foundation of working class politics'. It is on this basis they say, that many socialists have concluded (and Panitch and Gindin seem to agree), that it is through this specific location that the totality of the system is revealed, 'that the working class . . . is strategically positioned to lead the *struggle for universal liberation*.'[13] Here, in a slightly different rendering, human nature is posited as a potential to be realized, but once realized, it will enable the working class to become the agent of universal liberation.

It is also relevant here to recall that despite their claims to the contrary, even Hardt and Negri ultimately resort to the fiction of a 'being-against' as some sort of innate trait of human beings. Despite their claim to affirm the 'death of Man', they end up simultaneously asserting, 'The will to be against does not seem to require much explanation' because 'Disobedience to authority is one of *the most natural* and healthy acts.'[14]

We can see then that Eagleton's 'moral certainty' of popular revolt and Panitch and Gindin's claim that the 'socialist utopian goal is built around our potential to be *full human beings*', on the one hand and Hardt and Negri's 'revolt of the multitudes' on the other, are based upon a continuing investment in some 'human essence'—a sort of 'natural proclivity' of human beings to revolt against oppression, an innate desire for freedom. As we have noted above, however, this construction of 'natural proclivity' is the product of a specifically nineteenth century European historical experience of numerous revolts and rebellions. This was immediately buttressed philosophically by the Hegelian-Marxist tradition where the idea of a Universal class, with a certain ontological privilege, could become the privileged agent of historical necessity. Even though Hardt and Negri come from an explicitly anti-Hegelian tradition, in the last resort their certainty of revolt too leans on such a notion of a 'universal class'.

This belief in an innate human nature has its attendant hazards—not the least being that it cons us into believing that 'things will eventually be fine'. Eagleton, Panitch and Gindin or Hardt and Negri for that matter, could call it optimism, but we could also call it, paraphrasing Marx himself, the opium of the revolutionaries. Such beliefs in an innate human nature have always left revolutionaries gasping each time the 'masses' moved in their millions towards fascist parties. The only way they could then explain this 'aberration' was through resort to dubious notions like 'false consciousness'.

There is, of course, another serious issue here. Such attempts at recovering optimism, as those discussed above, tend to resolve philosophical questions through enunciation of political stances. There are three assumptions at work here, which we will merely note. First, that what is politically desirable must also be philosophically true and the second, that the political enjoys absolute privilege over the philosophical, such that we can always resolve a philosophical question by merely gesturing to its supposed political implications (by making statements such as: 'this stance will only lead to pessimism' or 'this is a recipe for surrender to identity politics'). Clearly, this makes a travesty of any philosophical argument. The third assumption, which requires a brief comment, is the patently false assumption that one and only one politics can possibly emerge from any given philosophical/epistemological position. The sheer empirical diversity of political positions that emerge from any philosophical position should tell us that such is not the case. Hegel's political proclivities for instance, did not prevent Marx and Engels from drawing very radical conclusions from his philosophy. It gave rise to both Left and Right Hegelians in their time. Or consider the way in which Nietzsche and Heidegger have inspired radically different political stances both on the Right and the Left. And we need only think of Jean-Paul Sartre or Herbert Marcuse on the Left to be able to see how absurd it would be to link Heidegger's influence on them with his politics.

At any rate, we should always bear in mind the fact that actual movements on the ground need neither metaphysical grounding in some absolute Truth, nor necessarily any grand vision of 'changing the world'. We therefore need to ask why do 'we' *need* utopias? What happened to earlier ones? How did they die? Who killed Utopia? Was it perhaps, the non-utopic 'everydayness of being' that killed it—or did the Utopian Ideal kill itself in its desire to mould the world in its image? Is this desire to mould the world the reason why every 'utopia' has so easily turned into a dystopia? Are we then seeing the end of an epoch whose imagination was framed by a kind of millenarianism, forever awaiting its Godot? Or is it still possible to reinvent it in some form? If so, in what form? These are complex questions as, it seems, it is *only the modern secular eschatologies* that have died, while religious ones, especially radical Islam, Hindutva and other religious (or religion-inspired) utopias for instance, seem to have gained ground at their expense in the last two or three decades. If this is really the case, what is it that accounts for the power and longevity of a religious utopia, in an era that is more generally marked by the 'incredulity towards metanarratives'? We are still far from having an answer to this question. One thing however, seems clear: the problem of Identity is a question that we ignore only at our own peril.

In this context, one might need to seriously interrogate some of the ways in which the writings discussed in this chapter frame their quest for a new Utopia. For, it is here that despite their immense insights, these accounts tend to remain deeply problematic from the postcolonial point of view.

## 'Empire', 'No Logo' and the Problem of Identity

As will be evident from the juxtaposition of the two quotes in the epigraph to this chapter, it is the vexed question of what has dismissively come to be termed as 'identity politics' that has now acquired a critical place and which must be negotiated in this post-utopian world. While marxists (and Leftists in general) have sought to dismiss these questions in old familiar ways, as diversionary and as deflecting the movement from its *main aim* of challenging global capital, the problem nevertheless remains. There is however more to this dismissal of 'identity politics' than mere marxist prejudice and as I have argued elsewhere, it is the continuing modernist investment in Universalisms that makes illegitimate all such articulations of identity—for it is inbuilt into the very structure of modern universalisms that they must privilege the unmarked 'human' subject as the foundation of all their theoretical endeavours. I have suggested that this play of universality and difference has been very much a part of marxism's own history as it came to the postcolonial world. The so-called 'Eastern question' or the 'national and colonial question', both in the early USSR and the colonies, was basically an expression of this problem: the language of universalism was always the language of the white European, while the communist from Soviet Central Asia or from the colonies had to always fight for a recognition of his/her own cultural difference. Recent scholarship has shown that such modern universalisms are only available to those who occupy the position of the dominant and hegemonic cultures—for those whose dispossession has to do with the colour of their skin or with the caste or gender they were 'born' into, such universalisms can often appear as extremely oppressive.[15]

It is in this context that I propose to discuss some aspects of the arguments made in both Naomi Klein's *No Logo* and Hardt and Negri's *Empire*, particularly the latter. Naomi Klein presents her account of the struggles against corporate globalization by setting it up against the 'culture wars' of the eighties (in North America and Canada). Her argument is presented in the form of a self-interrogation. She talks about 'my generation's campus identity politics' which, according to her 'boiled down, in the end, to a set of modest political goals that were frequently (and deceptively) cloaked in immodest rhetoric and tactics.'[16] She claims that though she is proud of the small victories that were won, like better lighting on campuses, more women faculty members and a less Eurocentric curriculum (which she qualifies as a phrase from her 'PC [Politically Correct] days'), she sees it as merely re-arranging the furniture, while the house burned down.[17] Her complaint is that poverty was not much of an issue in those days. She further claims that the basic demands of identity politics assumed an atmosphere of plenty: 'In the seventies and eighties that plenty had existed and women and non-whites were able to battle over how the collective pie would be divided.' In other words, now that the pie is shrinking it does not make sense to keep fighting about a share in it. However, a little reflection will show that it is *not the fight for a share* in the shrinking pie that disturbs her: What she now finds so problematic is that this struggle should be fought, *not along class lines* but along lines of identity. This is a point that is not sufficiently recognized when conventional Left wing arguments seek to present struggles around identity as 'mere' [?] questions of 'recognition' ignoring altogether the redistributive claims that are today quite central to such assertions.

However, if one looks more closely at the struggles around 'identity', say the Dalit movement or feminism/women's movement, how can one escape the fact that these have centrally concerned the question of property—at least in India. The women's movement has continuously fought for property rights for women in the last three decades. In fact, one might usefully recall that the Bodh Gaya land struggle in the late 1970s, almost split on the issue of women demanding equal claim to redistributed land. It is interesting that while the Left parties were earlier opposed to this claim and the titles distributed during communist sponsored land reforms in Kerala and West Bengal went only to male heads of the family, in recent years they have changed their position, impelled by pressure from the women's movement. The Left Front government in West Bengal has now introduced separate titles in land for women family members too. Equally important in this respect is the position adopted by the Dalit movement in the landmark Bhopal Declaration. This declaration adopted in a huge conference, held in Bhopal in early 2002, clearly stakes out an economic agenda for the movement that involves claims both on land and capital. It is important to note that all these struggles around property are quite central to what Klein and others like Hardt and Negri derisively call 'identity politics'; that struggles over 'property' are not simply translatable into the language of 'class' and 'class struggle'.

There is a certain sense of unease that attaches to Naomi Klein's reference to those days of 'politically correct identity politics' and she feels immediately called upon to disclaim that PC-ness. But what I want to underline here are two other claims made by her above: (1) That representation of women and non-whites in the faculties (and maybe corporations) and formulating less Eurocentric curriculums, merely 'amounted to re-arranging the furniture while the house burned down'. It is worth pushing this revealing metaphor a bit here. For, it seems, it does not really matter whether a particular chair is here or there; they are after all 'all chairs'! Such an assertion betrays an inability to understand the ways in which social structures of power and knowledge operate between races, castes, communities and genders. Unlike the relationship between chairs and tables, these are relationships of the structural distribution of power—and therefore of property and resources. (2) That such struggles assumed an atmosphere of plenty and so it was all right to battle over how the collective pie was to be shared. What if one were to argue that it is precisely when the collective pie is shrinking that struggles over who gets how much, really becomes more urgent and intense? What if one were to argue that the struggle over property (and economic resources, more generally) is not simply a struggle between the bourgeois and the proletarian but equally one between the white and the black, the woman and the man, the Dalit and the upper caste? What if, as the Indian case suggests, the question of class might become an upper caste ploy to deflect claims made by the Dalits and backward castes?[18]

In fact, the situation at least in our contexts, seems to be much more complicated, though I suspect, it is not quite so simple in America or Canada either. Certainly, recent evidence of indigenous people-based Left wing movements in South America reveals how central the question of identity has become for contemporary struggles. In our context, for example, questions of class cannot be seen any more as separate from those of gender, caste or community. The industrial working class, for instance reproduces within itself all the hierarchies of gender and caste, and happens to be for the most part, Hindu. In fact, as Thomas Blom Hansen's work shows, the Muslim workers of Mumbai are continuously discriminated against in subtle and not-so-subtle ways by both the Hindu workers and the employers—and it took a Muslim trade unionist to articulate this unspeakable problem before Hansen. We also know from a lot of recent work how Dalits continue to be employed in the lowest paid and socially demeaning jobs. In a sense, the emergence of leaders from indigenous populations in the new democratic upsurges in South America, displacing the hegemony of the former creole/mestizo leadership, illustrates a different aspect of the same question of identity and representation in the struggle for equality and dignity.[19]

By merely invoking the question of poverty, as Klein does, we cannot even begin to address the magnitude of the problems involved. However, let us leave Klein's text here for the moment and proceed to discuss in somewhat greater detail, the argument made by Michael Hardt and Antonio Negri.

Hardt and Negri devote a substantial part of their discussion to colonialism, and what they call 'postcolonial and postmodern theory'. They see both postcolonial and postmodern theory as responses to the colonial experience—though emanating from different quarters. Their argument is centrally framed around the idea that, in the postmodern era, sovereignty is reconstituted in a fundamental way. The old paradigm of modern sovereignty (expressed in the form of colonialism), gives way to a new imperial sovereignty (the sovereignty of Empire), and crucial to this passage from the one to the other, is their idea that there is no centre any more (there is no Rome, as they put it), nor any outside. Unlike the colonial order, Empire is an expanding realm that incorporates all and everything within its open frontiers. This idea has of course, been critiqued by many, arguing that the continuing domination of America over this new global sovereignty is very much a fact and in such a condition, to claim that 'there is no Rome', is to hide this brutal reality. However, this is not the point of my contention here. What is important from the point of view of my argument is that they consider "the various postmodernist and postcolonialist theories that have emerged in the 1980s' as giving the 'first view of this passage'—from modern to 'postmodern' or imperial sovereignty.[20] However, they see the perspectives offered by postmodern and postcolonial theories to be quite limited, because according to them, they are still fixated on seeking liberation *from past forms*: 'the lingering influence of the Enlightenment' (in the case of postmodernism) or 'the remnants of colonialist thinking' (in the case of postcolonialism). They suggest that both theoretical tendencies 'may end up in a dead end because they fail to recognize adequately the contemporary object of critique', *the new form of imperial sovereignty*. What does this mean? In the first place, it means, in their view, that both postmodernism and postcolonialism were probably adequate responses insofar as the object of their critique was modern sovereignty. They make a somewhat sweeping claim that it is modern sovereignty, symbolized by colonialism for instance, that produces the binary of the Self and the Other, of the White and the Black.[21] They argue that colonialism 'produces identities and alterities, imposes binary divisions on the colonial world'; it 'homogenizes real social differences to the absolute and then subsumes the opposition under the identity of European civilization'.[22] As opposed to this form of exclusion and Otherness characteristic of the modern paradigm of sovereignty, in the new imperial form, such overtly exclusionary mechanisms no longer hold. They invoke Etienne Balibar's recent work on racism where he suggests that racism now no longer operates on the notion of an intrinsic biological difference and suggests that instead, culture is now made to fill the role that biology once played, in the construction of the new, differentialist racism. Using this distinction, they go on to make the argument that imperial racism now adopts all the constructivist arguments of the postmodernists. 'In this way imperial racist theory attacks modern anti-racism from the rear, and actually co-opts and enlists its arguments'.[23] In doing this, they suggest, Empire works with differences and unlike the old paradigm of sovereignty, does not aim at 'complete cultural assimilation'. 'Contingency, mobility and flexibility are Empire's real power. The imperial "solution" will not be to negate or attenuate these differences, but rather to affirm them and arrange them in an effective apparatus of command.'[24] This highly reductive attempt at periodization is permeated by the desire to place the bewildering array of identity-based political struggles into a single ordering frame and thus attempts to produce another metanarrative by reference to which all specificity can be subsumed.

We may note in parenthesis that this sweeping theorization is based on a virtual ignorance of the workings of colonial regimes in the era of what they call modern sovereignty. Colonialism, at least in India and Anglophone Africa, was not interested in assimilation or homogenization but on the contrary, worked precisely with the kind of affirmation of difference, 'arranging them in an effective apparatus of command' that Hardt and Negri see as a distinctive feature of Empire. This was precisely what irked the Indian nationalists, for example, who saw this kind of playing off of one cultural community against another as the colonialist strategy of 'divide and rule'. This entire exercise was often based on fairly rigid and essentialist notions about native cultures. The extent to which cultural difference was 'affirmed' by colonialism is notorious, especially in the case of apartheid South Africa but none of these enter Hardt and Negri's theorizations.[25] And yet, it is on the postulated newness of this strategy that Hardt and Negri build their entire case regarding postmodernism and postcolonialism, which in their rendering, despite having played an important part in the critique of modern sovereignty, now stand as mere apologies for 'identity politics'. Thus they ask: What if the dominating powers that are the intended object of critique have mutated in such a way as to depotentialize any such postmodernist challenge? What if a new paradigm of power, a postmodern sovereignty, has come to replace the modern paradigm and rule through differential hierarchies of the hybrid and fragmentary subjectivities that these theorists celebrate? 'Power', they contend, 'has evacuated the bastion they are attacking and has circled around to their rear to join them in their assault in the name of difference.'[26] Valorization of cultural difference, in other words, is crucial to the new strategies of Empire.

It is worth underlining here that there is no single or fixed way in which questions of cultural identity relate to power and if contemporary post-structuralist critiques alert us to anything, it is to the danger of drawing such large and unsubstantiable correlations and making rigid periodizations. However, if one were to leave aside their reading (or lack of it) of the actual workings of colonialism, it is not difficult to see that this laboured exercise is directed at arriving at a way of getting around the vexed question of identity. In this long and complicated way, the authors attempt to actually consign the question of identity and cultural difference once again to a realm where it need not be discussed any more. While they do recognize that postmodernism 'provides important resources for those who are struggling to challenge modern discourses of patriarchy, colonialism and racism' and that 'the postmodernist insistence on difference and specificity defies the totalitarianism of universalizing discourses and structures of power',[27] they at the same time would like to place all questions of identity raised by it, in the realm of the past: it was all right to raise such questions when modern sovereignty ruled but now that imperial power has taken over the banner of difference, we can go ahead with our task—that is the task of fighting Empire and global capital.

Questions of identity do not disappear simply because radicals do not want to confront them. In the case of Hardt and Negri, it is all the more surprising because at times they do seem to have a more complex understanding of the question of identity and one of its most difficult manifestations, namely, 'fundamentalisms'. I put the term here in quotation marks because it is not an accurate description of the phenomenon under question and as many people struggling within their own communities have repeatedly pointed out, the new right-wing political resurgence in the name of religion is not really about going to the theological fundamentals of the religion concerned. Whether or not we agree with this reading, it is important that we recognize that for those fighting from within—say Islamic feminists, liberal Hindus or liberation theologists—it is a gesture of critical importance and needs to be strengthened by those fighting against such tendencies from outside, that is from within modern secular spaces. One of the important points where Hardt and Negri recognize the complexity of this phenomenon, appears in their claim that 'fundamentalism should be seen not as the re-creation of a pre-modern world, but rather *a refusal of the contemporary historical passage* in course'.[28] In that sense, they consider 'fundamentalisms' too, like postmodernism, to be symptoms of the passage to Empire. They go so far as to assert that 'fundamentalisms' should be seen, not as pre-modern but as postmodern projects. 'The postmodernity of fundamentalisms has to be recognized primarily in its refusal of modernity as a weapon of Euro-American hegemony—and *in this regard Islamic fundamentalism is indeed a paradigmatic case.*'[29] Here they touch the really crucial point: the resurgence of many such struggles around identity, especially the more xenophobic ones, are inextricably linked to the history of imperialist ravages in the colonial world and are very much located in modernity. This should lead us to think differently about them and about ways of fighting against them. However, it is a sign of the attempt to short-circuit the real and almost intractable problems posed by questions of identity (and 'fundamentalism') that despite such an understanding of the phenomenon, the authors can still see, or are possibly forced to see the Iranian revolution of 1979 as 'resurrecting an ancient order'.[30]

At this point, it might be necessary to briefly consider the label of postmodernism that Hardt and Negri attach to 'fundamentalisms'. They acknowledge that the two intellectual currents, namely, postmodernism and 'fundamentalism'—are in a sense diametrically opposed to each other: one justifies hybridity, the other purity; one insists on difference while the other is based on a most rigid sense of identity; one represents mobility, while the other stasis. How then do they see fundamentalisms as postmodern? They resolve this problem of simultaneous convergence and divergence between the two by suggesting that the two in fact, represent two different responses to the same condition but see them as arising at opposite poles. Postmodernism, they suggest appeals primarily to the winners in the process of globalization while fundamentalism appeals to the losers. It seems to me that there is a conflation here between the 'condition' that they loosely call 'postmodern' and the intellectual current that has come to be known by the same term. If one accepts that there is such a thing as the postmodern condition, then 'postmodern theory' should be seen to stand in the same relation to it as marxism stands to capitalism: Just as marxism takes capitalism as its theoretical object, one could say that postmodern theory takes the postmodern condition (the exhaustion of the metanarratives of emancipation, the insurrection of little selves, splitting of earlier national identity formations, etc.) as its object of reflection. Postmodernism, as a body of theoretical reflection, is nothing if not a critique of the attempts to fix and freeze identity rather than a celebration of it. It is easy to see the 'postmodern' insistence on—and may be celebration of *difference*—as a celebration of *identity* itself. Conflation of the two, however, involves a non-sequitor. It should be evident that *difference*, or more precisely *differa´nce* (as Derrida would put it) is *Identity delayed, deferred*. Identity, on the other hand, is the self-presence of meaning, of the transparence of the subject to herself. *Differa´nce* is the insistence that the subject is always-already plural, multiple—irreducible to any single self-evident Self. If all subjectivity is discursively constituted, and each individual resides at the intersection of any number of contending discourses, as I would argue following Derrida,. then Identity can only be a 'postmodern' theoretical object in the sense in which capital is the theoretical object of marxism. Hardt and Negri in fact, seem to be conflating the distinction that Louis Althusser once laboured hard to make us aware of—namely, the distinction between the theoretical/representational object and the real object itself.

One of the differences between radicals brought up in the old radical traditions of universalism and those who argue with a postmodern sensibility is that where the former would dismiss all anxieties about identity in some form or the other (false consciousness, secondary, diversionary, appropriated by imperial sovereignty, etc.), the latter would urge that they be taken seriously as they possibly speak to some experiential core—even while insisting that this core itself needs to be deconstructed. The philosophical underpinnings of radical thought of the past came from realist epistemological premises, which assumed a sharp disjuncture between 'appearance' and 'reality', 'phenomenon' and 'essence'—and had the happy option of understanding all unhappy things as 'symptoms' of a deeper malaise. For it, therefore, 'identity' was always the superficial 'appearance' or the 'epiphenomenon' whose real meaning lay embedded in some class structure. To the postmodern radical, however, it is the reality of the 'appearance' itself that needs to be taken seriously. Taking seriously however, does not mean always endorsing it, much less celebrating it.

## Different Worlds, Different Languages

Resistance, transformation and utopia, in all conventional radical accounts (like anarchism, marxism, and more recently in Hardt and Negri) then, are spelt out solely in relation to the rule of capital and from the fictional standpoint of a world divided into two camps—that of the oppressors *versus* the camp of the oppressed. Needless to say, this presents an extremely oversimplified picture of the contemporary world where alliances and solidarities are being forged in extremely complicated ways. Such a vision almost always, by default, tends to concentrate *on points where the global tension is the highest.* Further, this tension, almost always, is rendered in purely economic terms as that between capital and the Rest. It tends therefore, to overlook the possibility that there might be other stories, other conflicts and questions that are constantly playing themselves out and might need to be dealt with as urgently—even for the coalition against capital to gather strength. At best such a vision overlooks the serious anxieties about identity; at worst it sneers at them as something parochial and narrow. All the illusory, if grand, visions of 'the multitude' rising in revolt, or the popular forces across the world joining together in a massive battlefront against the rule of capital emanate from such fantastic visions. Such visions, predicated upon the idea of an apocalyptic moment of revolutionary rupture, are the precise secular analogues of the religious millennial expectation. They can never really ever deal with the present. In fact, it can be argued that religious millenarianisms have more room for the everyday, living present, which might precisely account for their powerful appeal.

To illustrate how the other processes at play often work against this expectation of the simultaneous global revolutionary rupture, let us return to the moment of 11 September and its continuing reverberations across the world. From early 1994, when the Zapatista rebellion in the Chiapas mountains of Mexico burst forth upon a capitalist world still euphoric over the collapse of socialism, the movement against corporate globalization was gathering more and more adherents—different and discrete currents but all sharing the poetry of a future liberation. We have noted the signposts along that path: Seattle, Melbourne, Quebec, Genoa on the one hand, and Brazil, Venezuela, Argentina on the other. It was then that 11 September happened. What had till then seemed to be a 'local' problem—a mere preoccupation with identity, now burst forth in the citadels of world capitalism, but in a form scarcely recognizable even to the anti-capitalist warriors as a struggle against capitalism. In a sense, it was not. It was a movement directed, not against the economic logic of capitalism but against the cultural and colonialist logic of imperialism, a logic that comes couched, always, in the language of universalism: imperialism as the flag bearer of democracy, freedom and human rights. For those who can see only the logic of economic exploitation, the other stories of oppression embedded in this history are but uncomfortable irritants. The two currents had to collide. Anti-globalization movements were put on the back foot and many protests were shelved, as bloodlust in American society rose.

For better or for worse, this is the world we live in. The global is no longer immune from the workings of the local. The local, of course, has never been immune from the global. Thus it is critically important to recognize that the discourse of an Osama bin Laden is, among other things, a discourse of 'anti-imperialism'. It is a discourse that is inseparably bound up with continuing imperialist ravages in the erstwhile colonial world. It is this that makes possible the appearance of the image of bin Laden alongside that of Che's in the buses and walls of the Bolivian capital. It is equally important to recognize that when 'the people' in these parts act against imperialism and the rule of capital, it is not always in ways that revolutionaries expect of them. In other words, the anti-capitalist Utopia rarely manages to catch the imagination of people in these parts of the world—except in certain contexts of extreme crises. In our context, one might even argue that the anti-capitalist utopia itself acquires very different, romantic overtones of nostalgia for the lost world. There is thus a deep chasm between how the same object (is it really the same?) is experienced by self-proclaimed revolutionaries on the one hand and by ordinary people on the other. The languages in which this experience is articulated are also radically different. This is the moment that we need to address. It is a moment of incommensurability of different languages and different worlds.

This, it seems, may have become the central intellectual-political question of our times. On the one hand, there is the language of modernity, including the language of radical/revolutionary politics that is spoken by the enlightened radical elites; on the other, there is the life-world of the 'masses' with their cultural resources and narratives of historical encounters through which they make sense of the world. It is important to note in this context, that Osama bin Laden was not always a radical Islamist cleric. On the contrary, it is precisely the transformation of the once Westernized bin Laden into an Islamic radical that we need to contend with. Increasingly, radical political theory will have to confront the problem of being radical in different contexts. Is it possible for radical political practice located in the Islamic world, for instance, to act upon *its* present without entering the particular discursive world of contemporary Islam that is already structured in not-so-hospitable ways for it? And yet, enter it must, if it has to be effective. Or to put it more sharply, it must in fact *emanate* from there; it cannot be transported from some Archimedean outside. And once it is part of that discursive world, can it simply act upon it without, in some way being, affected by it? This means that there will be different kinds of radical political practice—not all of them easily recognizable as radical in the same way.

A few instances might illustrate this point better. Aziz Al-Azmeh, for example, talks of sections of the 'Middle Eastern' intelligentsia, some of them of marxist persuasion, who combine theories of dependency with a 'Muslim primitivist' utopia to produce what they call a 'Muslim Left'. Al-Azmeh argues that this political tendency is actually a kind of hypernationalism rather than an 'Islamic primitivism'.[31] In an earlier time, Maxime Rodinson had discussed the phenomenon of Pan-Arabism whose influence had spread throughout the Arab world and became immensely popular. Rodinson had noted then that this ideology 'borrowed from marxism the characterization of its main enemy as imperialism', which often accepted the idea of 'a necessary evolution towards various rather vaguely thought-out socialist structures'.[32] In another context, he also noted that 'among the less enlightened masses [*sic*], who still keep to the faith and piety of their ancestors', 'curious reinterpretations' were often made to accommodate the idea of communism. They assumed, he argues, that communism could not be contradictory to faith.[33] Elsewhere, I have discussed the ways in which communists from such societies sought to find a way of keeping a dialogue between the two worlds open (Nigam 1999). What these observations draw our attention towards is crucial in terms of formulating a future radical project: that there is no *pre-existing thing called radical politics* that then enters societies that it wants to transform, *from the outside* as it were. Radical politics is really *that which grows from within a determinate social world* as a force which challenges its dominant structures of power and the modes of knowledge and thought that sustain it. In doing so, it opens itself out to different currents in the world of ideas—from marxism to Enlightenment-inspired ideals of equality and rights—but its allegiance to these ideas notwithstanding, it is forever marked with the sign of an 'impurity'. It is this kind of radicalism that we will need to reckon with more and more in the future.

Let me take another recent instance from an entirely different context. Nicholas Higgins presents a fascinating study of the experiences of the Zapatistas in the Chiapas region of Mexico, especially as articulated by the enigmatic Sub-Commandante Marcos in long conversations and interviews. It all began in 1983, when a band of city-bred revolutionaries arrived in Chiapas to found the Zapatista National Liberation Army. Fired with the ammunition of Marxist-Leninist theory, they began organizing the local people. Marcos arrived there in 1984 and soon they were taking classes on complex political and social questions. Says Higgins: 'Marcos talked of entering these communities and trying to teach "the absurdities that we had been taught; imperialism, social crisis, the correlation of forces and their coming together, things that nobody understands, and of course, neither did they".'[34] Keen to spread the political word, says Higgins, the ground that the revolutionaries sought to engage them on was nearly always centred around the question of history. The initial conversations themselves increasingly revealed 'misunderstanding and incomprehension', for it became clear that the indigenous held a different conception of time. Marcos recalled, 'You weren't always sure about which era they were speaking when they spoke they could be talking about a story that happened that very week, or that happened five hundred years earlier, or even when the world began.' Marcos explains that 'It's very difficult when you have a theoretical scheme that explains the whole of a society and then you arrive in that society and you realize that it explains nothing.' From this point on, 'the mestizo Zapatistas realized that their problems were not simply problems of translation' and that 'the Indian language had its own, different referents, its own cultural markers . . . .' Their notions of nation and national history were shaken. The local history revealed just how partial were non-Indian claims to a national history and to a large extent, the Zapatistas learned first-hand what it meant to be erased from the history books. It was then, listening to the Indians' own history of exploitation, of humiliation and racism, that they 'found the key stones upon which to build a new politics'. It was through this process, according to Marcos, that the idea of revolution itself underwent a transformation. 'Everything that was socialism in broad brush-strokes, but re-directed, enriched with humanitarian elements, ethics, morals, more than simply indigenous': the revolution now became an ethical call for a just world. Dignity was the new axis along which the idea of revolution now redefined itself.

This then was another blend. It was not purely indigenous in an inward-looking sense; but it was also no longer the revolution that the Marxist-Leninist revolutionaries went to the mountains to 'foment'. As in the case of the Muslim Left, the Zapatista movement is made up of impurity. The purity of the Rationalist revolutionary doctrine does not exist any more. Nor is it defined in any clear-cut way as a struggle simply against the rule of capital.

The purity of the universalist revolutionary doctrine in fact exists nowhere. Impurity is present not only in Eastern or postcolonial marxisms, where the 'impure' element is quite apparent, but even in the 'original' Western ones. Consider analogously, the history of Christianity, with the persistence of various 'corrupting' influences on the purity of the doctrine. Such repeated corruptions of the doctrine point to the continuing difficulties faced by all utopian/proselytizing projects: the persistence of the everyday—or what one might call, after Lyotard, the persistence of *paganism*. 'Paganism' then, needs to be rethought outside of and away from the purely theological or proselytizing frame, as that *recalcitrant particular* that refuses incorporation within any universalist frame. The pagan is both the particular and the local.

One of the critical questions, theoretically speaking, that the problem of universalism turns upon, is the question of time, as we can see in Marcos' accounts above as well as in a number of other ways which we shall repeatedly encounter through this book. A brief digression into my use of the concept is, therefore, in order.

## The Semantics of Historical Time[35]

One of the critical assumptions that underlies the modern notion of time that Marcos finds to be so much at odds with indigenous notions is that of its singularity and linearity. Time is One and it is irreversible; it always moves forward, such that at any given point, there can be only one Present, that is, the privileged present that is coterminous with that of the 'most advanced social forms'. That is to say that the Present only exists in the arena of the global. All other presents (or the 'presents' of all other societies) are remnants of an earlier epoch—the past. What should be evident here is that this notion can only function on the assumption that the world is a single entity. Jawaharlal Nehru put it brilliantly in his *Discovery of India*, while speaking of the relationship between India and the World:

> We in India do not have to go abroad in search of the past and the distant. *We have them here in abundance. If we go to foreign countries, it is in search of the present.* That search is necessary, for isolation from it means backwardness and decay. The world of Emerson's time has changed and old barriers are breaking down; *life becomes more international.*[36]

It could hardly be expressed better. The Present is Elsewhere; 'we' live in the Past. As old barriers break down and life becomes more international, we all become One entity, with a single past and a single present. 'Past' and 'Present' here are not mere markers of time; they refer to states of being. For purely in terms of 'time', wherever we are at *this* point of time is our present. In order to understand Nehru's—and thus the modern—conception of Time, we must understand the notion of Totality. For only when we begin to think of the time of the Totality, does a statement such as the above begin to make any sense to us.

Nehru says in so many words that his own society is the repository of 'the past and the distant'. And this sense of his is linked profoundly to the 'becoming international' of the world. 'We' lose our own sense of Self. We begin to see our present as a remnant of some bygone era. For Nehru, however, this was not a matter of regret; this *was the way to be modern*—and thus to be celebrated.

We know from the work of scholars of time that this is a state that comes into being with the new consciousness of time inaugurated by modernity. The idea of a single, linear and irreversible time, wedded firmly to the modern notion of Progress, is what creates this anxiety of being 'left behind', of becoming obsolete. Colonialism was the first crucial moment of that 'becoming international' within this new notion of Time. It inserted us into a whole new grid where we were no longer to be self-determining subjects. We were to be determined and judged by where we stood on the continuum of the new 'homogenous empty time' of modernity, to use Walter Benjamin's well-known characterization of this new conception. To be sure, as many scholars have pointed out and as we will see later on, there *were* earlier moments in history when life became 'global'; what is different in the colonial moment is that it, for the first time, set universal standards of what it meant to be 'modern' and therefore 'Present,' that is, not a relic of 'the Past'.

Reinhart Koselleck suggests that this operation becomes possible through the invention, in eighteenth century Europe, of the concept of World-History. This World-History was (and still is) seen as a single totality that is governed by a single logic and temporality. Through this conceptual device, the colonies became the Past of this new entity—World-History. World-History was now made of different existences all mapped on to the new framework of simultaneity, the co-presence of the Past and the Present.

In dealing with this secular-modern notion of 'empty time', scholars and philosophers of time have inevitably ended up with an aporia. That is, thinking the co-presence of the Past in the Present. Koselleck calls this the 'contemporaneity of the non-contemporaneous'. In a sense, Benedict Anderson encounters a similar problem when thinking of the possibilities of the imagination of 'nationhood': the idea of 'simultaneity' that is a condition of possibility of imagining the nation, only becomes possible once this modern notion takes firm hold. And in that process, Anderson also refers to the 'discovery', in the sixteenth century, of 'grandiose civilizations' like those of China, Japan, South East Asia, the Indian subcontinent, Aztec Mexico and Incan Peru—which 'suggested an irremediable human pluralism'. How could the European, he asks, deal with these different entities 'whose genealogies lay outside of, and were unassimilable to, Eden?' Anderson's suggestion is that *only homogeneous, empty time 'offered them' accommodation*: that is, by making possible the idea that others too could exist alongside 'us' [the Europeans], *in the same time.*[37] This charity extended by modernity's homogenous, empty time had, in the event many other consequences that we have only begun to realize in recent decades.

Koselleck also shows the emergence of the notion of Progress in the same period in Europe, which, we can see, supplemented this notion, by firmly entrenching the idea of 'backwardness' as Past. Not very far behind was the notion of Development and taken together, 'World-History,' 'Progress', and 'Development' could now place all societies in a single linear continuum.

This notion of time has been seriously questioned in recent decades and though this is not the place to go into a disquisition on the philosophy of time, we need to pursue the implications of this idea a little more since it is crucial to my argument. What does Anderson, for instance, mean when he says that 'only homogeneous empty time could offer accommodation' to these other, non-European societies? His discussion suggests the notion of time as an empty container through which all societies necessarily move. From that angle, we could say that we do live in the same time. We could then argue, with Johannes Fabian, that it is not that we really exist in 'different times' but that Western Man and anthropology as a discipline (for that is the locus from where Fabian speaks), '*deny coevalness*' to non-Western societies.[36] In other words, we could paraphrase Fabian and say that Western anthropology by assigning non-Western societies the status of a past, thus refuses to accept that there could be different presents existing in the same time. Both Anderson and Fabian work within the framework of homogeneous empty time, but where Anderson sees it 'offering accommodation' to non-Western societies, Fabian sees a 'denial of coevalness' or what he calls 'allochronism'. What both of them share however, is the idea that this conception of time becomes a mode of incorporation of these non-Western societies into 'World-History'.

Yet, it is clear that whether we see it as 'offering accommodation' or 'denying coevalness', the terms of this incorporation are set by what is considered to be the Present of World-History, which is none other than the present of the West. This incorporation cannot but be then, simultaneously, the subordination of these societies to the logic of Western modernity. Time becomes the trope of domination and power. Thus, Fabian remarks: 'In short, *geopolitics* has its ideological foundations in *chronopolitics*' (Fabian 1983: 144).

We could also look at the question from another angle. When we say that 'time is irreversible', are we not really speaking of a different notion of time—one that is not 'empty' in a sense, but 'full': for are we not suggesting that what is irreversible is *what happens in it*? Take out the content of time, take out the different ways in which we mark its existence with dates, calendars and events, and every hour, every day and night is like any other—endlessly repetitive and one might say, circular.[39] Manuel Castells' rendering of Leibniz's notion of time as the 'order of sequential existences' is of this kind; it is not some *thing* which is independent of existent things.[40] Castells thus pushes the point to its logical conclusion: if 'time is the order of succession of things', then without 'things' there would be no time.[41] We could push the question in another direction. That is to say that the idea of World-History can really be maintained only by positing a single series of successions. The moment we begin to see histories in the plural, rather than a single History, with a plurality of successions, we would have to start seeing time too as plural. The plurality or heterogeneity of time then becomes not an objective datum but is intertwined with notions of

Selfhood and emergence of newer and different histories. Time in this sense also becomes experiential. Witness for example, the emergence of Dalit or women's histories that have emerged in the recent past which seek to fill in the period of nationalism with different histories of doing, marked by different events from those of nationalist narratives.[42]

For our purposes, when we deal with time, we are actually dealing with this latter, *historical time*. In that sense, we could say that time is the time of the subject's doing. And as Louis Althusser was at pains to tell us, this notion of Time 'cannot be *read* in the continuity of the time of life or clocks'; 'it has to be constructed' (Althusser and Balibar 1975: 101). Discussing the 'time of economic production' as 'a complex intersection' of the different times, rhythms, turnovers, etc.', he underlines that it 'is only accessible in its concept' and like every concept, is never given but must be produced or constructed (ibid.: 101). The problem of course, becomes more critical, as Althusser realized, as one moves into a whole range of questions related to 'contemporary economic and political practice', especially when dealing with notions like 'underdevelopment', 'backwardness' and 'survivals'. This prolonged and deep meditation on the problem of Time, became one of the key elements in *Reading Capital* and importantly from our point of view, represents marxism's most significant attempt to deal with this problem. At this point the political project of marxism, as we will see in a subsequent chapter, was beginning to encounter the question of time as a political problem of utmost urgency. The 'coexistence of modes of production', the idea of a 'social formation' and 'uneven development' undergirded the entire world of marxist debate in the 1960s, 1970s and 1980s. Etienne Balibar puts it well in a subsequent essay, when he says that epochs like the 'ancient', 'modern' and the 'postmodern' 'do not supplant one another like the scenes of a play … they are all still present in a disunified totality, *in a noncontemporaneity that is the very structure of the current moment*' (Balibar 1994: 59).

Seen from this angle, the tendency to decree as illegitimate and obsolete, all that is not in sync with the 'Present', is to endorse the founding violence of the modern world. When one looks at modernity in relation to different temporalities then, we are alerted to the continuing presence of this violence in the global, and this recognition imposes upon us the responsibility to think the present in radically different ways.

It is at this point that we enter a really difficult terrain. For a critique of modern time-consciousness does not open for us any possibility of a return to traditional or non-modern modes of being. This return is never possible. And yet, the question remains. What if, unlike in the West, these other forms of life have not simply disappeared? E. P. Thompson once said that in writing his unconventional *Making of the English Working Class*, he was merely trying to rescue the artisan who perished in the storm of industrialization 'from the enormous condescension of posterity'. In a sense, this was a happy possibility available to him: to occupy the position of a critic who came late upon the scene of 'History', when all was already done. What if, unlike Thompson, we live in times like ours—and in worlds like ours—where we are witness to all that 'History' conceals in its sleeves? In a sense, all of Western marxism was born and emerged as a political practice, when in Marx's own words, the very memory of the dispossession of agricultural communities had been lost. More importantly, its understanding that there was a certain historical inevitability to the destruction of the old and the institution of the new (and the 'new' was always, eventually Progress), stood it in good stead with regard to this critical question. All subsequent debates within and concerns of that marxism, therefore, bear a mark of this circumstance. (The Althusserian moment could mark a break from that logic to some extent, primarily due to its entanglement with maoism but that is another question).

The questions for us, in the postcolonial or Third World is that fundamentally, our context and situation does not afford us the luxury available to the critic-come-late. We must deal with the different forms of life that mark our present, as contemporaries; as they are, all on-stage, all-at-once, to use Balibar's trope.

At another level, however, the question of the 'Past' itself remains problematic—even, that is, in the case of *what we know* to be the past. We know after Nietzsche, Foucault and Derrida among others, that 'the past' is never ever accessible to us in any unmediated form, that 'we' are all 'always already' constituted by the present.[43] Further, the very instability of the subject-position denoted by the 'we', places 'us' in extremely complicated positions vis-à-vis the 'past' and the 'present', for we never really occupy singular historical times. If Time is also about subjectivity, then we can never really ever be only 'woman' or 'Dalit'; 'worker' or 'Indian'; 'Bengali' or 'Muslim'. Derrida will of course, argue that the very conception of time belongs to the domain of metaphysics, and represents the 'domination of presence'.[44] He will find the entire philosophical tradition grappling with this problem of time, running from Aristotle through Hegel to Heidegger, as an attempt to deal with an aporia. For, to him 'presence' itself involves a meaning deferred—which he attempts to capture in his term '*differance*'.

As he would put it, even though we might begin, 'strategically, from the place and the time in which "we" are', in the last analysis, this move is not justifiable, since it is only on the basis of *differance* and its history that we can even begin to know 'who we are and where we are' and 'what the limits of an "era" might be.'[45] This reference to Derrida is important for two reasons. First, in attempting to disinter the modern conception of time as empty and homogeneous, we must resist the temptation to posit plurality and heterogeneity as given and fixed. Notions of subjectivity—the 'we'—must not be seen as defining a self-evident and self-present entity. This interrogation of the modern notion of time should rather be seen as a move that helps open out a space of thinking the subjectivity of the Other—in this context, we can use the Derridean impulse to think the being of those relegated to the status of [the West's] 'pasts'—as always open subjectivities. Second, as Derrida would propose, we must think this subjectivity, this 'Being', 'without nostalgia, that is, outside of the myth of a purely maternal or paternal language, a lost native country of thought'.[46] In invoking this Derridean gesture then, we can find a way of escaping the predicament of an endless search for an authentic past. Therefore, apart from the fact of the well-known oppressions and violences of the past, which in many cases make such a desire for return undesirable, Derrida advances more profound reasons why nostalgia may not be the best way to deal with this predicament. He then suggests that we affirm this condition but in the Nietzschean sense: 'in the sense in which Nietzsche puts affirmation into play, in a certain laughter and a certain step of the dance'.[47] A critique of modern time-consciousness then, imposes upon us the responsibility to think against the hegemonic modern, but at the same time, away from nostalgia for lost origins. It calls upon us to think of different ways of being, different forms of life.

The practical political question can nevertheless be raised here: What about [non-modern] forms of life that are under attack daily, right before our very eyes? How do we see the struggles of the adivasis of Narmada valley or the people of Tehri; the struggles of the peasantry against dispossession from land for the purposes of corporate/capitalist development, whether accomplished under the banner of private capital, as in India or under the garb of the state sector and the party-bourgeoisie as in China? In this context, it is necessary to underline that from the point of view of our discussion so far, these forms of life do not belong to the past; the struggles around these issues therefore, do not take place under the banner of nostalgia. However problematic such struggles might be from the point of view of a rampaging corporate capitalism, they are struggles that, in our contemporary, belong to the future. At the heart of these struggles is not a yearning for a lost past but also the articulated or unarticulated vision of a different future. Nostalgia for the lost world is, if anything, the preserve of the intelligentsia or the elite, which is inevitably bound to their search for authenticity and purity.[48]

An interrogation of the modern notion of Time and the difficulties of thinking identity and different forms of life, obliges us to rethink our entire idea of Progress and the place of the supposedly non-modern in the imagination of a different future. For if the present is not simply to be understood as the elimination of all 'existing-but-outmoded' forms of life and beliefs, then the very idea of Progress as we understand it today has to be either abandoned or, at the very least, completely redefined.

## NOTES

1. The subsequent fate of the Lula government should not detract from the overall significance and novelty of the Brazilian experience of municipal government and participatory budgeting—as well as a unique experiment with the party-form that is the PT.
2. I am grateful to Sinclair Thomson for this information.
3. I owe this expression to Shuddhabrata Sengupta.
4. Among the recent attempts to resurrect such a revolutionary subject or messiah, Slavoj Zizek's name certainly comes to mind. See his essays on what he calls 'repeating Lenin', especially Slavoj Zizek, 'Repeating Lenin', 2001. This essay is also available on the Internet: http://www.lacan.com/replenin.htm Also see Zizek, 'Can Lenin Tell Us About Freedom Today?', e-text, http://www.lacan.com/freedom.htm 2002, Also see Michael Hardt and Antonio Negri, *Empire*, Cambridge, Massachusetts and London, Harvard University Press, 2001, England, and Hardt and Negri, *Multitude—War and Democracy in the Age of Empire*, New York: Penguin Books, 2004. Hardt and Negri's idea of the 'multitude' though is far more complex than Zizek's metaphysical 'proletarian subjectivity'.
5. This slogan, as well as the WSF itself has been recently attacked in India by a section of self-styled maoists as being 'too amorphous'. The WSF in particular,

has been attacked as being a 'tool of imperialism' by this section that held its own separate 'road show' by the name of Mumbai Resistance in January 2004. This critique has in fact all the elements of the old stalinist left imaginary and need not detain us here. As will be clear in the course of this book, much of the argument here is precisely against such a way of looking at forms of movements, platforms and struggles as, at once, readymade and finished forms.

6. Naomi Klein, *No Logo*, London: Flamingo, 2001; Michael Hardt and Antonio Negri, *Empire*, Cambridge, Massachusetts and London: Harvard University Press, 2001; Leo Panitch and Colin Leys, (eds.) *Necessary and Unnecessary Utopias*, in *Socialist Register 2000*, London: Merlin Press and Calcutta: KP Bagchi, 2000 and John Holloway, *Change the World without Taking Power: The Meaning of Revolution Today*, London, Virginia: Pluto Press, 2002, are some of the volumes that directly address this question, in some way or the other.

7. Being a collection of different essays (*Necessary and Unnecessary Utopias, Socialist Register 2000*), emerging from diverse concerns and experiences like feminism, ecology, etc., there is no necessary coherence in the theoretical frameworks of the different contributors. What binds them, however (barring the two opening theoretical essays), is the fact that they seek to recover a utopian ideal that is at once detached from millennial visions and located in the everyday practices of different kinds, including those of academic disciplines and social movements. Diane Elson's essay on 'Socialized Markets, not Market Socialism'—as opposed to market socialism, in fact, argues for a third way—a way between the plan and the market (p. 68). She argues for a vision of a future that builds upon alternatives that are rooted in current experiences, rather than on grandiose schemes of social engineering (p. 67). Kate Soper writes on 'Other Pleasures: The Attractions of Post-consumerism', arguing that utopias are necessary, among other things, as 'stimulants of desire and hence contributing to the development of new forms of political subjectivity' (p. 118). Johanna Brenner talks about 'Utopian Families', exploring the ideas of democratic community and family life—beyond the heterosexual, monogamous family. In his essay 'Outbreaks of Democracy' Ricardo Blaug provides a critique of representative democracy and attempts a reconceptualization of democracy, following Steven Wolin, as a 'mode of being' rather than as a set of institutions or a form of government. Judith Adler Hellman writes on 'Real and Virtual Chiapas: Magical Realism and the Left', while Colin Duncan presents the vision of an ecological utopia which would recover the centrality of agriculture ('The Centrality of Agriculture: History, Ecology and Feasible Socialism'). Then there are essays on health and the dystopia of modernity, on the havoc of genetic engineering technologies,

on NATO's war on Yugoslavia, on the rise of private armies in the USA. Taken together these do point to a different possibility—that of *utopias of the everyday*. They point to the possibility of thinking of that unachieved good life which does not, rather need not, await the coming of a millennial or apocalyptic moment to realize itself.

8. Terry Eagleton, 'Utopia and Its Opposites', in *Socialist Register,* 2000, p. 37, emphasis added.

9. It is not possible to enter into this question in the space of this chapter, but it certainly needs to be stated that there are many complicated layers of problems to be studied here. As Craig Calhoun's work *The Question of Class Struggle* indicates, the most militant struggles against capitalism were launched in the nineteenth century, *from the outside*, by artisans resisting incorporation in the system. Once incorporated in the system, working class struggles became more and more domesticated and concerned themselves with bargaining on economic question. Seldom did their protests challenge the system itself. The anti-colonial movements and peasant struggles too, have not yet been studied adequately in their own right—theoretically that is—but have generally been subsumed under the narrative of socialism and anti-capitalist struggles. Even the Russian revolution was, in many ways, as Gramsci notably put it, a revolution against *Das Kapital.* In a sense, a proper study of these struggles will only become possible if we stop looking at them as mere adjuncts of the history of socialism or the 'working class movement'.

10. Eagleton, op. cit., p. 37.

11. Leo Panitch and Sam Gindin 'Transcending Pessimism: Rekindling Socialist Imagination', *Socialist Register,* 2000, pp. 3-4.

12. Ibid., p. 5., emphasis added.

13. Ibid., p. 13, emphasis added.

14. Cited in Ernesto Laclau, 'Can Immanence Explain Social Struggles?', *Diacritics*, Winter 2001, vol. 31, no. 4, pp. 3-8, Baltimore.

15. For the Dalit question, see Aditya Nigam, *The Insurrection of Little Selves: The Crisis of Secular-Nationalism in India*, New Delhi: OUP, 2006, Chapter. 5; for the discussion on marxism, see Aditya Nigam, 'Marxism and the Postcolonial World: Footnotes to a Long March', *Economic and Political Weekly*, vol. 34, nos 1 and 2, 9 January 1999.

16. Naomi Klein, op. cit. p. 121.

17. The citations in this section are from pages 121-3.

18. I have discussed this at great length elsewhere and will not enter into that discussion here. Suffice it to note that throughout the period from the 1950s, when the Kaka Kalelkar Commission was constituted in the 1950s, right up to the time when the Mandal controversy errupted in all ferociousness, all upper caste claims were made in the name of 'class' and economic backwardness. The RSS position on this issue is the best example of this.

19. See Jorge G. Castaneda, *Utopia Unarmed—The Latin American Left After the Cold War*, New York: Vintage Books, 1993, pp. 92-4 for a discussion of this dynamics in Mexico and Guatemala and Forrest Hylton and Sinclair Thomson, 'The Chequered Rainbow', *New Left Review*, Sept.-Oct. 2005, pp. 41-64 for a discussion of Bolivia.

20. Unless otherwise stated, the discussion in this paragraph is based on Chapter 2.4, 'Symptoms of Passage', in Hardt and Negri, op. cit., pp. 137-59.

21. Ibid., see p. 128.

22. Ibid., p. 128.

23. Ibid., p. 190.

24. Ibid., p. 200.

25. See Mahmood Mamdani, *Citizen and Subject: Decentralized Despotism and the Legacy of Late Colonialism*, Delhi: OUP, 1997.

26. Ibid., p. 138.

27. Ibid., p. 139.

28. Ibid., pp. 146-7, emphasis added.

29. Ibid., p. 149.

30. Ibid.

31. Aziz Al-Azmeh, *Islams and Modernities*, London and New York: Verso, 1993, p. 101.

32. Maxime Rodinson, *Marxism and the Muslim World*, New Delhi: Orient Longman Ltd, 1980, p. 83.

33. Ibid., p. 54.

34. Nicholas Higgins, 'The Zapatista Uprising and the Poetics of Cultural Resistance', *Alternatives*, vol. 25, no. 3, July-Sept. 2000, pp. 359-74.

35. This phrase is taken from the subtitle of Reinhart Koselleck's well-known work; see Koselleck, *Futures Past: On the Semantics of Historical Time*, Cambridge, Massachusetts, and London: MIT Press, 1985.

36. Jawaharlal Nehru, *The Discovery of India*, New Delhi: Jawaharlal Nehru Memorial Fund & OUP (1946/82), p. 565. All emphasis added.

37. Benedict Anderson, *Imagined Communities*, London and New York: Verso, 1991, pp. 22-31.

38. See Johannes Fabian, *Time and the Other—How Anthropology Makes Its Object*, New York: Columbia University Press, 1983.

39. Here we are not discussing the physicist's notion of time though even there, time begins to be marked through notions of change, e.g. the expansion of the universe. For a fascinating discussion see, Stephen Hawking, *A Brief History of Time*, New York: Bantam, 1988.

40. For an interesting discussion see, Charles M. Sherover, *The Human Experience of Time: The Development of Its Philosophic Meaning*, New York: New York University Press, 1975. For this reference see p. 106.

41. Manuel Castells, *The Rise of Network Society. The Information Age*: Economy, *Society and Culture*, Volume I, Oxford: Blackwell Publishers, 2000, p. 494.

42. I have discussed the emergence of such different histories at greater length in Aditya Nigam, op. cit.

43. This is clearly an oversimplification of the problem, as we shall see in the brief discussion that follows.

44. Jacques Derrida, *Margins of Philosophy*, Brighton: The Harvester Press, 1982, p. 63.

45. Ibid., p. 7.

46. Ibid., p. 27.

47. Ibid., p. 27.

48. For a discussion of the constitution of the subjectivity of the colonized and the yearning for the past, see Nigam, op. cit., pp. 188-95.

# 2

# GENEALOGIES OF GLOBALIZATION

## Unpacking the 'Universal' History of Capital

With the battle over 'industrialization' in West Bengal intensifying, the CPI(M) general secretary Prakash Karat evoked the memory of a supposedly heroic marxist encounter with the narodniks in nineteenth century Russia (Karat 2007). In a note at the end of an article published in the party newspaper, Karat defines the narodniks thus:

> Narodniks in late 19th century Russia believed that with the overthrow of Tsarism, a traditional village based communal system could go towards socialism. Considering capitalism and industrialization regressive, they idealized the old peasant-village economy. Ultimately they resorted to individual terrorist actions against the Tsar and lost the sympathy of the peasants who were horrified by their actions.

This description of the narodniks is revealing in more ways than one—not the least of these being the figure of the 'maoist' or the 'naxalite' lurking somewhere in this representation of a nineteenth century Russian phenomenon in twenty-first century India. One should not miss the references to 'going over to socialism', bypassing capitalism and industrialization or to 'individual terrorist action'. Anybody even vaguely familiar with Mao's *Critique of Soviet Economics* and his insistence on China bypassing the capitalist path, should be able to see the resonance of this 'narodnik' idea in the very history of Third World marxism. The CPI(M) has always been uncomfortable with this position, but it never really mattered till recently, when it actually became a practical question.

It might be worth recalling that in the final years of the nineteenth century, Lenin had effected a final closure to that debate, arguing that capitalism and industry were inevitable (Lenin 1899/1977).

West Bengal chief minister and Polit Bureau member Buddhadeb Bhattacharya repeated the article of faith about the inevitability of industrialization and capitalism in his response to marxist historian Sumit Sarkar's critique of Bengal's industrialization policy. Bhattacharya said: 'The process of economic development evolves from agriculture to industry. The journey is from villages to cities.' In a more dramatic assertion of this faith in the historical inevitability of capitalism, he underlines that *'it is incumbent on us to move ahead, otherwise there will be the end of history'*.[1]

Let us remind ourselves that what is at work here is a certain narrative of Progress and History that derives from a certain rendering (or reading) of Marx. This narrative involves a well-entrenched notion of what we might call the 'universal history of capital'—a notion shared by both bourgeois economics and this particular brand of marxism. Economics as a discipline is of course so thoroughly constituted by capital and capitalism (which is why 'socialist economics' is destined to remain an oxymoron), that there is no way of producing an 'economically rational' argument against capital. We can leave this matter for the time being, as that is not our immediate purpose here, though this is something for any future socialist project to ponder over very seriously.[2]

It is true, however, that a very real problem faces the Left Front and the CPI(M) in West Bengal—as indeed it does the Left in South Africa, Brazil, and now many other parts of the South American continent: how to produce more livelihoods that do not merely stop at reasserting the value of simple subsistence economies. Whether wage-slavery and 'jobs' in the bourgeois sense of the term are the best option is of course, open to question. I will also insist here upon the recognition of a trivial historical fact that every child knows but no adult dare acknowledge: as far as unemployment goes, industrialization is the problem rather than the solution. Marxists apparently knew this long ago but seem to have forgotten it since. For instance, in 1938 a publication of the Communist Party of Great Britain noted: 'Unemployment is a problem as old as the industrial system itself . . . . The fact that the workers need employment in order to live finds no place in the consideration of the employing class when they hire workers.'[3] Remember the 'industrial reserve army' that Marx talked of? This all-too-obvious link between industrialization and unemployment has now been forgotten by most marxists, lost under the accumulating deposits of (bourgeois) economics, might one say? Unemployment is created by capitalism and industrialization, and yet they are blindly assumed to be the solution to a problem they necessarily create.

The problem of 'unemployment', as we will see below, is the fundamental axis around which the current crisis of the Left and of labour movements revolves. The time has come, therefore, to take a closer look at this crisis. In this chapter, I wish to argue for a re-reading of Marx as a critical historian of capital and a reassessment of his legacy. I also wish to re-read the received history of capital, in order to interrogate the common sense that has come to dominate our understanding in this respect.

## The Mobility of Capital

It may be worthwhile to remember that the current crisis has to do with *the extremely heightened mobility of capital alongside an equally extreme immobility of labour*. We have seen in our own experience how this works against labour struggles. Pre-World War II capitalism was fixed to *place* and was relatively far more immobile, given the predominance of the large factory system. Earlier successes of the working class movement were based on this fact: just like the landlord was tied to the land, so was the capitalist. The situation has changed fundamentally now with global production circuits, subcontracting and flexible forms of industrial organization.

Let me take just two instances of how this earlier immobility of capital has both affected and has been affected by the workers' movements. One, the militant workers' struggles in West Bengal in the late 1960s and early 1970s. It is well-known that it was precisely the militancy and the immediate success of those struggles that led to one of the most significant impulses for deindustrialization and massive flight of capital to relatively peaceful states elsewhere in the country. So devastating was the consequence of this flight (in terms of aggravating the unemployment situation and the weakening of even simple wage struggles) that by the time the Left Front (LF) government assumed power in 1977, it had learnt a lesson: henceforth it would rein in workers' militancy and try to lure capital back into the state. Only rapid industrialization would be able to provide jobs to the unemployed and for that capital was indispensable—so the LF and the CPI(M) argued. Consequently, capital now finds itself strong enough to dictate terms. So powerful has been the hold of this imagination that the marxist-led government of the state has decided to dispossess the peasantry and acquire huge tracts of agricultural land for making them available to capital. This is the logic that lies behind the whole range of new developments from Singur to Nandigram, which has been rehearsed once again in Bhattacharya's letter to Sarkar.

Two, take another, global example. Consider the debate on the social clause more closely. Contrary to what many marxists believe, the 'social clause' is not just an imperialist conspiracy, meant to browbeat something called the 'Indian nation'—or Third World nations—into submission. A closer look will immediately make it clear that this move of the Western governments was and is solidly backed by the trade union and labour movements in those countries. And the entire position of northern/western trade unions and left wing groups in favour of higher labour standards for Third World workers has all along been propelled by the need to prevent 'their own capital' from moving out.[4] There have been instances of extreme abjection where some sections of German workers, for example, even took wage-cuts to prevent 'their capital' from moving out to Asia.[5] When the Western governments placed the demand for including labour standards as part of international trade agreements, this was the imperative they were addressing—given the high social and political costs that heightened unemployment can have.

In both cases, the abjection of the working class was a direct consequence of its past victories. Equally importantly, it was a consequence of the flight of capital: it is worth underlining that beyond a point, capital did not fight back, it simply withdrew, it fled, and thus deprived the working class of its 'foundation', namely, wage-slavery. In a sense, the move from old-style Fordist methods of organization to post-Fordist ones has also been impelled by the same logic: it was becoming extremely expensive to keep workers employed and pay for their upkeep even in times of recession, or to keep up inventories of stocks, raw materials and so on. More to the point however, is the fact that those modes of organization tied down capital to a particular place. If capital had to acquire mobility and flexibility, then it had to restructure in a way that it could 'farm out' work and simply keep control in its own hands.

It is worth keeping in mind that through the 1970s, 1980s and early 1990s, manufacturing units relocated to Third World countries in a big way and it was only much later that services and call centres started moving out. If we look carefully we can see that in an immediate sense, this relocation was the consequence of at least three factors:

Firstly, the *profit squeeze* that capital had been facing during the post-war years of Keynesian welfarism and the New Deal, due to high wages and social security—in other words, *high labour costs*. Secondly, the intense *crisis of accumulation* that surfaced as high labour costs combined with strong environmental regulations, making corporations not only pay more (for cleaner technologies and the like) but also making them answerable to local communities for their air, water and other resources. It is important to keep in mind that *both these costs have been imposed on capital accumulation by the strength of movements*—in one case the labour movement (and the post-war attraction of the idea of socialism); in the other case, the powerful ecological movements that have made the states enact laws and take action.

There was a third factor as well, which falls chronologically speaking, between the first and the second and whose effects were first felt in the United States of America. This was the rise of Japanese corporations like Sony, Toyota and Nissan on the one hand and European corporations on the other, which created unprecedented pressures on US companies like General Motors, Ford and Chrysler—in a range of consumer manufactures leading to widespread closures and 'deindustrialization'. It is estimated that disinvestment and relocation of industries, in the 1970s alone, in the US led to the disappearance of thirty-two to thirty-eight million jobs (Bluestone 2003: ix).

And so it transpires, capital is not the sovereign, all-powerful entity that we think it is. It has acted on each of these occasions under pressure from the labour, environment and other movements. Moreover, its move to relocate operations in the Third World—where there is no infrastructure (abysmal power situation, bad roads), interfering governments and where everything becomes easily politicized—*is primarily a result of its crisis. It is fugitive capital that has run away from one part of the world.*

Yet, such is our conditioning as victims that we fail to see the strengths of the movements that challenge capital. The reason that makes the LF government of West Bengal or the communist government of China woo capital and that makes Western trade/labour unions demand universal labour standards and take wage-cuts, really happens to be the same: *the complete dependence of labour on capital.* And yet, this dependence is not a natural fact; nor is it something ordained by something called History (with a capital 'H').

## 'Universal' Capital

Let us be clear, however, that what we are dealing with here is not merely an out-of-date Indian edition of marxism which is yet to free itself from this universalist narrative of capital. This idea of capital and capitalism constitutes pretty much the dominant orthodoxies of economic and of global financial institutions. It should also be made clear at the outset that here we are concerned with the discursive object called 'capital' (and 'Capitalism'), that is the concept, rather than the thing-as-such and this concept has colonized our minds for close to two centuries. To borrow a statement from Gibson-Graham, 'it is the way capitalism is thought, that has made it so difficult for people to imagine its supersession'. I will argue that there are two different or alternative discursive constructions through which this hegemony is exercised.

First, the marxist, 'Progressivist' discourse of History and 'Capital' as its agent that unites the whole world into a new and modern universe, leaving behind the parochialisms and particularisms/narrow-mindedness of pre-capitalist existence. In this rendering, which suffuses the *Communist Manifesto* and many other marxian texts, we see capitalism performing not merely an economic function but also a world-historical one of bringing all history-less peoples and societies into the orbit of history and civilization.

Second, the bourgeois economist discourse, which makes no such world-historical claim, but bestows a kind of eternal quality to 'capital' and the 'market'. In this construction, capital and market (used as terms that *necessarily* go together) appear as the most *rational* forms of economy: market as the embodiment of economic and indeed some ontological Rationality. In some versions, it will even be claimed that these are the most natural forms as well, since they conform to a 'natural' human propensity to maximize self-interest.

Both these discourses underwrite 'Capital' as the Agent of Historical Progress and/or normatively desirable in different ways. For the present, I shall be concerned here with the first of these, assuming that the second does not really require any serious challenging except for those—capitalists and their hangers-on—who benefit from this dispensation. There are elements of the second discourse that will automatically come under scrutiny as we proceed with the first.

The idea of capitalism's inevitability virtually assumes the dimension of a Teleology whose enchantment or seduction is impossible to resist—especially for marxists. So much has this teleology come to determine our idea of capitalism that we literally begin to see capitalism as immanent in society from its very beginnings—the very day human beings begin to enter into relations of exchange.

Thus for instance, Fernand Braudel states: 'I have argued that capitalism has been potentially visible *since the dawn of history*, and that it has developed and perpetuated itself down the ages . . . .' (cited in Lachmann 2002: 44). Referring to the 'Industrial Revolution' and the 'formidable transformation' wrought by it, he claims that 'capitalism remained essentially true to itself' and what Marx, Weber and their successors describe as the beginnings of capitalism in sixteenth-century England was really no more than a 'shift . . . from the Mediterranean to the North Sea represent[ing] the victory of a new region over an old one' (Lachmann 2002: 43).

It is interesting that not merely someone like Braudel but even those who have lately been involved in writing alternative histories of capitalism, seriously challenging the received Eurocentric wisdom of Marx, his contemporaries and his followers, have resorted to this narrative of capitalism as a sign of Progress and Modernity. Thus, for John M. Hobson it is not enough to make the important claim that from CE 500 onwards, 'the Persians, Arabs, Africans, Japanese, Jews, Indians and Chinese created and maintained a global economy down to about 1800', in which major civilizations of the world were at all times interlinked (hence his term 'oriental globalization'). It is also not enough to underline that during this earlier globalization, the various regions were governed by rulers who provided a pacified environment and kept transit taxes low in order to facilitate global trade. It is as though it is almost mandatory to also claim that many of the methods and institutions that were put in place for ensuring the above were *capitalist*. Thus he goes on to say: '*a whole series of sufficiently rational capitalist institutions were created and put in place after 500 to support global trade.*' (32, emphasis added). Hobson cites Janet Abu-Lughod to underline the above point: 'Distances as measured by time, were calculated in weeks and months at best, but it took years to traverse the entire [global] circuit. And yet goods were transferred, prices set, exchange rates agreed upon, contracts entered into, credit—on funds or on goods located elsewhere—extended, partnerships formed, and obviously records kept and agreements honoured' (32). And this is said as though it is self-evident that these are the signs of capitalism.

Let me take another instance, nearer home. Jairus Banaji, in a fascinating recent essay, 'Islam, the Mediterranean and the Rise of Capitalism', undertakes, it seems to me, a twofold task: (i) that of writing an *international* history of capitalism and thereby rescuing it from what Paul Sweezy once accused Maurice Dobb of, namely, passing off the West European transition experience as the history of (world) capitalism as such. (ii) Equally importantly, rescuing Islam from the West-imposed stigma of being a 'backward' religion. In doing so, Banaji traces the history of 'mercantile capitalism' in the Arab world through the ninth to the fourteenth centuries in order to show that Islam and the Islamic world was indeed a pioneer of capitalism, for that alone would rescue it from the stigma of backwardness. He therefore says: 'But when these joint-stock companies [i.e. the Dutch and English East India Companies] were formed on the eve of the seventeenth century, they in turn built on the legacies of earlier and possibly less internationalized forms of merchant capitalism whose origins lie—in Europe around the twelfth century, and elsewhere—in the Islamic world and China—even earlier.' Continuing further on the 'Arab Trade Empire', Banaji says:

> Concepts of profit, capital, and the accumulation of capital are all found in the Arabic sources of the 9th to 14th centuries. For example, Shāfi'ī (d. 820) defines the function of partnership as the 'expansion of capital' (*namā' al-māl*). *Al-māl* was primarily capital not money, and whenever it is translated as 'money' it means capital in money-form or money-capital. Again, discussing the discretion allowed to agents under *commenda* agreements, Sarakhsī (d. 1090) writes, 'the investor's aim in handing over the capital to him [the agent] is the achievement of profit'. In another passage where he defends the usefulness of such contracts, Sarakhsī says the contract is allowed 'Because people have a need for this contract. For the owner of capital may not find his way to profitable trading activity, and the person who can find his way to such activity may not have the capital. And profit cannot be attained except by means of both of these, capital and trading activity'. A later writer Kāsānī (d. 1191) distinguishes the 'creation of capital' from its further expansion, arguing 'the need for the creation of capital takes precedence over the need for its augmentation' and defining partnerships as a 'method for augmenting or creating capital' (*tarīq namā'al-māl aw taḥṣīlihi*).

Banaji claims further that the fact that 'this vocabulary was part of the wider cultural world of Islam and not confined to the legal schools is shown by other writings'. He cites the tenth-century geographer al-Iṣṭakhrī as saying of the traders of Fars in southern Persia that they had a 'passion for the accumulation of capital' (*maḥabbat jam'a al-māl*). 'In the *Kitāb al-ishāra ilā maḥāsin al-tijāra*, "Handbook on the beauties of commerce", a manual on trade probably written in the 11th century, the author refers repeatedly to the capitalist as *ṣāḥib al-māl* ("owner of capital")'. Banaji even finds, in Ibn Khaldūn (d. 1405), 'a clear resonance of the labour theory of value (or *a* labour theory of value)'. According to him, in the *Muqaddimah*, vol. 2, Ibn Khaldūn states clearly, 'labor is the cause of profit' (*sabab al-kasb*). '[H]uman labor is necessary for every profit and capital accumulation', while gold and silver are the only socially acceptable measures of value 'for all capital accumulations'. He also defines profit (*ribḥ*) as the 'extent by which capital increases' (or is increased), and commerce as the 'striving for profit by means of the expansion of capital' (*muḥāwala ilā al-kasb bi-tanmiyat al-māl*).

Banaji's problem, however, is that marxism has no theory of commercial capitalism. That capitalism to it *remains industrial capitalism*. This is what prevents it from recognizing the world-historical role of Islam: 'Thus Islam made a *powerful contribution to the growth of capitalism in the Mediterranean*, in part because it preserved and expanded the monetary economy of late antiquity and innovated business techniques that became the staple of Mediterranean commerce (in particular, partnerships and commenda agreements), and also because the seaports of the Muslim world became a rich source of the plundered money-capital which largely financed the growth of maritime capitalism in Europe.' In this essay, written in honour of marxist economist Ernest Mandel, Banaji cites Mandel himself to the effect that 'the accumulation of money-capital by the Italian merchants who dominated European economic life from the eleventh to the fifteenth centuries originated directly from the Crusades, an enormous plundering enterprise if ever there was one'. In Mandel's and Banaji's description then, we find another kind of 'primitive accumulation'—not one based on the expropriation of the peasant but one based on loot during the crusades. It is Banaji's argument that only if marxism is amended in a way that allows for a broader understanding of capitalism than industrial capitalism, in other words, one that can incorporate mercantile or commercial activities of the previous centuries, into the history of capitalism, can there be any possibility of rescuing either Islam or even the non-European world from ascriptions of 'backwardness'.

In other words, in what I consider to be the absolutely crucial and important work of these scholars, there is an assumption that we in the postcolonial world must claim some kind of capitalism in our own history in order to challenge the accusation of backwardness. In the bargain, we might of course, broaden capitalism to mean so many things that the very term seems to me to lose its specificity.

## What is Capitalism?

We have seen Hobson's and Janet Abu-Lughod's argument that there existed a global economy for many centuries prior to the rise of Western hegemony. In Hobson's words, 'the key development' was the emergence of a series of interlinked world empires that enabled a broadly peaceful environment, conducive to global trade. In his opinion: 'The rise of T'ang China (618-907), the Islamic Ummayad/Abbasid empire in the Middle East (661-1258), as well as the Fatamids in North Africa (909-1171) were crucial to the emergence of a sufficiently extensive global trading network.' He cites Philip Curtin to underline that 'the simultaneous power of the Abbasids and the T'ang made it comparatively easy for long distance traders to make the whole journey across Asia and North Africa'. He also references the work of Jack Goody, Andre' Wink and Nigel Harris to state that 'global connections went as far back as 3500 BC, and insists that all agree that the big expansion of global trade occurred during the post-600 period' (35).

Writing of China, Hobson says, 'China's "industrial miracle" occurred over a period of 1500 years and culminated in the Sung revolution—some *six hundred years before Britain entered its industrialization phase.*' He goes on: 'The Chinese industrial miracle is worth focusing upon in some detail because it was the single most important event in the history of global intensive power between 1100 and 1800. For it was the diffusion of the many Sung Chinese technological and ideational breakthroughs that significantly informed the rise of the West.' (51)

Among these technological and ideational breakthroughs, Hobson mentions the development of iron and steel technology (600 BCE to CE 1100); water borne transportations through canals; use of petroleum and natural gas as fuels; creation of a tax system based on cash; invention of paper money in the ninth century, which evolved into 'true' paper money by the tenth century; paper and print technology; a general rise of a commercialized economy. (54)

Hobson also buttresses his point by invoking Francis Bacon on the antecedents of the 'navigational revolution' to the effect that the three most important world discoveries, those of printing, gunpowder and the compass were all invented in China. Noteworthy too, he says, citing Bacon, is the fact that it were the Chinese who discovered around AD 1000 that magnetic north and true north were not one and the same, which led, by the fifteenth century, to the construction of the most accurate maps then known. (57)

The point I wish to underline here is this—the development of trade, technology and the knowledge that it presupposes, the invention of paper money or an elaborate taxation system—none of these are necessarily specific to capitalism. It is possible to have all these and not have capitalism. Taxation, more specifically, is a matter related to statecraft. I wish to argue that what was specific to capitalism as we know it, was a particular development that took place in eighteenth-nineteenth century Europe—in the same milieu that gave birth to both bourgeois economics and marxism. This was *the disembedding of markets and the economy from social relations*—the emergence of what Karl Polanyi calls the 'self-regulating market' that transforms land and labour into commodities up for sale in the market. It is, in other words, a reification of the market, its elevation to something that stands above society and social relations and establishes thereby a different relationship with production, state, money wealth and so on. This development is of course impossible without the institution of the bourgeois property form—the individual owner whose wealth and property is meant primarily for exchange, investment and accumulation. The reified market can exist only to the extent that bourgeois property has taken root.

The emergence of this new configuration transforms the very logic of production, irrespective of whether it can actually transform the organization of production. Once this happens, production increasingly takes place for the 'world market' rather than for local/domestic consumption. This is an altogether new development that even high levels of trade, exchange and industry of the past did not do. The problem with the fascinating accounts discussed earlier is that they all tend to reduce all the earlier history of enterprise, industry and exchange to the realm of the pre-history of capitalism. Capitalism remains the immanent Telos, the destiny; and all these different episodes from non-Western history can only acquire legitimacy if they can be shown to tend towards capitalism and through it, towards Universal History.

Marxists have celebrated the demise of the old world and the complete victory of capitalism. This means that all other ways of life and modes of living are destroyed, installing capital as the only form of property (ownership)—thus also as the only employer. The only other form of ownership that has been thought about—state ownership—is, of course, a model that has come to be in serious crisis, apart from being implicated in totalitarian political structures. The state as owner and employer is, also for very sound economic reasons, not a viable proposition. However, from our point of view, the really relevant point here is the first one: what is it that authorizes (or legitimizes) such a celebration of the destruction of all other ways of life and modes of being and the reduction of the entire world to the logic of wage-slavery? The answer to this question provided by both neo-liberals and marxists is very much the same: it lies in this very idea of historical inevitability, the idea that there is a Universal History that has already played itself out in the West that we cannot but repeat here. We might be prepared now to argue that the history of modernity is not one; that there are alternative trajectories, indeed alternative modernities but when it comes to the history of capitalism, we are still overpowered by this idea, thanks in no small measure to Marx himself, the chief historian and theorist of capitalism. That is an idea I wish to unpack here. Not the least because, just when marxists thought they had defeated the narodniks, the ghost of narodism would begin to track them and follow them, right into the twenty-first century—arising now within the marxist or socialist universe itself.

## Primitive Accumulation and the Law of History

Since the onset of globalization, a lot of writings by marxists have rehearsed and cited many times over, the celebrated passages from the *Communist Manifesto*, where Marx and Engels talk about the 'revolutionary' role of capital in exhilarated terms. Recall those famous passages where they talk of 'all that is holy is profaned' and 'all that is solid melts into air'; the passage where they claim that the 'bourgeoisie cannot live without constantly revolutionizing the means of production' and of 'building a world in its own image'. The triumphalism of a certain nineteenth century understanding of capitalism that sees the whole world being rapidly modernized in the same way as was Western Europe, is palpably evident in these passages. And this is what has been canonized as marxist orthodoxy over the last century and a half or more. However, as is known today, at least some fragments of an alternative reading of this history are also available in Marx. Let me follow that alternative reading for a while in order to lay out the contours of my argument.

In this alternative reading, let us underline that the rise of capitalism is not the result of an inexorable historical law of Progress that must be celebrated. Marx opens his discussion of primitive accumulation, in the last section of *Capital, Volume One*, by asserting that the origins of capitalist private property lie in '*conquest, enslavement, robbery, murder*'.

He describes the process of primitive accumulation as '[T]he process . . . that clears the way for the capitalist system . . . [and] takes away from the labourer the possession of the means of production', as 'a process that transforms, on the one hand, the social means of subsistence and of production into capital, on the other, the immediate producers into wage-labourers.'

This so-called primitive accumulation, he asserts, is nothing else but the historical process of divorcing the producer from the means of production. Marx recognizes that while this process frees the serfs 'from serfdom and from the fetters of the guilds', it simultaneously produces this new form of enslavement and dispossession. He pours scorn over 'our bourgeois historians' who recognize only the emancipatory side of this process. In other words, even when he sees the emancipatory dimensions of Progress and Development, his moral revulsion against the violence and injustice of this process remains apparent. Thus his indignation: 'the history of their expropriation, is written in the annals of mankind in letters of blood and fire'.

In the rest of the discussion, Marx takes up the specific case of England for discussion. It is important that through this reading of English history, he lays bare the way in which capitalism came to its own through the forcible dispossession of the erstwhile peasant communities. Unfortunately, once again, he universalizes that process with disastrous consequences but let us leave that aside for the time being. He traces the history of the usurpation of common lands first by individual feudal lords through the late fifteenth and early sixteenth centuries. The eighteenth century marks a fundamental change in the process, in Marx's perception. While the fifteenth and sixteenth centuries saw the process being carried on through individual acts of violence, the 'advance made by the 18th century shows itself in this, that *the law itself becomes the instrument of the theft of the people's land*'. This is embodied in the Acts of parliament for the enclosure of the Commons.

By the time we reach the nineteenth century, he remarks, 'the very memory of the connection between the agricultural labourer and the communal property had vanished'. The so-called 'clearing of estates' is then described by him as the 'last process of wholesale expropriation of the agricultural population from the soil'.

There is a ring of the surreal, as one feels in his reflections on nineteenth century England the reverberations of twenty-first century Bengal: 'To say nothing of more recent times, have the agricultural population received a farthing of compensation for the 3,511,770 acres of common land which between 1801 and 1831 were stolen from them and by parliamentary devices presented to the landlords by the landlords?'

Let us underline that the purpose of this exercise of reading Marx and his rendition of English history is not meant to uncover some ostensible Universal History in operation. On the contrary, it is to underline that once presented as Universal History by Marx and his generation, it becomes a self-fulfilling logic. Thereafter, marxists can only act in one way that is commensurate with this logic; every other way is deemed to be reactionary and against the logic of History. What we will need to excavate from the debris of the political practice of the past two centuries is the manner in which the belief in certain logic of History, operating as Scientific Knowledge, already laid out the contours within which one could act.

Marx also goes on to discuss the ways in which, from the end of the fifteenth century onwards, bloody legislations were enacted to keep the displaced population in check. The population which was rendered destitute was 'disciplined and normalized', to use a Foucauldian expression, through these laws. The 'free' proletariat, created by the 'forcible expropriation of the people from the soil', which 'could not be absorbed by the nascent manufactures as fast as it was thrown upon the world', was turned '*en masse* into beggars, robbers, vagabonds, partly from inclination, in most cases from the stress of circumstances'.

## Marx and the Crisis of Universal History

Marx certainly cannot be exonerated from the responsibility of having produced the Universal History of capitalism that we are, in a sense, reeling under. However, this was only one side of Marx. Already in 1853, while he was working on and producing this Universal History, he found himself caught in a deep bind—that of explaining the irreducible heterogeneity of the world in his time. Following Eric Hobsbawm's interpretation of the *Grundrisse (1857-58)*, as outlining a 'non-consecutive' map of historical development that allowed for 'three or four alternative routes out of primitive communal systems', Teodor Shanin suggests that Marx was 'already aware' of the difficulties of this universalism and had therefore 'worked out and put to use concepts of Oriental Despotism and of the Asiatic Mode of Production' (AMP).[6] Of course, these were conceptual devices of trying to account for the heterogeneity of 'past', 'pre-capitalist' forms. In the end, Marx's position at this time would be to argue that capitalism would, as the first truly universal system, bring in these 'societies without history' into the orbit of World-History. The future was still One—all societies inevitably moving inexorably towards the *telos*, the final goal.

The very concepts of Oriental Despotism and the Asiatic Mode of Production refer back to a Eurocentric and in some ways an Asian-exceptionalist view of History. The notions of Time and World-History that were dominant and which he received from Hegel, provided an excellent way out of the problem posed by this irreducible heterogeneity, by suggesting that these societies represented 'past forms' that were to soon go out of existence.

More to the point is the strange episode of Marx's encounter with the Russian peasant communes first through some fortuitous circumstances and then more directly through Vera Zasulich and the Russian Marxists. The latter were involved in a furious debate with the narodniks who did not merely celebrate these past forms, but as Karat rightly concedes, *posed the question of their becoming the basis of a socialist future*. Teodor Shanin remarks that already in the *Grundrisse*, Marx had shown indications of taking peasant agriculture and 'communal land ownership' in 'pre-capitalist modes of production' and the problem of 'uneven development' seriously (14-15). What is crucially important is that this quest was not resolved in one fell swoop. It pre-occupied him more and more and in 1870-1, he started learning Russian and immersed himself in a study of the Russian social formation, including the writings of such narodnik theorists such as Chernyshevskii and others like Alexander Herzen. Shanin remarks that 'what followed was a long silence . . . Marx did not publish anything substantial until his death' (7). This, we might underline, was also the period of his intensive study of India and other Oriental societies.[7]

It was in this frame of mind, ten years into his studies, that he received in 1881, a letter from Vera Zasulich, a former narodnik turned marxist. As mentioned earlier, this group of marxists was engaged in a serious controversy with the narodniks over the inevitability of capitalism in Russia and of the significance of the peasant communes to the socialist project. Zasulich therefore wrote to Marx seeking his opinion on the matter. Japanese scholar Haruki Wada has unearthed the entire sequence of events around this episode.[8] Marx wrote four drafts of a reply to Zasulich but ended up not sending any. Finally, after his death, Engels sent the fourth draft to the Emancipation of Labour Group to which Zasulich belonged and which was led among others, by Plekhanov and P. B. Axelrod. The letter was never published, even though after as long as seven months, they replied to Engels that they would, now that the letter had been translated into Russian.

All of Engels' efforts went in vain. In 1911, the letter was discovered by D. B. Riazanov, who deciphered it with the help of Bukharin but then, once again it was left unpublished. In 1923, it was published by B. I. Nikolaevskii, a Menshevik in exile. Once it was published, it was immediately brought out that very year by Riazanov, where he prefaced it with a remark that 'the drafts merely exemplified a decline in Marx's scholastic capability'. It was the Socialist-Revolutionaries who enthusiastically picked it up as evidence that 'on the question of the future of the peasant communes, Marx was definitely on the side of Populism' (Wada 1983: 41-2).

Wada notes, in this context, that even at the time of the publication of the first volume of *Capital*, Marx's attitude towards Russian populism and the peasant communes was utterly negative. According to Wada, Marx viewed Herzen's contention that the peasant commune was unique to the Slavic world, as simply laughable (Wada 1983: 43). He cites Marx as saying that 'Everything, *to the minutest details*, is completely the same as in the ancient Germanic community . . . .' By the time the French edition of *Capital* was published in 1875, however, Wada notes that there was an interesting change. In this edition, in Chapter 26, 'The Secret of Primitive Accumulation' Marx struck out a passage about the expropriation of the agricultural producers which gave a sense of a more universal history and in its stead wrote: 'it has been accomplished in final form only in England . . . but *all other countries of Western Europe* are going through the same movement.' Thus, Wada suggests, Marx allowed for the possibility that Eastern Europe and Russia might not be following the same trajectory (ibid.: 49).

## Retarded Capitalism

It is in the 1960s and 1970s that this theme of capitalism in the peripheries or the Third World comes to the fore and the debate on the AMP is resumed. Unfortunately, the entire story of this episode was eventually brought to light in English much later. The 1960s debate, except in Japan, remained by and large untouched by the knowledge of this important engagement. Thus for instance, Susanne D. Mueller could argue in the *Socialist Register* as late as in 1980, writing on 'Retarded capitalism in Tanzania', that it was the 'reactionary utopianism of Russia's Narodniks' that Lenin had effectively demolished a hundred years ago, that was being 'institutionalized' and 'labelled as socialism' by Nyerere.[9] It is interesting that Mueller's critique of Tanzanian 'socialism' was that the state, in the name of socialism, was acting 'to forestall the development of a bourgeoisie and a proletariat by basing accumulation on the expansion of middle-peasant household production' (Mueller 1980: 203). Even more interesting is her assertion (which she underlines by citing another marxist scholar of Africa, M. P. Cowen) that 'by forestalling "the direct separation of household producers from their means of production", the State has "fettered the accumulation of indigenous capital within smallholding production"' (ibid.: 203). Lest we miss the point, it should be underlined that what is being lamented here is precisely the attempt to preserve the property of the peasantry, even if that meant 'fettering accumulation' within 'smallholding production'. This reading of Tanzania's specific history is predicated upon a desire for the replay of European history and is clearly unable to ask the question as to what the Tanzanian leadership might have been doing with the idea of socialism. In claiming that 'capitalism, exploitation, classes and class struggle' were 'a unique product of Western colonialism' (ibid.: 206), was Nyerere possibly trying to do something else—say argue that the bourgeois notion of property was really not commensurate with notions of property or the socio-political conditions extant in Africa? Could his insistence that self-reliance, via a strengthening of the 'already socialistic' traditional economy have been something more than merely 'cultural' in a narrow sense?[10] Was his insistence and Mueller's attempt to draw a parallel with the narodniks, ironically, not very far off the mark, in that case? One could read similar anxieties into the experiments undertaken in China under Mao Tse-tung, which attempted to find a balance between 'ten major relationships', which included most centrally, that between agriculture and industry. The slogan of 'walking on two legs', in retrospect, was an attempt to avoid the violent decimation of agriculture and populations dependent on it. Those experiments may have failed, sometimes disastrously, but they nevertheless signal in a direction that 'scientifically' inclined marxists have tended to ignore. Much like Chernyshevskii who argued that Russia could benefit from the 'relative advantages of its backwardness', Mao too emphasized that the fact that the Chinese people were 'poor and blank' could be to China's advantage. Hence his argument, much like that of the narodniks', that China could avoid the capitalist path and pass on to socialism directly. It is true that the attempts to build steel furnaces in backyards in villages, undertaken during the Great Leap Forward, were completely misplaced and ended up as a disaster. However, the logic of that attempt was clearly to find a more decentralized model of development, and one where the peasants themselves would become capitalists—a bit like Nyerere's Tanzania. It is also very easy to dismiss the violent and genocidal Pol Pot regime without further ado but the question that the Cambodian tragedy poses too, may linger for a very long time. For once again the desire to inscribe 'socialism' (that is, anti-capitalism, embodied in the abolition of money and market relations) in ancient Khmer glory seems to underline another violent rejection of bourgeois property relations. All these instances are indicative of the fact that the so-called Universal History of capital and its self-fulfilling logic may have produced anti-capitalism in more forms than we recognize; they are also indicative of the fact that this logic may not be all that universal after all.

We also know that during the 1960s and 1970s, there was another very significant debate that raged among marxists—the debate on 'underdevelopment', that argued from within a marxist universe that capitalism does not necessarily produce capitalism and development everywhere. The name of Andre Gunder Frank is associated with the position that 'underdevelopment' in the peripheries was not simply a 'lack' of development; that it was rather the product of 'development' in the centre/metropolises. Undoubtedly, in those debates, there was a tone of lament in the fact that capitalist development in the countries in the periphery could not take off or was arrested due to structural connections with the metropolises. But that is precisely the point that interests us here: capitalist development did not simply emerge everywhere out of some inexorable law of history. Even a few centuries of colonial expansion could not really succeed in implanting it everywhere in the world, though colonization did fundamentally alter the logic of integration of colonized economies into the so-called 'world economy'.

More recent historians of capitalism have thus made the point that 'the transition [from pre-capitalist forms to capitalism] is too long to have any real meaning as a transition . . . .'[11] They recall the early critiques by Ernesto Laclau and Robert Brenner of Andre Gunder Frank and Wallerstein, where Laclau, for instance, argued that 'although capitalist relations of exchange had been universalized across the globe since the sixteenth century, capitalist relations of production were much more unevenly distributed, having a far denser presence in the core than in the periphery'. This problem of large parts of the world, deeply integrated and implicated into a world market and yet resistant to a transformation of the actual mode or organization of capitalist production has dogged marxist thought right from Marx's own time. We know that this problem was sought to be explained through the distinction between 'formal' subsumption of labour under capital (e.g. integration into the world market) and 'real' subsumption (reorganization of production along capitalist relations). The idea was used to argue that the whole world, once integrated into capitalist exchange relations, is already irrevocably capitalist; it is thus a matter of time before this formal subsumption is transformed into real subsumption. At one level therefore, this conceptual device helped to mask the very provincial, Western European origin of capitalism and produce it as a Universal norm. Thus it was the rest of the world—more than three fourths of it that refused to obey the supposed Universal norm of capitalist development—that remained the 'exception' that required explanation.

If this was a way of understanding the 'lack' of capitalist development in the so-called peripheries of the world-system, how exactly was development explained, where it did take place? We know that in many of the late-industrializing countries of the 'periphery', it was the state that built capitalism and virtually produced a capitalist class. Here again, the project of building capitalism was the project of a state elite that believed that that was the only way to be in the modern world. To explain the rise of state capitalism in states like Brazil and South Korea, marxist as well as non-marxist scholars influenced by marxism deployed the notion of the 'relative autonomy of the state' (Fox 1980; Amsden 1990). This 'relative autonomy' was defined by E. V. K. Fitzgerald in Brazil's context as a 'state's capacity to take action against the interests of any one fraction of capital (or even of national capital as a whole at any one point in time) in order to promote the long-run survival and expansion of capitalism as a social formation'.[12] Alice Amsden's study of South Korea shows that were it not for the state, there would neither be capitalism nor a bourgeoisie; it was the state that put the country on the high road to capitalism.[13] And we know today that where the 'state' as such failed to spawn and develop capitalism, international financial institutions, especially the IMF and the World Bank, and lately, the WTO, have played that role of transplanting notions (and institutions) of property and market that are commensurate with industrial capitalism. And yet, despite these direct interventions, not to speak of a few centuries of direct colonial rule, capitalism has not yet managed to entrench itself in large parts of the world.

## Decentring Capital

However, capitalism as a universal phenomenon continues to structure our understanding of history till this day, partly because not enough has emerged so far by way of producing alternative histories of capitalism that put its rise in perspective. Concepts or formulations such as 'retarded capitalism', 'dependent capitalism', 'arrested development' simultaneously produced capitalism as the norm and the histories of the periphery as histories of Lack, in much the same way as our modernity is a history of Lack—always waiting to be incorporated into the 'full-blooded bourgeois' order. That the exception/s were spread over such a large part of the world was not of any consequence in reconsidering the premises of the theory itself. In fact, throughout the world, marxists were debating about the potentialities of capitalist development in their respective societies before colonialism came along and stunted that growth.

It is interesting in this context, to revisit the well-known Maurice Dobb-Paul Sweezy transition debate and find the latter insisting that what Dobb refers to as the 'classic' form of feudalism, would be better described as West European feudalism. It is also interesting to see that in this debate on the transition (origins of capitalism), we can see the difficulties encountered by the protagonists in maintaining a logic of the evolution of the feudal mode into the capitalist mode of production. Thus Sweezy says: 'The transition from feudalism to capitalism is thus not a single uninterrupted process—similar to the transition from capitalism to socialism—but is made up of *two quite distinct phases* which present radically different problems and require to be analysed separately.'[14] Those familiar with the debate might recall that Sweezy was trying here to emphasize that 'feudalism in Western Europe was already moribund' *before* capitalism was born. His argument was that the growth of commodity production had already 'undermined feudalism' and that there was a prolonged intervening period of 'precapitalist commodity production', before capitalism actually came into existence.

Whether one agrees with this analysis or not, one must recognize this disjunction that Sweezy seeks to register. Maurice Dobb did not fundamentally disagree with Sweezy on the point that this period between the fourteenth and sixteenth centuries was a period of transition—even if he would resist the suggestion that it was neither feudal nor capitalist.

We need to also remind ourselves that the concept of the mode of production became, in the practice of marxist theory, more and more difficult to sustain, precisely for the reasons outlined by Sweezy and not quite contested by Dobb himself, namely, the prolonged coexistence of different 'modes' within the same time-space. Thus was invented the concept of the social formation—the actually existing form that expressed an articulation of more than one mode of production. What Sweezy and Dobb agree was a two-century long transition in Western Europe, would appear to be an endless one, if one were to look at the 'world-system' as a whole. A closer look thus reveals that this process of the 'rise of capitalism' is rather contingent and not a universal law.

If theoretical marxism remained entrapped, by and large, within the self-fulfilling logic of this Universal History, practical marxism did struggle to find a way out, as we saw in the instance of Mao. While the revolutionary struggles of the twentieth century broke out invariably in the colonial world as peasant insurrections, theoretical marxism, especially in the West and the former Soviet Union, started expressing deep unease at this 'corruption' of marxism by 'peasant consciousness'. Any number of studies of that period that deal with the Chinese and Vietnamese revolutions can be cited as evidence of this fact. Not only did Western and Soviet marxism take this route, even the doctrinal variants adopted by many Third World movements [for instance the CPI(M) in India], continued to see their own existence as a sort of illegitimate child of a backward society.

Theoretically speaking, it was in the writings of Louis Althusser and Etienne Balibar, who were among the very few Western marxists to have taken Mao seriously, that the entire question of the history of capital and the question of so-called survivals of 'past forms' was reopened in some essays in *For Marx* and later in *Reading Capital*. Balibar's essay in *Reading Capital* argues persuasively, on the basis of his reading of the *Grundrisse*, that capitalism arises out of the contingent conjunction of two independent and discrete histories—that of free labour and that of capital or 'men with money'. In other words, Balibar suggests that it is not the 'feudal mode of production' that evolves into the 'capitalist mode', but the different elements that comprise the 'structure' called capitalism, that come together to form capitalism.[15] It is thus the history of the elements that one must look at rather than the history of the structure. Althusser returns to this question in his elaboration of his 'philosophy of the Encounter' and poses the question explicitly as one of the contingency of capitalism.

In the *Philosophy of the Encounter*, Althusser returns with a different gaze as he scans the history of capitalism in Europe and Marx's understanding of it. Commenting on the coming together of labour and capital and their 'taking hold', he says: 'We can go even further and suppose that this encounter occurred several times in History before taking hold in the West', as happened at least once in the thirteenth and fourteenth century Italian states. 'The elements do not exist in history,' he says, 'so that the mode of production may exist, *they exist in a "floating" state prior to their "accumulation" and "combination"*, each being the product of its own history . . . .' (Althusser 2006: 198)

In the light of his new philosophy Althusser reads the problematic, teleological parts in Marx as arising out of a conflation of the accomplished fact (capitalism) with its taking-hold or being accomplished—that is, the process of becoming capitalism. This conflation, he suggests, results in seeing the structure as preceding its elements and reproducing them. For the late Althusser, capitalism is never a fully accomplished fact. It is thus from this angle that he reads the chapters on primitive accumulation and finds them already coloured by the teleology of capitalism's inevitability—even though he considers it to be the 'true heart' of *Capital.* He goes on to suggest: 'Here we witness the emergence of the historical phenomenon whose result we know—the expropriation of the means of production from an entire rural population in Great Britain—but whose causes bear no relation to the results and its effects.' The element of contingency and uncertainty arises from the fact that we do not really know what the reason for this expropriation was. That it was eventually diverted by the 'owners of money' looking for impoverished manpower, appears to him as rather accidental and the mark of the non-teleology of this process.

The other interesting question that Althusser raises is regarding the 'owners of money': where does their money come from? It could it be usury, colonial pillage or mercantile capitalism, he ruminates. But it is the phenomenon of mercantile capitalism that is, according to him, a great mystery—a capitalism before the emergence of a capitalist mode of production and the exploitation of free wage-labour. This riddle of the bourgeoisie, 'this strange class—capitalist by virtue of its future, but formed well before any kind of capitalism, under feudalism—known as the bourgeoisie' is something that intrigues him.

If these are the kind of questions that can be asked with reference to Europe—and there are any number of historical investigations that substantiate Althusser's questions—what about the so-called Third World? What if, after the Late Althusser, we now ask, why must all exchange relations, and money be necessarily seen as part of some prehistory of capital? The fact that there are relations of exchange need not at all imply existence of any form of capitalism. Exchange, entrepreneurship and by extension, market and money have been present in fairly ancient societies too and are not linked to capitalism in any way. This is a question, we might do well to remember, that intrigues and puzzles Marx too. Merchant 'capital' does not always sit easily with capitalism and we could recall the oft-quoted discussion conducted by Marx in *Capital Volume Three*, of the phenomenon and how it could in fact, even impede the growth of industrial capital. This is not the place for an extended discussion of mercantile capitalism. Suffice it to say that a lot more lies buried beneath its history than is visible to the 'naked eye'; a history that is yet to be excavated once the deposits of the teleology of industrial capital's supremacy are done away with. We might then be able to see the existence of markets, exchange and entrepreneurship in their own right, not merely as the pre-history of capital. We might then be able to see why newer, post-capitalist forms of property and ownership need not be predicated on a dissolution or decimation of either individual ownership, or indeed common property. We could very easily imagine a society with large sectors of agricultural production that works in tandem with a certain kind of industry, rather than one dominated by an abstract thing called Industry—irrespective of whether it produces poison, nuclear hazards or automobiles—which can only arise by decimating agriculture.

## Capitalist Property, Private Property and Common Property

We cannot however, conclude our argument in this chapter without referring to more recent theorizations of property by the ideologues of capital. In a strangely perverse way, they lead us to a very interesting insight into the contemporary crisis of capital as well as to the difficulties of instituting bourgeois property rights as the sole form of ownership. I am thinking here of Hernando de Soto, whose work has provided new impetus to international financial institutions like the IMF and the World Bank as well as to a whole new range of NGOs, obsessed with the idea of instituting formal property titles and 'documenting' all property into deeds. The Title of Hernando de Soto's book is telling: *The Mystery of Capital - Why capitalism Triumphs in the West and Fails Everywhere Else.* As the title itself shows, the book investigates what it sees as capitalism's colossal failure ('failed everywhere'). What de Soto means by this 'failure' of course, is precisely that the bourgeois property form has failed to take root everywhere, *frustrated by the modes of living and being in the Third World*:

> Imagine a country where the law that governs property rights is so deficient that nobody can easily identify who owns what, addresses cannot be systematically verified, and people cannot be made to pay their debts.

> Consider not being able to use your own house or business to guarantee credit. Imagine a property system where you can't divide your ownership in a business into shares that investors can buy, or where descriptions of assets are not standardized.

This, in de Soto's view, is the general picture of life in the 'developing world,' home to five-sixths of the world's population. He believes that life in these parts of the world shows how, contrary to the Western perception that sees capitalism as the answer to global underdevelopment, *it hasn't even been tried* here yet. For, 'in a capitalist economy, all business deals are based on the rules of property and transactions which do not even exist in the Third World. Their property systems exclude the assets and transactions of 80 per cent of the population, cutting off the poor from the global capitalist economy as markedly as apartheid once separated black and white South Africans.'

This last bit might lead us to believe, as it has misled many well meaning NGOs, that the intention here is to draw the poor into the charmed circle of development. 'The poor's assets can also be legally titled and the potential capital trapped inside can be released,' he says. Nothing of the sort is actually intended. The real problem, it seems, is that capitalism has entered a serious crisis, largely because, in most of the world it does not have the kind of 'market' it wants. This is a very specific market; not a market of consumer goods.

This is best understood in de Soto's own rendering. Some years ago, Hernando de Soto was invited by the Indonesian government to advise it on identifying the assets of the overwhelming majority of Indonesians living in the 'extralegal sector'—said to account, according to him, to close to 90 per cent of the population. Though no expert on Indonesia, he says, as he strolled though the rice fields of Bali, he noticed that a different dog would bark as he entered a different property. The dogs knew very well which assets their masters controlled. To determine who owned what in Indonesia, he advised the Cabinet to begin by 'listening to the barking dogs.' One of the Ministers responded, he says, by exclaiming: 'Ah, jukum adat—the people's law.'

Indonesia represented to de Soto all that is wrong with the Third World economies. It was the great merit of capitalism in the West, he believes, that governments adapted the 'people's law' into uniform rules and codes that all could understand and respect. 'Ownership once represented by dogs, fences, and armed guards is now represented by records, titles and shares.' This was what transformed the entire logic of capitalism in the West. With titles, shares and property laws, houses were no more mere use-value (as shelter); they could now be used as capital (security for credit to start or expand a business). (From 'The Hidden Architecture of capitalism', http://www.ild.org.pe/eng/articles_en1.htm).

This is of capital importance. It is not enough to own individual or family property. If it remains simple use-value, it is simply 'dead capital'. Every bit of property should be able to live a double life—as credit security, as share and such like. If we are really interested in understanding what happened in the West that was really different from previous centuries of trade and industry in other parts of the world, this is where we should look.

The astute eye of de Soto is quick to realize that '[T]hroughout the Third World and the formerly communist countries, neighborhoods buzz with hard work and ingenuity. Streetside cottage industries have sprung up everywhere, manufacturing anything from footwear to imitation Cartier watches. There are workshops that build and rebuild machinery, cars, even buses. In many countries, unauthorized buses, jitneys, and taxis account for most public transportation. Often, vendors from the shanty towns supply most of the food available in the market, from carts on the street or from stalls in buildings they built themselves. The new urban poor have created entire industries and neighborhoods that have to operate on clandestine connections to electricity and water (De Soto, *Citadels of Dead capital*, http://www.reason.com/news/show/28018.html). But alas! All this remains dead capital till it is brought within the fold of the formal economy.

To conclude, it will be worthwhile to reflect briefly on the words 'dead capital' a bit. To be sure, from de Soto's own descriptions, this capital is anything but 'dead'. It is very much alive and happens to provide a livelihood for millions of people across the globe. More importantly, this 'capital' is a source of constant anxiety for both 'formal capital' and the state, though for different reasons. To 'formal capital' it poses a threat to its profits, especially in the figure of the 'pirate' that has now become a pervasive metaphor for the illegal, the unruly and the unregulated.[16] The pirate today is one who copies, multiplies and distributes or sells with scant respect for the original except as object of consumption. The pirate produces the 'copy' or the 'fake' and throws it alongside the 'original' into the market, duping the original branded producer. Often, though, s/he who is called the pirate, merely shares information and products with others. In more recent times, the really sharp conflicts around this issue have taken shape around the new possibilities of copying and sharing made available by new digital technologies and the Internet. In this context, 'intellectual property', copyright and trademark have become the new banners of capitalist aggression—as it stands threatened by such pirate or *contraband capital*—its own cheap copy. To the state, it poses another kind of threat by depriving it of what it believes are its legitimate revenues—all the transactions in this domain being completely 'off the record'. Considering the vastness of this domain, this must surely be a huge loss!

Given all this, in what sense then, can we understand this contraband capital to be dead? Precisely in this, that by being outside the pale of the formal economy, it eludes the mechanisms of disciplining and policing that are put in place by state elites in countries like India in order to bring the entire 'economy' within the domain of the 'formal'. For that alone can ensure that the owners of such capital pay taxes or save and make their money available for investors to play with. This might sound too far fetched but if the experience of countries like India is any indication, big corporations and sections of the bureaucracy have colluded to openly loot such public money that has been kept in their custody as savings.[17] Calculations like de Soto's underline the scale of money and stocks that can become available for states and financial players were these to be made 'formal' and be documented in titles and deeds. It is precisely because it is not available today that ideologues like de Soto would consider such capital 'dead'. I am not suggesting a conspiracy here but pointing to the fact that contemporary capitalism is today in one of its most serious crises—not in the conventional marxist sense of an imminent breakdown or collapse but rather in that it may have run against the limit of its own development and expansion, living continuously on the artificial respiration of credit and individual small savings for its capital needs.

## NOTES

1. See Buddhadeb Bhattacharya, 'Thousands of young people want jobs . . . they will shape the country's future', *Indian Express*, 19 January 2007, p. 11. For Sumit Sarkar's critique, see 'A question marked in red', *Indian Express*, 9 January 2007. p. 11. It is interesting to note that the term 'narodnik' has been made into such a word of abuse among marxists that even Sarkar and other Left critics thought it necessary to clarify recently in a press conference, upon their return from Nandigram, that they were marxists and not narodniks.

2. 'Socialism' here must be understood as a project, a search for a world beyond capital, rather than any specific historical form. It is this sense, I believe, that animates the formation of something like the 'Movement for Socialism' in Bolivia, whose leader Evo Morales was recently elected President. The Movement for Socialism is like most other South American new Left formations (e.g. the Zapatistas), a movement of the indigenous people rather than a classically marxist and modernist one.

3. See, Wal Hannington, *A Short History of the Unemployed*, London: Victor Gollancz Ltd, 1938.

4. That this is not even a position widely shared by 'capitalists' and their spokespersons is also equally revealing. See for instance Lou Dobbs (2004). Dobbs, who hosts CNN's *Lou Dobbs Tonight*, has been scathing in his television programmes as well as in this book against the attempts to outsource America's jobs to Asia. He sees this as an assault on middle class Americans and all this while claiming 'I am a lifelong Republican . . . I am a capitalist . . . I have not only been a journalist for three decades but also an executive, a businessman and an investor', Lou Dobbs, *Exporting America: Why Corporate Greed is Shipping American Jobs Overseas*, New York and Boston: Warner Business Books, 2004.

5. See Samuel Brittan, 'Globalisation depresses western wages', http://dictionary.reference.com/browse/oxymoron, accessed on 9 November 2006.

6. Teodor Shanin (ed.), *Late Marx and the Russian Road: Marx and the 'peripheries of capitalism'*, London, Melbourne and Henley: Routledge and Kegan Paul, 1983, pp. 28-9.

7. This renewed intellectual search—if not a crisis—for Marx is partly occasioned by the fact that it was during the 1860s and 1870s, according to Raphael Samuel, that an important breakthrough in the social sciences, the discovery of prehistory, 'was to lengthen the notion of historical time by some tens of thousands of years, and to bring primitive societies within the circle of historical study' (cited in Shanin, ibid., p. 6).

8. Haruki Wada (1983), 'Marx and Revolutionary Russia', in Shanin, ibid. This volume details the events and texts related to this episode through a fascinating documentation.

9. See Susanne D. Mueller, 'Retarded Capitalism in Tanzania', *Socialist Register 1980*, http://socialistregister.com/socialistregister.com/files/SR_1980_Mueller.pdf . Mueller's essay should merely be seen as an indication of the fact that

even in well-informed marxist sections, this was the common knowledge about narodism.

10. This might link up with Karl Polanyi's argument that markets and exchange relations always existed but were embedded in existing social relations and thus not acultural matters. What he saw as distinctive of capitalism was the disembedding of markets—and the transformation of 'the economy' into abstract, acultural spaces.

11. John T. Chalcraft, *Radical History Review*, issue 91, Winter 2005, pp. 13-39.

12. Cited in Jonathan Fox, 'Has Brazil Moved Toward State Capitalism?', *Latin American Perspectives*, vol. 7, no. 1, Winter 1980, p. 65.

13. Alice H. Amsden, 'Third World Industrialization: Global Fordism or a New Model?', *New Left Review*, 182, July-August 1990, pp. 19-25.

14. Paul Sweezy, 'A Critique', in Rodney Hilton, *The Transition from Feudalism to Capitalism*, London: Verso, 1980, p. 50.

15. Louis Althusser and Etienne Balibar, *Reading Capital*, London: New Left Books 1977, pp. 297-81.

16. On this question, my understanding has been fundamentally influenced by the work of the Sarai Programme in the CSDS, Delhi, the Alternative Law Forum, Bangalore and of Ravi Sundaram and Lawrence Liang in particular.

17. One can immediately think of what *The Indian Express* called the 'Great Indian Bank Robbery' involving leading corporates who owed something to the tune of Rs. 110,000 crore to nationalized banks, waiting to be written off as 'non-performing assets' (see Samar, Halarnkar, Ritu Sarin, Sucheta Dalal and George Mathew, 'Rs. 11,00,00,00,00,000: The Great Indian Bank Robbery', *The Indian Express*, 1 December 2002, front page). Similarly, the scandal of the Unit Trust of India's US-64 savings scheme which wiped off crores of rupees worth of savings of small household investors (see, Praful, Bidwai, *Frontline*, 21 July-03 August 2001). Allegations were rife that the savings of small household investors were unscrupulously played in the stock market. And then of course, there is the classic case of the theft of the workers' provident fund money to the tune of crores of rupees, by the owners of West Bengal's jute industry.

# 3

# TIME AND THE REVOLUTIONARY IMAGINATION

If the socialist revolution in the 'twenty Latin Americas' cannot be unified, then neither can its timing. The national fragmentation of the Latin American revolution is matched by the way its political calendar is fragmented into quite unconnected rhythms and upheavals. In each country the process has its own time clock: whether armed or not, the class struggle will always be at a different moment in Caracas and Buenos Aires, and again different in Guatemala city. Vanguards can see far and wide: it is this that makes them the vanguard . . . . Vanguards decide on their present action in view of the 'far-off socialist ideals' with which, by theoretical anticipation, they become contemporary. But it is pointless for them to set their watch to Caracas time in Buenos Aires (or Hanoi time in San Francisco for that matter). The people who make history are living by the time not of a continental, or world, revolution, but of the material living conditions of the area, the town or the country, which their horizon is bounded by.

—Regis Debray[1]

In the Austro-Hungarian monarchy there are examples of all the economic forms to be found in Europe, including Turkey . . . . What exists in the International as a chronological development—the socialism of artisans, journeymen, workers in manufacture, factory workers, and agricultural workers, which undergoes alterations, with the political, social or the intellectual aspect of the movement predominating at any given moment—takes place contemporaneously in Austria.

—Otto Bauer[2]

## 'Staging' a Revolt

An 'extraordinary' event took place in May 1967, in a small area of north Bengal. Known in the annals of Indian political and cultural history as the Naxalbari revolt, it acquired its more popular identity as the 'naxalite movement' (in its anglicized rendition). A peasants' armed struggle to begin with, Naxalbari represented a utopian burst of revolutionary energy as rebels from within the CPI(M) challenged the cautious pragmatism and *realpolitik* considerations that had come to mark radical political practice of that period. Formally, the main plank of the movement was its complete rejection of all parliamentary politics and a call for armed seizure of power. Located within the global conjuncture of the rise of Left wing radicalism and anticipating the May 1968 upsurge in the West by a full year, the revolt was formally inspired by maoism and the ongoing Cultural Revolution in China.

Maoism, of course, had a longer history dating back to the 1940s, especially the period of the Telengana peasants, struggle (1946-51), in the then princely state of Hyderabad. Parenthetically, it is important to state here that in the context of Indian politics, we must make a distinction between this generic-maoism and the other species-maoism that emerged as a specific political current in the early 2000s.[3] Individual characters changed sides, different permutations and combinations took shape but the attraction of maoism continued to grow through these decades. The idea of a peasant revolution always presented an attractive option to many radical youth. These sections were always at loggerheads with the dominant urban-based leadership of the CPI and later the CPI(M). To this leadership, the lure of parliamentarism has always proved too great to resist—this was the perception among the rurally oriented Maoists. These issues have formed the bases of a range of disagreements between different factions of the CPI and the CPI(M) from the Telengana days and became a fundamental point of rupture in the case of the naxalites.

As the years went by, internal differences within the CPI reached a point of no return. It is important to remember that after Independence the CPI had emerged as a significant electoral-political force at least in some states, and within a decade was able to form the first elected communist government anywhere in the world, namely, the one formed under E. M. S. Namboodiripad's chief ministership in Kerala in 1957. In some other states like Andhra Pradesh too, the CPI performed reasonably well. While these experiences strengthened the parliamentary perspective within the party, they were also leading to increasing restlessness among sections that were beginning to see these moves as abdication of the revolutionary path. The debate within the CPI, which eventually led to the split and the formation of the CPI(M) in 1964 involved thus a whole range of issues connected with the understanding of Indian state and society, the nature of its 'bourgeois' democracy, the strategic perspectives of the Indian revolution and such other matters. That the CPI(M) leadership following the split failed to discuss and take a position on many of the issues concerned, certainly helped the more youthful and restless sections to gradually move away from the leadership. It was in precisely such a situation that once again the newly formed 'revolutionary' party, namely the CPI(M), was presented with the opportunity to form coalition governments in the two states of West Bengal and Kerala. The party decided to go ahead with the task of forming governments in these two states.

It was at this juncture that the rebels decided to strike. In fact, it was on the very day that the new government in West Bengal was taking the oath, in 1967, that the first 'incident' was reported from Naxalbari. Thereafter, the matter simply escalated. That the Chinese Communist Party hailed the struggle as the 'burst of spring thunder' over India and lent its support to the rebels, only added to the escalation.

Very soon, what had begun as a by-product of an internal debate within the CPI(M), became a public Event of major significance. It unleashed a debate in society at large about matters that might have had little to do with the 'path of India's revolution'. It is significant, for instance, that the maoist moment of the 1960s, signalled in a way that is yet to be seriously studied, a major crisis of what we can call 'political modernism' in India. For, it was this moment that, in positing 'the rural' and 'the peasant' as the fount of all revolutionary creativity, ironically reactivated an earlier gandhian ethos of the critique of technology and urban life. However, it is something else that I wish to gesture to here.

In a sense, the Naxalbari revolt was literally 'staged'—intended to serve as an aid, more powerful than words and treatises could, in the inner-party struggle. However, as happens in most such cases, the protagonists of the revolutionary message/line had also really started believing what they were saying. Nothing was said for mere effect. The rebels really thought that the 'Indian revolution' was round the corner, that the people were ready but it was the 'revisionist' and reformist leadership of the CPs that was holding them back. The maoist dictum 'a single spark can start a prairie fire' was understood to be valid for the India of the late 1960s and 1970s, to the extent that Charu Mazumdar could exhort—and most naxalite rebels would believe and follow him—to make 1970s the decade of liberation.

As time went by, the rebels realized what their predecessors, the cautious pragmatists of the CPI and the CPI(M) had realized during the years of the Telengana struggle: a militant armed struggle, even of revolutionary proportions, could not hold out in one small and isolated region. If Regis Debray, cited in the epigraph to this chapter, saw a fragmentation of the Latin American revolution along national lines, 'following quite different and unconnected rhythms', the Indian communists have seen this time and again within the huge landmass of the 'nation-state' called India.

The actual revolt did not last very long—in fact was surprisingly short-lived. But soon the idea of Naxalbari caught on—initially within the peripheries of the existing CPs, mainly the CPI(M), eventually spreading outwards in society at large. There were Naxalbari-type peasant revolts in different parts of the country—Lakhimpur Kheri in UP, Debra and Gopiballabpur in Midnapore district of West Bengal and later in Musahari in Bihar. In fact, an important and much more intense armed struggle was already on at that time in the Srikakulum area of Andhra Pradesh but such was the semiotic significance of 'Naxalbari' that it only began attracting public attention *after* it formally allied itself to the Naxalbari path (Dubey 1994). There were incidents in some parts of Kerala too. This extended period, between the crushing of the Naxalbari revolt and its spread to other parts, primarily in the form of a peasants' armed struggle, covered something like two years. By the time the revolutionaries had regrouped and formed 'the party', namely, the CPI(ML), the movement in its first phase was well on the way to being over. This was April-May 1969—the party being formed secretly on 22 April, Lenin's birthday and announced publicly at a May Day rally that same year. This was the time when the second United Front government came to power and released the naxalite leaders who had been arrested after the fall of the eight-month long first UF ministry. The second UF ministry lasted about two years.

It is also well-known that within these two years, that is, by this time, the naxalite movement in West Bengal at least had become an almost exclusively urban affair, attracting to its fold some of the brightest students from the most elite backgrounds. Only later did the more underprivileged students from vernacular backgrounds start joining it. In this phase, the movement had already exceeded the intentions and control of its authors, some of whom watched in bewilderment, as brash young students went about demolishing the statues of respected figures of the Bengali renaissance. Already, the movement had started degenerating into mindless killings in the name of 'annihilation of the class enemy' and it acquired a particularly grotesque form at this time. All in all, at this time it presented a picture of anarchy and directionlessness.

Nonetheless, by this time Naxalbari had become an 'idea', a metaphor, a call to arms and more; it became a call to ruthlessly critique the legacy of colonial rule and everything that went with it, extending to a critique of the postcolonial Indian state's own very significant continuities with the colonial. And it was then that, as colonial rule came under the scanner, even the role of important Bengali leaders and intellectuals was found to be wanting in that respect. They were all seen as collaborators—or at least as not sufficiently strong and resolute in their opposition to colonial rule. The naxalite characterization of contemporary India as a 'semi-feudal' and 'semi-colonial' country, even though it drew its poetry from Mao's formulations on pre-revolution China, served to underline aspects of continuity with colonial rule, which stood in sharp contrast to the insistence of the mainstream CPs, on the break and discontinuities following Independence—of which too there were many. The point here is not whether the naxalite characterization of India as semi-colonial was correct or not; what was of crucial importance was that it enabled a wholesale re-examination of certain aspects of our intellectual and political heritage. The youthful impetuosity witnessed in the iconoclasm of that period is only an exaggerated and irreverent form of what was to be undertaken later by scholars in their reassessment of the Bengal renaissance in the early 1970s.[4]

Despite all this, in its stated intent, the naxalite movement wanted Revolution in the marxist sense of capture of state power. That was the reason for its impatience with the cautious pragmatism of the leaders of the traditional communist parties. And whatever their poetry of 'protracted peasant warfare', they wanted instant revolution. Thus the call to make the 1970s the decade of liberation. Thus the impatience with anything that would prolong this period of revolutionary transformation. It was the return in a different form, of the 'original' notion of Revolution as Apocalypse, drawn in the marxist imagination from its deep roots in Judaeo-Christian culture. This secularized eschatological idea of revolution as an apocalyptic moment of rupture has had a long innings in marxism, which, in its leninist form, recast and reconstituted this imagination quite substantially. This leninist reconstitution, as we know, was based on a rendering of the idea of the 'current situation' or conjuncture and the related concept of the 'weakest link'. The 'current situation' in all its specificity was the crux of Lenin's understanding and he was astute enough to understand that revolutionaries could not simply wish a revolutionary situation into existence. In naxalite discourse, however, the 'current situation' or the revolutionary conjuncture takes a different form. For by insisting that in countries like India, the 'objective' situation *is always revolutionary*, it sought to shift the terms of debate to the 'subjective' aspect—the essential non-preparedness of the CPs to take on the task of revolution and revolutionary mobilization. The characterization of India as a 'semi-feudal' and 'semi-colonial' country served to emphasize the point that such a regime could not but be isolated from its people, being basically a parasitical and narrow stratum which ruled simply by virtue of support from its 'imperialist masters'. Hence the only thing required was determined action by a revolutionary vanguard and people would readily lend their support to it.

The entire movement—at least its first phase (1967-71)—should be seen more as a performance; it should be seen as a performative critique, at once, of the waning radicalism of the mainstream Left parties and of 'actually existing Indian democracy' whose failure to deliver was increasingly becoming evident in those days. However, tragically, the participants and actors of the revolt also really believed what they were saying. And thus the inevitable happened.

Like hundreds of such struggles that have died out waiting for synchronized countrywide revolutionary struggles to develop, naxalism too died out. At least for the time being. Eventually, it took rebirth in the late 1980s, with considerable regrouping and rethinking, as it got down to the more long-term task of building a movement. Not surprisingly, most groups eventually reconsidered their attitude to elections and democratic institutions opening the way to different forms and degrees of parliamentary participation. Today, with the exception of one, the recently renamed CPI(Maoist), most of the naxalite groups have decided to participate in elections and parliamentary politics in some form.

## The Ghost of 'Uneven Development'

Staying with the manifest discourse of any movement [of the naxalites, and indeed, of other parties like the CPI(M)], let us suspend, at least for the time being, all questions of intentionality. We must assume that all of them genuinely and sincerely wanted to bring about a revolutionary transformation of Indian society. That they failed must then have to do with something more than just 'betrayal' or foolhardy romanticism. There may have been elements of both in the numerous failed revolutions across the world, but revolutions still happen despite them—when they do, that is. Most often, however, they do not happen. Most radical movements are then faced with one of the two choices: *either* face marginality and live the life of a minor 'revolutionary sect'; *or*, enter the parliamentary democratic arena and eventually be co-opted. There are literally hundreds of instances of both kinds across the world, reduced in different ways, to the same fate: complete inefficacy with regard to their 'revolutionary objectives'.

We might then need to ask a very different question here: why is every revolutionary movement so persistently haunted by the spectre of 'reformism' and 'betrayal'? A recurring motif in all attempts to 'explain' such 'failures' is that of 'uneven development'—gesturing to *the virtual impossibility of a synchronized and simultaneous* attack (of different regions, different classes, different social groups, etc.) on state power with a view to 'capturing' it.

As a matter of fact, it will not be an exaggeration to say that the global history of the communist movement, has been continuously ridden with this anxiety of dealing with the ghost of 'uneven development'. The dream of world revolution floundered and died on the rock of 'socialism in one country'. The initial years of the Russian revolution in Lenin's lifetime were marked by this anxious wait for the European revolution that never happened and 'socialism in one country' had to be reluctantly accepted as a reality. The Chinese revolution had to await, among other things, the crisis of imperialism and the Second World War, the overall process of decolonization—in other words, the simultaneity of the war and anti-colonial revolutions—in order to finally take control of state power. Even the Russian revolution, we know, was made possible by the peculiar conjuncture of the First World War when all the social contradictions fused together into an explosive unity. Trotsky's formulation of the 'law of combined and uneven development'—and the related idea of 'permanent revolution'—was an attempt, among many others, to deal with this heterogeneity or non-simultaneity, which I shall discuss at greater length below.[5]

The Left's experience in India, likewise, has revealed a continued tension brought forth by this 'uneven development' of the revolutionary situation. There were at different points of time, different points of conflagration and intensity of class struggle but they could never add up to a materialization of the dream of an all-India upsurge. The sharp debates around the Telengana peasants' struggle in the late 1940s in the

Communist Party centred on the same question: whether to continue the peasants' struggle that began in the princely state of Hyderabad, and was directed against the feudal classes of Razakars and Deshmukhs, even after Hyderabad became integrated into the central state power of independent India. That is, a revolutionary situation existed in Hyderabad prior to independence, but once the state was merged in the Indian Union and Nehru's army marched in, the situation underwent a qualitative transformation.[6]

More to the point, of course, was fact that in the rest of India the nationalist fervour of the anti-colonial struggle was now being directed towards the new task of nation-building. Other 'discordant voices' of the days of the nationalist movement, namely, the Dalit movement and the Muslims who decided to remain in India, had to struggle to find a place for themselves in the new dispensation. Different currents of the pre-1947 days were now coming together through complex negotiations, in the entity of the new nation. In the midst of these different stories, the desire for an armed insurrection could only have sounded thoroughly out-of-tune. The disastrous ultra-Left line of insurrection in 1949, known more popularly as the BT Ranadive line, proved exactly that. Eventually, the CPI, on the advice of the CPSU, had to call off the armed struggle in Telengana. Legend has it that when the CPI delegation met Stalin, he asked them to point out Telengana on the map. Looking at it in amazement, he is said to have exclaimed that they must be crazy to think that from there they could capture the whole of India!

It is worth mentioning here that the 1951 meeting with the CPSU leaders yielded two important documents, one being the first-ever *Programme* of the CPI, which was to become redundant very soon, with a rapidly changing situation. The second document, known as the *Tactical Line* (the *Statement of Policy*, in its legal version), underlined this aspect of 'uneven development' with great emphasis:

> It must be realized that because of the vast area of India, *because of the uneven level of mass movement in different parts of the country, uneven acuteness of the agrarian crisis* and uneven strength of the influence of the party itself, *the peasant movement cannot develop at the same tempo everywhere.* Premature uprisings and adventurist actions of every type must be avoided . . . . (Cited in Basavapunnaiah 1985b: 38)

In the history of the CPI(M), the question surfaced repeatedly in the course of the 1960s, 1970s and 1980s. This time round the question on the agenda was not 'revolution'. On these occasions, there was no armed struggle anywhere. Yet the intensity of popular mass struggles in the preceding decades in Bengal and Kerala had provided a secure place to the communists. In the rest of the country their presence was on the whole, negligible. For the communists, this was a difficult situation. For they have never had any clue about what to do when 'revolution' was not on the immediate agenda. Lenin had told them that in such circumstances they could and must participate in elections and enter bourgeois parliaments and carry on the struggle within—to complement and strengthen the struggle without. But what if this participation led, as it did in the late 1960s, to the possibility of their forming governments? Not to take the responsibility would be an abdication of the trust of the people who voted them into power.

The first crisis thus came when the party decided to actively form a state government in West Bengal, in a coalition of about 14 parties. That was when a section of the ultra-Left, the naxalites, broke away from the party accusing it of betraying the revolution. The naxalites' tragedy was that they still had the visions of an armed revolutionary struggle 'maturing' all over India in the near future. This was not going to happen. Eventually this movement was to undergo a series of splits and dissipate—until its rebirth in an entirely different form later. For the majority of those who remained in the parent party, entering the government was merely a holding out operation. They were still 'waiting for the situation to mature' in the rest of the country—so that they could go back to where they belonged. The stance of the CPI(M) towards the two United Front governments of the late 1960s, in West Bengal and Kerala was therefore that these governments had little real powers; that they should be seen as 'instruments of struggle' rather than as real governments. The simultaneous 'maturation' of the revolutionary situation was the dream that propelled them but the cruel fact of the matter was that this was not to happen. Fortunately for them, till the Left Front government finally came to power, they were rescued each time from this predicament by the ruling party's intolerance which saw to it that none of their governments lasted more than a couple of years at best.

After 1977, things changed dramatically, much to the discomfort of the communists. By this time, three things had happened: First, the massive explosion of pent-up democratic aspirations after the Emergency made it difficult for the ruling parties to topple the Left Front government, especially as there were no internal dissensions of any significance that they could exploit. Second, the LF turned out to be a much more homogeneous front, with the CPI(M) alone having absolute majority. Third, it seems that the Congress party itself had probably learnt that it would be best to let the communists run the government and pass that more difficult test of resisting the lures of power.[7] A fourth thing had also happened. A section of the CPI(M) in West Bengal had realized that all the gains of the land struggles of the late 1960s, for example, could be overturned, almost overnight, by the ruling party at the Centre, once they were out of power. Such would also be the case with many other issues. They therefore had to devise methods that would be legally and constitutionally sustainable. This further strengthened the hands of people like Jyoti Basu and E. M. S. Namboodiripad, who were less instrumental in their relationship to parliamentary democracy.

The manifest and official discourse of the party however, remained 'revolutionary'—which effectively meant that it entered parliamentary institutions in bad faith, with a cynical attitude to them. As I shall argue later, the problem of most 'revolutionaries' with regard to democratic processes and institutions is precisely that of bad faith but for the time being I wish to return to our narrative.

The first few years of the CPI(M)-led LF government were spent in the expectation that they would be toppled soon. With that perspective, the government initiated some popular measures like a token allowance for the unemployed, food-for-work programme in the villages, hikes in salaries of teachers and government servants and so on. The LF government of the day was clearly not expecting to be in office for long and had not thought through the financial implications of these measures—that could be left to the government that followed. This was not to be—with its own hands it had to revoke some of these measures. Very soon the party had to come to terms with the fact that this time round it would be tested on a fundamentally different ground. This was another effect of 'uneven development'. There was even a time, as late as in 1985, when important sections within the West Bengal CPI(M) demanded that paragraph 112 of the party's *Programme*, which provided for the party's participation in state governments, be deleted (Basavapunnaiah 1985b). The understanding was that being in power was corrupting the party and since there was no sign of the party growing in the rest of the country such that it could make an all-India impact, it should return to where it belonged.

In a sense, long after the party had become comfortably ensconced within the parliamentary set-up, the inner-party debate in 1996 around participation in the Central government (the famous 'historic blunder') was still haunted by this spectre of uneven development (Menon and Nigam 2007: 103-5).

This repeated reappearance of the ghost of uneven development points insistently in one direction: the impossibility of synchronized and simultaneous assault on state power. It points to the irreducible heterogeneity of the 'present moment', or what Louis Althusser called the category of the '*historical present*'. It points to the 'unconnected rhythms and upheavals' and the difficulties of unifying the political calendar that so troubled Regis Debray in the South American context. This was after all what cost Che Guevara his life: South America was not Cuba and the revolutionary movement could not simply be wished into existence. A 'revolutionary situation' in the leninist sense, is the rarest of rare occurrences in history; for the most part there are what one might call 'non-revolutionary times', that is, times marked by the extreme heterogeneity of the present moment. Experience also shows that revolutionaries do not really know how to deal with such 'non-revolutionary times'. They know—or believe they do—what the conduct proper to revolutionary situations or times is or should be. And whatever else, it is certainly not the lack of a will to fight or the courage and determination that they lack.

The problem really is that revolutionary imagination is predicated upon the notion of a simple and homogeneous, singular present—that is a Present (or a revolutionary conjuncture) where all the different presents merge into a single ruptural moment. The revolutionary lives for that time. All other times are times out of joint, where s/he must simply wait for that moment or at best act in ways that hasten its arrival. This desire for a homogeneous present, of a simultaneous revolutionary upsurge, it should not be difficult to see, is closely tied to the pursuance of the chimera of the 'state'. It is *because* the state must be *captured* that the revolutionary imagination invests so much in a synchronized mass action. But, what if the 'state' were not some 'thing' to be captured? What if the state were not simply an 'apparatus' but a condensed expression of class and other relations (patriarchy, caste, race, community) and practices existing at any point of time? Does the fact that mere 'capture of state power' in any of the 'socialist' countries did not lead to a change in any single practice in any significant way, say something about the thing called the state itself? What would such an understanding mean for political practice? We will return to this important question later but for the present, let us simply note that the notion of politics outlined above, is a profoundly anti-political notion of politics that takes away from politics that which is constitutive of it—its contingency that is fundamentally linked to what Lenin called the character of the 'current situation'.

## Multiple Struggles and the 'Current Situation'

This brings us to the question of 'politics' as such. Every politics should be understood in relation to its object. Every politics addresses a specific object, which it acts upon and seeks to transform. In that sense, all politics is about transforming the 'present' in some way and yet, the present of every politics is different; each has a different history, not reducible to the history of capital-labour relations or to some notion of 'class struggle'. So for instance, Dalit politics or feminism address their own specific objects, namely, caste oppression and patriarchy, which they seek to transform.

When the revolutionary imagination speaks of the 'present', however, it refers almost exclusively and solely to capital and capitalism and the mythical entity called 'the working class'—an entity that has little to do in fact, with the 'empirical' working class. As we have seen, in the vocabulary of the Old Left, revolutionary times were understood as times of large-scale mass upheavals that, in one ruptural moment burst forth on the political scene and led to transformations of political regimes. Lenin described a 'revolutionary situation' as one marked by a 'considerable increase in the activity of the masses' that moved them into 'independent historical action'. He would always insist that revolutionaries cannot simply wish a revolutionary situation into existence; they had to always act upon a *given situation* – the 'current situation', even if they themselves constitute important elements of that situation. It is the attributes of this 'current situation' that all revolutionary/radical political action needs to first comprehend. However, there is one problem: this 'current situation', as Althusser rightly pointed out, is a situation of complex determinations, comprising the accumulation and fusion of innumerable different 'contradictions'. He called it the 'overdetermination' of contradictions. We can paraphrase his point thus: it is not a simple 'maturation' of the 'principal contradiction' within the totality called 'global capitalism' or the 'world economy' that will lead to a revolutionary rupture but the *fusion of a number of different 'contradictions'* into an explosive unity that will define a 'revolutionary situation'. How else, asks Althusser, could the class-divided popular masses (proletarians, peasants, petty bourgeoisie) throw themselves *together*, into a general assault on the existing regime?[8] We could add to this list of class-divided 'popular masses' today, a whole range of other groups and sections engaged in struggling against different kinds of oppressions—patriarchy, racism, casteism, and the nation-state/capital's displacement/dispossession of communities from their land. The popular masses, in other words, are not merely class-divided but also divided along innumerable other axes and for all of them to come together, there has to be a truly 'exceptional' situation—a revolutionary situation—in existence. In other words, there has to be a recognition from within these different kinds of movements of the immediacy of the need to rally *against the same forces*, usually represented in some centralized institution like the state, or one imperialist centre. But this is precisely what happens very rarely in history. What is more, the experience of past revolutions shows that the outcome of such apocalyptic transformations is not always the same for all the forces that came together to 'take state power' in the first instance. A mere change of political regimes does not lead to the transformation of all those power relations, the struggle against which animated the 'popular masses' in the first place. In most cases, the initial success of the revolution leads to the dissipation of popular unity, as is evidenced by the experience of innumerable movements the world over.

A certain hierarchy of antagonisms is inherent in such an understanding, for the point of articulation of different forces has to be a privileged one, where all or most conflicts get 'fused'. It is impossible, for instance, to think of such a ruptural unity around the question of patriarchy or caste oppression. Feminism or the Dalit movement will always remain *specific* antagonisms for they have to do with specific mechanisms of micro-power within society at large. Nevertheless, it is possible to imagine the feminist and Dalit movement, under certain circumstances, joining forces with labour or other movements in order to fight the onslaught of capital and state power. Such a coming together of the otherwise divided 'popular masses' therefore, has as its focus one single object: the capture of state power that supposedly embodies the interests of capital. The success of the 'revolution', understood as 'capture of state', is synonymous then with the dissipation of the very entity called the 'popular masses': At the precise moment when the revolution achieves its success, the different social groups that came together lose the very rationale of their unity. Overdetermination thus leaves intact the independent logic of the other 'contradictions' in their discrete existence.

The leninist programme of revolution as capture or 'transformation' of state power, then, is a very restricted one and needs to be rethought. Since such a revolution always acts upon one privileged present—at the point where the political tension at any given moment is the highest, all other presents are subsumed, all other questions deferred, in order to strike at the state power in question. Once the regime change has taken place and the immediacy of the moment is lost, the revolutionary energy dissipates, leaving only the most Jacobin elements within the revolutionary bloc to take control of the newly constituted power.

Rethinking the idea of revolution in this sense involves a rethinking of the very idea of *a 'present'*, defined by a singular logic of the totality. The old radical project—the project of the pre-Althusserian Lenin for instance—was premised on such an idea of a singular present, defined by a certain notion of *totality* that was governed by a single organizing principle or logic. 'World capitalism' was understood to be a single whole and all the nation-states, differentially incorporated into it were seen to be, despite certain specificities, moving towards a fuller incorporation in it. The idea of an international working class movement, expressing the common interest of an undifferentiated class, and even all humanity, was clearly based upon this notion of a global totality animated by a single logic or, in the Old Left lexicon, the 'principal contradiction'. The leninist-maoist moment, in recognizing the crucial significance of national liberation struggles in breaking the chain of imperialism, did rupture this understanding to some extent but it did so only in a practical form. It did so by positing peripheral national liberation struggles/revolutions and subsequently, nation-states, as critical players in the overarching struggle against imperialism, and therefore against world capitalism. In the schematized form in which this question was debated within the communist movement, it was the 'principal contradiction' that provided the governing logic and all other contradictions, though recognized, always had a secondary place. After the Second World War, for instance, it was argued by dominant sections of the Old Left that the principal contradiction was between capitalism and socialism, and that would determine the fate of all other social contradictions. Other 'contradictions' like that between capital and labour in the 'advanced' capitalist countries, the contradiction between imperialism and national liberation struggles, inter-imperialist contradictions and such others were recognized as secondary. In practice, there were different versions operating among different sects of the marxist Left. In one rendering the principal contradiction was the contradiction between international capital and the international working class, in another the capitalist world versus the 'socialist camp' and in yet another, between imperialism and national liberation struggles. Nevertheless, it always had to be *a single defining contradiction that would determine the fate of all others.*

Needless to say, the catalogue of social contradictions enumerated by the different communist parties/groups was in itself quite restrictive and took no cognizance of the innumerable other conflicts that were already playing themselves out, particularly in the eighties and nineties in the postcolonial world, not to mention other conflicts that had already broken out in the metropolitan countries. Important among these conflicts were those that were articulated around issues of identity, gender, race, sexuality and the impending ecological disaster. These issues were either considered to be the product of some ruling class conspiracy or at best, matters that would be resolved automatically once the basic class questions were resolved. Their 'resolution' had therefore, to be infinitely deferred to some future socialist society. That the new society could itself reproduce all the old structures of domination had to do, critically with the fact that the very understanding of revolution was based upon the notion of a single, homogeneous time and restricted its imagination to the macro-structural level. Micro-power and the everyday always eluded the revolutionaries because their eyes were fixed on the large structures of capitalism and state power. In the event, of course, the global history of 'actually existing socialism' was to show that even capitalism could not be transcended in any fashion by these means.

Radical politics then, it seems to me, cannot be seen as *a specific kind of politics* that only defines itself in relation to the present of global capital. As evident from the above discussion, there are always, any number of different oppressions, and modes of domination and power that operate, against which different kinds of political practices emerge. Since none of these different oppressions are ever reducible to each other or to any common denominator, there can never be any single thing called Radical Politics. What we have rather, is an extreme heterogeneity of the historical present; times that are utterly unsuitable for any kind of revolutionary project of the kind we have been discussing so far. We could call them 'non-revolutionary times'.

## Non-Revolutionary Times

We could try to understand these non-revolutionary times with reference to Lenin's understanding of a 'revolutionary situation'. Lenin, as we have noted, repeatedly points out that revolutionaries cannot simply call a revolutionary situation into existence or create it out of nothing; they must always *act upon a given situation*. Thus his assertion, in the context of the collapse of the Second International, that 'to the Marxist it is indisputable that a revolution is impossible without a revolutionary situation' and that not every revolutionary situation need lead to a revolution.[9] Lenin also points out that one of the critical signs of a revolutionary situation is a 'considerable increase in the activity of the masses' as a consequence of which they are drawn into '*independent historical action.*'[10] We might need to reflect more seriously on the specific phrase used here: 'independent' historical action, that is, spontaneous action not 'mobilized' by vanguard/s. It is this sense that prompts Lenin's own response after the defeat of the 1905 revolution and especially after 1908, the period of Stolypin reaction: they would have to wait for the 'new revolutionary upsurge'. Reading Lenin's formula in reverse then, a non-revolutionary situation is a situation where the 'masses' or 'people' are not active as one singular political entity. Altering Lenin's terms somewhat, we might also say, it is a situation where the 'masses' or 'people' *do not yet exist*, that is, exist as so many different classes, social groups, communities, or cultural groups—yet to be constituted into a revolutionary subjectivity through political practice. The 'people' does not exist prior to the political practice that constitutes it as such—a political practice that acts upon an *overdetermined* and explosive present.

In this context, it is useful to consider the argument made by Laclau and Mouffe in their important work, *Hegemony and Socialist Strategy*. Laclau and Mouffe show convincingly that the early twentieth century responses to the 'crisis of marxism'—especially those of Rosa Luxembourg and Eduard Bernstein—reveal a very different notion of class unity from those of more conventional renderings like those of Karl Kautsky. Unlike Kautsky, they begin with the premise of an *initial fragmentation* of the working class, which is located in the very structure of the economy, that is to say, capitalist production necessarily fragments the working class rather than unites it. Its unity emerges, or must emerge through political practice, or what could be called in Laclau and Mouffe's terms, through hegemonic practices. The 'unity of the working class is not an infrastructural datum constituted outside the process of revolutionary overdetermination'.[11]

If this is the case with the working class whose theoretically posited unity was becoming increasingly difficult to sustain, then Laclau and Mouffe suggest, the matter is infinitely more complicated in relation to what Althusser calls the 'popular masses'. 'The concept of hegemony', they suggest, 'will emerge precisely in a context dominated by the experience of fragmentation and by the indeterminacy of the articulations between different struggles and subject positions.'[12] In their discussion, Laclau and Mouffe also distinguish between what they call *democratic struggles* and *popular struggles*. Very schematically, democratic struggles refer to struggles like feminism and anti-racism, which are predicated upon a proliferation of antagonisms, as distinct from popular struggles which are based on the division of the political space into two camps. The latter, we can see, is a defining feature of the revolutionary or insurrectionary moment. There is a point in this way of delineating the notion of 'popular struggle' or what Poulantzas called a situation of 'dual power', especially if we consider this formulation in the specific context of Third World *revolutionary and national liberation struggles* through the twentieth century. Here the moment of rupture is not one 'insurrectional' moment but develops over a prolonged phase extending over decades. Thus reworked, the idea of overdetermination can help us understand the meaning of such struggles, where the revolutionary situation does not 'mature' in one apocalyptic moment but proceeds through a series of protracted hegemonic struggles and where the political space is already divided into two camps.

It is instructive in this context to look at Mao Tse-tung's reading of the situation of the Chinese revolution. With Mao we repeatedly get the feeling that the continuous emphasis on 'protracted warfare', on the prospect of a long-drawn out struggle over decades, as against the search for the sudden insurrectional moment of rupture in Lenin, has to do with *a different sense of time*. Russia, to Lenin, was the 'weakest link' in the imperialist chain, which could be ruptured with decisive proletarian action, at the moment of crisis. This was possibly because Russia was situated at the intersection between the European imperialist (modern) and the colonized Asian (premodern) worlds. This intersection was certainly a spatial one in the sense that literally, the Russian empire straddled both worlds. But it was also a 'temporal intersection' in terms of the development of capitalism, a modern proletariat, links to the European world, on the one hand and the vast mass of Asian populations who lived, as it were in a different time. But what *determined* Russia's future was its European part—for that part was *where history was*. The Asiatic part of the Russian empire never really figured in Lenin's revolutionary imagination.[13] China, on the other hand, was not merely geographically isolated but, like the Asiatic parts of the Russian empire, lay outside the 'frontiers of history' and therefore also *temporally outside the domain of the present of World-History*.

The prospect that Mao was dealing with was that of 'long term survival' 'of one or more areas under "Red political power" completely encircled by a white regime'.[14] Mao was clear that such localized 'Red power' could survive only because of two crucial conditions (among other things): (i) China was neither an imperialist country nor 'a colony under imperialist rule'—in other words, lacking in a centralized state power.[15] Equally importantly, this survival was made possible by internecine wars among warlords—and this was a consequence of China's being a localized agricultural economy and not a unified capitalist economy, alongside its division into different spheres of influence.[16] This provided the revolutionary forces the possibility of moving between these different areas and escape the repression of a centralized state machinery. (ii) More importantly, for our purposes, the survival of this power also depended upon whether the *nationwide revolutionary situation* continued to develop. He stated unambiguously that 'if this nationwide revolutionary situation does not continue to develop but stagnates for a fairly long time, then it will be impossible for the small Red areas to last long'.[17]

What is the notion of a revolutionary situation implicated in this formulation, where clearly a 'local Red power' can take shape but which may or may not find a nationwide resonance? What is the disjunction that Mao seeks to register here? Let us return briefly to the passage from Regis Debray, cited as the epigraph to this chapter. Debray speaks of *national fragmentation* of the Latin American revolution, with which he discerns a certain symmetry of the different temporal rhythms: 'in each country the process has its own time-clock'. This formulation suggests a certain *uniformity of temporal experience within a nation/state structure* that differentiates it from others. The 'people' ('who make history'), according to Debray live in the time of the area, town or country which their horizon is bounded by, in contradistinction to 'the vanguards', who *by theoretical anticipation* become contemporary with the time of continental or world revolution. Mao's China, lacking in a single, centralized state structure lacked in a singular time. Different temporalities marked its different constituents. The revolutionaries in China, therefore, did not have the possibility of the kind of revolutionary situation that the Bolsheviks had in Russia, which as we saw, was articulated around a centralized state structure. What is more, China did not even have a unified capitalist economy; it was but a huge landmass with warring warlords. The vanguards in China, therefore, lived the time of world revolution, almost entirely by theoretical anticipation.

The project of the modern state becomes closely entangled at this stage in the search for nationhood and a hoary past, a Great Tradition of the incipient nation. It is this that Poulantzas referred to when he suggested that, '[T]he State establishes the modern nation by eliminating other national pasts and turning them into variations of its own history.'[18] Poulantzas' discussion is still framed by old categories of nation, which are in some sense assumed to be already there, as for instance when he says: 'the modern nation-state also involves eradication of the tradition, histories and memories of the dominated nations . . . .' (Poulantzas 1978: 113). This however does not reduce the significance of his observations cited above. The state, according to him, thus monopolizes national tradition, 'storing up' the memory of the people-nation. In much the same way as Laclau and Mouffe see the fragmentation of the working class into so many different sections as an initial condition, so too does Poulantzas see the 'spatiality and historicity of each [national] working class' as a variant of the time-space of its own nation—and not of the 'working class' as some supra-national or 'anational' original essence, subsequently assuming contingent national forms.[19] This discussion of the state/nation and its relation to time has a direct bearing on our understanding of Mao's 'China' and Regis Debray's Latin America: the non-existence of the state in China and the existence of different national states in Latin America account for a very different kind of idea of a revolutionary situation from the one Lenin encountered in Russia.[20]

None of the above, however, exemplifies 'non-revolutionary times'. The instances in the above discussion merely point towards different kinds of revolutionary situations from the Russian—or French—kind. But they do show how even these depend critically upon the development of a *simultaneous revolutionary* situation for their success. That is precisely what Mao calculates for in China, and what eludes Debray in Latin America. When Otto Bauer (in the second epigraph to this chapter) asserts that forms that appear as chronological developments in the international context, are actually contemporaneous in the Austro-Hungarian empire, he is, in fact, pointing to the fact that given these different forms, the idea of revolutionary intervention in the old framework of acting upon *a single present* becomes extremely problematic. It requires the spelling out of a different notion of revolutionary intervention. To quote Bauer: 'To see the processes of transformation of capitalist society no longer as following the tempo of a unified and homogeneous logico-historical mechanism, but as the result of a multiplication and proliferation of endogenous factors of mutation of the relations of production and power—this implies . . . at the political level, a supersession of the mystifying alternative between "reform" and "revolution".'[21]

It is worth recalling that Trotsky's formula of 'combined and uneven development' attempts to deal, at a global level, precisely with what Otto Bauer is trying to grapple with in the context of the Austro-Hungarian empire—with of course, very different conclusions for theory and revolutionary strategy. He says: 'Unevenness, the most general law of the historic process, reveals itself most sharply and complexly in the destiny of the backward countries. Under the whip of external necessity, their backward culture is compelled to make leaps. From the universal law of unevenness thus derives another law which, for the lack of a better name, we may call the law of combined development—by which we mean a drawing together of the different stages of the journey, a combining of separate steps, an amalgam of archaic with more contemporary forms.'[22] As Lowy rightly notes, the presupposition of this formulation is a specific idea of human history: '*with the appearance of capitalism as a world system, world history becomes a (contradictory) concrete totality* . . . .'[23] The very idea of 'unevenness' presupposes a totality; it assumes that the different entities involved here are parts of a larger whole—capitalism and World-History. This idea clearly resonates with Koselleck's rendering of the emergence of the idea of 'World-History'. The second law, that of combined development, posited by Trotsky, however, produces a notion of a totality that is at once threatened. For, in the passage above, the totality of world capitalism confronts a 'backward culture' *as an externality*, which it then forces to transform under its whip. 'Savages [*sic*] throw away their bows and arrows for rifles all at once, without travelling the road which lay between these two weapons in the past', says Trotsky, suggesting that in the process something entirely unexpected and new has come into being—a combination of the archaic and the contemporary. Does this 'backward culture' or 'backward country' thereby become *fully integrated* into the totality of world capitalism? Clearly, if it were the case, and Trotsky were dealing with a unified and homogenous capitalism, he would not need to posit this 'law'. The problem is that he has to deal with the fact that the 'totality' of world capitalism he is confronted with is *never really complete.* As Lowy remarks, this idea (of combined and uneven development) 'enabled Trotsky to transcend the evolutionist conception of history as a succession of rigidly predetermined stages and to develop a dialectical view of historical development through sudden leaps and contradictory fusions'.[24] It enabled him to argue against the evolutionist conception of the marxism of the Second International that held that the socialist revolution could only, legitimately take place in the countries of advanced capitalism. This move effectively problematizes the very idea of a totality whose existence is supposedly governed by an *internal rationality*. In a sense, Lenin's idea of the totality too, is one that is effectively decentred, given his insistence that the centre of world revolution can shift unexpectedly and need not coincide at all with the centre of world capitalism. Here the argument of the 'weakest link' put forward by Lenin becomes the mode of his displacement of the Centre of the totality of world capitalism. Both

Trotsky and Lenin then, see *a relation of externality between capitalism and pre-capitalist societies*, which takes place through the problematic agency of colonial annexation and war.

How does the problem of permanent revolution raised by Trotsky now appear from this standpoint? It seems to me that while he is correctly able to challenge an evolutionist view of history, and thus overcome the 'stagist' mindset by arguing for *socialist revolutions* in 'backward *capitalist* countries', the continuing hold of the category of 'totality' forces him to still see world capitalism as a single closed entity, moving towards a common destiny. It is not difficult to discern here the idea of a *single logos*, a governing principle, an internal logic at work that compels all countries to move towards the common socialist future of all humanity. It is this that makes him see all these 'backward' countries as already '*backward capitalist* countries'. It is this ideological *a priori* of the category of totality that subverts the possibility opened out by his reading of world capitalism as an incomplete whole.

Thus, while the problem of temporality is recognized by both Lenin and Trotsky at the practical level, it never becomes a theoretical problem leading to a rethinking of the category of totality and its specific instance—world capitalism. This is a problem shared by all shades of marxists. What if we deny the very possibility of a fully formed, internally coherent totality, that is to say, we recognize the problem of different historical presents and different times? What kind of implications does it have for our understanding of radical and revolutionary politics in the 'capitalist periphery'?

In the first place, such a move would call attention to the ways in which revolutionary movements and radical politics are, and have been, discussed in the postcolonial world as merely some (other) version of a socialist/proletarian revolution. Even Mao, who challenged the Comintern and stalinist orthodoxy in very significant ways, continues to talk of the Communist Party of China as a 'working class' party and the Chinese revolution merely as a contingent of the International Communist Movement. Nowhere do we get a serious theorization of the peasant struggle and peasant militancy that constituted the backbone of many of these revolutionary movements like China and Vietnam. Movements like India's nationalist/anti-colonial struggle, of course, remain completely outside the pale of any theorization by marxists—seen at best as some kind of 'passive revolution' in some rare subsequent departures by some scholars. The Indian nationalist movement, which was another instance of protracted warfare, reveals some very specific characteristics as a struggle that has no telos—an open-ended contestation between different tendencies and currents, often within the same party (the Indian National Congress), but also more violent contestations say between the INC and the Muslim League or the Hindu Mahasabha. The model of the Indian freedom struggle is, in many senses, unique. But it is also a movement that shows how rare the possibilities of a synchronized political action can be and how many countercurrents and narratives can run side by side, calling for a very different set of negotiating mechanisms.

Secondly, if we understand a social totality as an articulation of different temporalities, of many different presents, we might better be able to appreciate how rare the possibilities of their fusion into an apocalyptic revolutionary situation can be. This will help us understand what I have been calling non-revolutionary times. If revolutions have not occurred in many parts of the world where we would have expected them to, the fault may not lie with the practice of revolutionaries so much as with theoretical illusions about the imminence and inevitability of the revolutionary moment. We will then be able to see 'uneven development' for what it is: *the explanation for the failure of that promised moment to arrive.*

Non-revolutionary times then, are times that are marked by this deep heterogeneity of different presents. They may not always be times of reaction and counter-revolution but are likely to be characterized by what Laclau and Mouffe call the proliferation of antagonisms and the emergence of different kinds of democratic struggles which resist the constitution of the subject position of the 'popular'. These are times that, therefore, call our attention to the framing of 'revolutionary politics' in the abstract, torn from all historical context; they direct us to reconsider the entire conceptual framework that sets up the absolute priority of some eternal revolutionary principles such that the only alternative outside its framework it can recognize is *reformism*. The dichotomous world of the old revolutionary framework erects the 'dual power strategy' as the sole form for transformative politics.[26] Consequently, it does not know what to do when such 'dual power' situations are nowhere on the horizon. It is the persistence of the dual power strategy that inevitably *poses the question of transformation in terms of an all-or-nothing option*. The binary of revolution *versus* reformism is a logical consequence of such a strategic outlook and blocks any possibility of new, creative forms being thought out, as every strategy that moves out of this frame of reference is *ab initio* illegitimate, even if sometimes necessary. 'Working within the system' can thus only produce varieties of social democratic surrender to the logic of the system. We can only have the pathos of a Biman Bose or a Benoy Konar who claim that they are only building capitalism in West Bengal *because that is all that they can do*! With this bad conscience, the revolutionary can never think the possibility of being and working *subversively* 'within the system'.

This is why all radical politics is always besieged by the threat of 'reformism'/co-optation and 'parliamentarism'. On the other hand, one could take a leaf from the book of feminist politics (or some strands of Dalit politics) to see how to be within a system subversively. One might then be able to see that radical politics can only exist in constant tension with itself, rejuvenating its transformative impulse by continually reinventing itself. For, subversion is not about arms and armed struggle. It is, above all, about continuously challenging the 'obviousness' of common sense, about challenging the truth-effects of power. The moment at which a radical politics freezes its categories into some eternal, timeless truths, it cannot but get caught in the mesh of domesticated bourgeois institutionalism. In order that radical politics is able to thus reinvent itself, it will have to be continuously alert to the ways in which newer subjectivities are taking shape and new challenges to the system are emerging on the ground in actual political practice.

## NOTES

1. Regis Debray, *A Critique of Arms, vol. 1*, Harmondsworth: Penguin Books, 1977, pp. 19-20, emphasis added.

2. Otto Bauer, cited in Ernesto Laclau and Chantal Mouffe, *Hegemony and Socialist Strategy: Towards a Radical Democratic Politics*, London and New York: Verso, 1985, pp. 27-8.

3. Elsewhere, we have referred to this tendency of species-maoism as the 'third phase of naxalism', even though naxalism itself is part of the generic-maoism of the 1960s and earlier periods. (See Nivedita Menon and Aditya Nigam, *Power and Contestation: India Since 1989*, London: Zed Books Ltd, 2007, pp. 115-23).

4. Ref. V. C. Joshi (ed) *Rammohun Roy and the Process of Modernization in India*, Delhi: Vikas Publishing, 1975.

5. For a detailed discussion of the genealogy of this idea, see Michael Lowy, *The Politics of Combined and Uneven Development—The Theory of Permanent Revolution*, London: Verso, 1981.

6. This is the official position of the CPI(M), which believes that it was correct to have withdrawn the struggle once this change took place.

7. Though the LF came to power during the tenure of the Janata Party government at the Centre, the JP government was very short-lived. Largely it was the Congress party that ruled at the Centre for the most part till the mid-1990s.

8. Louis Althusser, *For Marx*, London: Verso, 1969, p. 99.

9. V.I. Lenin, 'The Collapse of the Second International', *Collected Works* (*CW*), vol. 21, Moscow: Progress Publishers, 1977, p. 213.

10. Ibid., p. 214.

11. Laclau and Mouffe, *Hegemony and Socialist Strategy: Towards a Radical Democratic Politics*, London and New York: Verso, 1985/99, p. 13.

12. Ibid., p. 13.

13. Witness for instance the following from his criticism of the Mensheviks, where he claims that they do not understand that what is decisive in marxism is its revolutionary dialectics and adds: 'For instance, it does not even occur to them that because Russia stands on the border-line between the civilised countries and the countries *which this war has for the first time definitely brought into the orbit of civilization*—all oriental, non-European countires—she could and was indeed bound to reveal certain distinguishing features.' Lenin, *CW*, vol. 33, pp. 476-7. Emphasis added.

14. Mao Tse-tung, *Selected Works, vol. I*, Peking: Foreign Languages Press, 1977, p. 64.

15. Ibid., p. 65.

16. Ibid., p. 65.

17. Ibid., p. 66.

18. Nicos Poulantzas, *State, Power, Socialism*, London: NLB, 1978, p. 113.

19. Ibid., p. 118.

20. The existence of the state is a necessary though not sufficient condition for a unified and homogeneous temporal experience. The power and reach of the state into the deep recesses of society has other coordinates which we cannot go into now. But it is for this reason that even in countries like India, despite the existence of a centralized state, communists have always had to deal with heterogeneous times.

21. Otto Bauer, cited in Laclau and Mouffe, op. cit., p. 45. Bauer is also careful to point out while making the above point that this proposal of his '*does not involve an evolutionist type of option, as if socialism were realizable through homeopathic doses*'.

22. Ibid., p. 87.

23. Michael Lowy, op. cit., p. 87.

24. Michael Lowy, op. cit., p. 87.

25. I borrow this phrase from Poulantzas, op. cit., pp. 257-60, who borrows this expression from Lenin who used it to designate the situation in Russia where the power of the soviets confronted the power of the state, but generalizes it to describe a strategic perspective of the kind we have been discussing above. For my purposes, both kinds of perspectives—that is the Russian and the protracted war—can be seen as instances of dual power.

# 4

# EMPIRE, NATION AND MINORITY CULTURES

## The Postnational Moment

It might be appropriate to begin this chapter by referring to two striking images of recent times. The first, an image of the Kurdistan region of Iraq on the eve of the American attack, beamed in the Western media, with an air of moral righteousness. This was the image of Kurdish men and women, arms in hand, preparing to 'welcome' the US forces, as the television commentator put it. The second, a photographic image, republished by the Indian book review journal *Biblio*, of young Afghan girls playing football, with their *hijab* off, at least with their faces uncovered, in the aftermath of the fall of the Taliban regime. This image was part of the barrage of information in the media following the fall of the Taliban: stories of music and dance on the streets of Kabul, of the rejoicing artist who had concealed the human images on his paintings with an overlay of paint, now wiping it out to reveal the human forms beneath. The Western media even enlisted, in a manner of speaking, the support of the Revolutionary Association of Afghan Women (RAWA) for Empire, despite RAWA's repeated assertions that they did not support the US attack on Afghanistan.

Not very long ago, the Western world had witnessed a similar situation with NATO's 'humanitarian' bombing in Serbia/Kosova, with the Kosova Liberation Army (KLA) fighting with open support from NATO forces. Milosevic's brutal ethnic cleansing programme, it is well-known, had already marginalized and destroyed the old political leadership of the Kosovars, leaving KLA as the only force opposing the Milosevic regime. The bombing of Serbia thus ended up splitting the European Left down the middle on this issue.[1] Should the bombing be opposed? Short of military intervention, is there any way of reining in Milosevic? These were recurrent questions even among anti-war activists and they continued to reappear through the war on Afghanistan and Iraq. How do we 'refuse to choose' in this context, as it seems we must? The choice either way is a difficult one, for the fight is no longer between the Good and Evil, between Revolution and imperialism, or from the other side, between Freedom and Totalitarianism. Whether it ever was such a neat Manichean division, is in fact, debatable.

'Empire', say Michael Hardt and Antonio Negri, 'is materializing before our very eyes.'[2] The two important events that signal the emergence of Empire, they say, are the first Gulf War and the war in Kosovo. The events that they identify as critical in the construction of Empire, merely presaged the later wars unleashed in the aftermath of 11 September. Empire, suggest Hardt and Negri, is not just another name for globalization; it is a 'global order, a new logic and structure of rule', which is certainly coeval with and linked to the new global circuits of production but not reducible to them. Hardt and Negri read 'the declining sovereignty of nation-states' as one of the primary symptoms of the coming of Empire—a new form representing a new kind of sovereignty.[3] Crucial to this new sovereignty is the eclipse of conflicts or competition between several imperialist powers, and the overarching idea of a single power 'that overdetermines them all, structures them in a unitary way and treats them *under one common notion of right that is decidedly postcolonial and postimperialist*'.[4] This new form of sovereignty is presented as 'a global concert', 'a unitary power that maintains social peace and produces its own ethical truths'.

The really significant and persuasive part of Hardt and Negri's thesis is that Empire is not formed simply on the basis of force but on the basis of its ability to present force as being in the service of right and peace. 'All interventions of the imperial armies are solicited by one or more of the parties involved in an already existing conflict . . . . Empire is . . . called into being and constituted on the basis of its capacity to resolve conflicts.'[5]

All the instances cited above are those of direct war and intervention and they at least serve to illustrate, somewhat dramatically, what might be a more general condition, that I wish to discuss in this chapter. My interest here is in two questions, quite different from those of Hardt and Negri: my entry point is not that of Empire but that of (1) minority groups or cultures who almost inevitability appear as opportunist in their eagerness to welcome the powerful forces of Empire. (2) New kinds of political intervention, which often (though not always) deploy the rhetoric of universal human rights or that of a universal global civil society against the power of the nation-state without necessarily being complicit in the project of Empire. Lodged here, in these two kinds of political subjectivities might be a larger question, an exploration of which might allow us to pose the problem of the postnational moment in a way that looks beyond the binary of 'within' and 'without'. In the following section, I discuss the question of the 'postnational'—of thinking beyond the nation—as distinct from the shorthand term 'globalization'. I do this through a discussion of an exchange between Arjun Appadurai and Partha Chatterjee, some years ago. In entering the discussion through this debate, I attempt to steer clear of both—a celebration of the global (Appadurai) and an exclusive insistence on struggles within (Chatterjee).

There is something else here that needs to be underlined as well. In the stance of the Kurdish people or the desire of the young Afghan girls playing football or, for that matter, the artist in Kabul, we have instances of everyday life and desire. The people involved here are ordinary people, not 'Rightists' or 'Leftists'—and they are not obliged to be 'political'. In grappling with political subjectivites today, I do not wish to lose sight of such ordinary folk.

## Thinking Beyond the Nation?

In an early essay on the crisis of the nation-state, which explicitly delineated the contemporary moment as 'postnational', Arjun Appadurai laid out a programmatic imperative: 'We need to think ourselves beyond the nation.'[6] Such an exercise, Appadurai claimed, would help 'provide part of the apparatus of recognition for postnational social forms'.[7] He argued that there were already in existence a whole range of movements, which could be called postnational, which were floundering because of the lack of an adequate political language that would be able to provide them a way of 'thinking their way out of the imaginary of the nation-state'.[8] In identifying the actual formations Appadurai lists a vast range from terrorist organizations and transnational diasporic groups to organizations like the Amnesty International and Oxfam. 'We are looking at the birth of a variety of postnational social formations', he says.[9] There is a sense in his rendering that the world is now increasingly made up of diasporas, of refugees, tourists, guest workers, transnational intellectuals, and illegal aliens—all increasingly unrestrained by spatial boundary and territorial sovereignty, and that this is what determines the meaning of 'postnational' and the crisis of the nation-state in the contemporary—almost as though the distinction between national territories has dissolved. Here Appadurai's argument sounds like some prevailing romantic/anarchist neo-Deleuzian talk of nomads, rhizomes and flows (of populations, images, commodities), and of world citizenship, as though this were now the dominant experience of populations worldwide. Such celebratory rhetoric of nomadism and flows, seems to be quite innocent of the continuing sharp inequities of power between say the West and the non-West.

Such a notion of free mobility does not square with our own experience in the 'peripheries' of world capitalism, where struggles against displacement and dislocation of rural populations have become acute, as mass displacements through land acquisitions create ever larger number of mobile populations of 'development refugees'. Similarly, struggles over urban space have erupted with particular sharpness in recent years. The process of relatively freer flow of populations, *within the nation-space*, that was so characteristic of the decades following decolonization, and which made the postcolonial city a hospitable site for large numbers of people coming in search of livelihoods, is now sought to be halted, as nation-states prepare these metropolises for foreign capital and the consumerist middle classes.

On the global level too, analyses of the recent rejection of the European constitution by large sections of people in France and Netherlands, for instance, show that at least one of the major concerns behind it was the fear of immigrants and the 'lesser Europeans' trooping into these countries, throwing their societies into crises. And these crises have to do with material questions like jobs and resources, as much as they have to with questions of culture. Free mobility and the possibility of 'nomadism' are actually available only to the most privileged, who inhabit the 'uncluttered spaces' of anonymous, individuated modern existence. For the bulk of the populations, at least in the Third World, who live in the dense and cluttered spaces of rural and urban community life, the liberation from space has not yet come. The meaning of the postnational moment for these populations is not quite one of movements and flows but something very different, which I intend to explore below.

Partha Chatterjee has responded to Appadurai's suggestion with a certain sense of legitimate alarm. Chatterjee reads in Appadurai's discussion a possible argument for 'postnational forms of government'—which may not have been the latter's suggestion. This is however an argument that many others have made in recent times, as for example, the advocates of 'cosmopolitan democracy'. These advocates have already begun thinking in terms of 'world citizens' 'whose membership in world organizations would no longer be mediated through their nationality but would have popular representation in a world parliament through direct elections above the national level'.[10] There are different versions of this idea, including the cruder versions of 'world governance' advocated by many powerful international institutions like the IMF and the World Bank.

While Chatterjee might be unjustly reading all this into Appadurai's proposal, his alarm, it seems is because he also reads in Appadurai's essay—not without justification—a position which too has acquired increasing popularity among scholars and activists in recent years: a *case for a global civil society*. Chatterjee argues that 'a considerable part of transnational activities today take place in the domain of non-state institutions under the sign of a modernization of civil social formation'.[11] He further argues: 'These are the activities of a transnational public sphere whose moral claims derive from the assumed existence of a domain of universal civil society.'[12] These organizations, UN agencies, women's organizations, human rights groups 'act as an external check on sovereign powers of the nation-state and occupy the critical moral position of a global civil society assessing the incomplete modernity of particular national political formations'.[13] Chatterjee is rightly wary of such global civil society or public sphere activism based on the language of individual autonomy and the rights discourse, that is often deployed quite innocently alongside the more cynical use of such rhetoric by the US in its political interventions across the globe. In a lecture delivered after 11 September and the US 'War on Terror', for example, he likens these kind of activist efforts to the squirrel in the *Ramayana*, carrying pebbles one by one for building the bridgehead of Empire. Chatterjee is justly worried that the 'celebratory rhetoric' and 'high moral passion' associated with these visions of global modernity elide the political-strategic implications of such postnational formations. He likens the current phase of globalization of universal rights to the 'moral cultural drive to spread "modernity" throughout the world', associated with colonization. His argument provides another vantage point of viewing the phenomenon identified by Hardt and Negri—that of being called-into-being of Empire.

Chatterjee concludes his argument by arguing quite forcefully that the struggles within the nation-state, which are about democracy rather than modernity, therefore situate themselves on the site of the internal, national domain of political society, rather than that of a universal, global civil society. As opposed to this, in the latter sphere of transnational civil society, he suggests, the framing idea is that of *modernity* and this, he argues, will inevitably structure the world in a colonial pattern, based as its normative ideals are on those of Western modernity. The logic of contestations over democracy and representation in political society, on the other hand, often violate the 'universal modern conventions' of civil society.

The problem of course, is that despite the force of Chatterjee's argument, there is an equally insurmountable problem with an argument that seeks to confine struggles and movements to the space 'within the nation'. For now, on the other side, the argument against universalism and the rights discourse gets incorporated within the cultural exceptionalist, rather essentialist rhetoric of many tyrannical Third World regimes, who we know have strongly argued against human rights on this ground. In fact, this is precisely what Jurgen Habermas cites in his impassioned argument for the kind of global modernity that Chatterjee is arguing against. Habermas cites, in particular, the sharp conflict that came to the fore at the Vienna Conference on Human Rights where a number of Asian governments like that of Singapore adopted this line of argument. He also refers to the 1993 Bangkok Declaration jointly signed by Singapore, Malaysia, Taiwan and China.[14] This then is the scenario: the army of global modernity marching under the banner of Universalism (of Rights) confronting the indigenous oppressors of all hues, presenting their anti-imperialism under the banner of Cultural Exceptionalism.

It is, of course, incorrect to say that Chatterjee makes an argument for exceptionalism. On the contrary, he continuously points to struggles *within* these societies that challenge the inequities of power and resources, but reminds us repeatedly that these struggles can only be fought within the domain of national political societies. In her argument against the 'universalization of Human Rights' position, Nivedita Menon finds in Chatterjee's claim the openings of a third possibility: one that can steer clear of both the universalist claims of Human Rights discourse and the nationalist, anti-West rhetoric of the above-mentioned Third World regimes. She finds the notion of political society important in underlining the fact that we are dealing here with many different forms of modernity. She thus emphasizes that the notion of political society must be seen as neither modern nor traditional—a domain of contested modernities.[15]

However, this is a direction Chatterjee does not take—namely, the opening of a third possibility: the Kurdish men and women or the ordinary Afghan people, whose instance I cited above, cannot be seen, by any stretch of imagination, to belong to the normative world of Western modernity or global civil society. If anything, they must be seen as part of the 'national' domain of political society in a way that immediately throws the 'national' into crisis. This is where things start becoming messy. Transversal alliances, often fleeting and momentary, are being continuously forged between oppressed and subjugated populations in one part of the world, with what are sometimes the bigger oppressors than the more proximate ones.

In the following section, therefore, I will examine what I think is a more general condition, namely, the 'opportunism' of minority cultures/existence. This is also where the framing binary of empire and colony, espoused by postcolonial theorists, seems to me to fail to recognize other voices that are continuously, simultaneously at play—voices that do not fit into either term of the binary.

## Nations and Minority Cultures

Before we enter the vexed question of the 'opportunism' of minority cultures and their significance for understanding the postnational in a more complex and layered way, a brief discussion of the *paradigm of nationhood* will be in order. I would like to begin an exploration of this paradigm of nationhood by narrating two stories picked up at random from contemporary India, which suggest a different notion of belonging embodied in very different *lived* categories that structure the 'cognitive map' of the popular.

The first is the story of an old man from the 'East'—that is *eastern Uttar Pradesh*, a province in north India—a *purabiya* as 'easterners' are referred to in spoken Hindi. This man, Mata Badal, came from some village in the Awadh region and worked as a gardener in the house in Dehra Dun, where we grew up. Every other year he would take leave from my father to go to his *des* (literally country or homeland). He would tell us that he did not like life here in this *pardes* or foreign land, where he had been forced to come in search of livelihood. As children we used to laugh at his 'ignorance': how silly of him, we often thought, that he does not even know that his *desh* (country/nation) is the whole of India. What I did not realize then but have begun to feel increasingly now is that his *des* was emphatically not the *desh*; it was not a mere *apabhransha* or a linguistically 'fallen' form, of the purer, Sanskritik *desh*. On the contrary, it embodied a different mode of being and notion of belonging. Outside this *des*, he seemed to live like an exile. It is also interesting that this was/is not merely his idea of belonging but also of all those who would refer to him as an 'easterner', for implicit in the notion of the *purabiya* is the idea of the frontier or horizon outside of which what is East does not matter. Even

'Calcutta', which for instance, became the object of so many folk songs of separation for the inhabitants of east Uttar Pradesh, did not figure at all within the limits of the lived geography of the inhabitants of western UP (now Uttarakhand), till very recently.

My second story, that of Zubeida, is even more fascinating. This story is narrated by Nivedita Menon, who met Zubeida in the relief camps in Gujarat in June 2002, after the carnages, which had completely destroyed her bangle trade.[16] In the course of one of the conversations, Zubeida asked her, 'Have you ever been to Bindravan [*sic*]?'[17] On getting an answer in the negative, she asked yet again, 'Never been there? Not even for pilgrimage (*teerath*)?' and then wistfully added, '*woh hamaara vatan hai* (that is my land)'.[18] Zubeida, a Muslim woman from the land of Krishna, permeated with a Vaishnavite ethos, sitting in the camps of Gujarat, and barely able to pronounce the actual Sanskritik name of her land—and yet, she thinks of it as *hers*. Contrast this attachment and sense of Zubeida's belonging to Vrindavan to her relationship to the 'nation' that is India, where she is a perpetual outsider—always a potential traitor or a Pakistani agent. Vrindavan never demands any demonstration of unflinching loyalty of her in the way that India does. Vrindavan, her *vatan*, like Mata Badal's *des*, is never overcome by the sense of crisis that the nation is perpetually threatened by, in relation to its inhabitants. It needs no continuous reiteration of loyalty; it simply *is*. The nation, on the other hand, as Ernest Renan, that ardent champion and theorist of nationalism, famously put it, *is a daily plebiscite*.[19] Loyalty for the nation must be rehearsed and reproduced, every day, every hour.

What is the relationship of Mata Badal's *des* and Zubeida's *vatan* to this entity called 'India that is Bharat'? It is easy to explain these terms away as ignorance—and that is precisely my point. The *spirit of Indianness*, the idea that one belongs to some larger landmass with specific cultural contours, *has to be inculcated* through the massive pedagogical enterprise of national education. Only then can one become a national citizen.

At one level, these are not unusual stories. In other time/s, in other place/s, there have certainly been many such instances. Miroslav Hroch mentions the instance of the district of Polesie in interwar Poland. When its inhabitants were asked in the Census of 1919 about their nationality, 'most of them just replied: from hereabouts'.[20] Or take the instance of France in the 1880s when General Georges Boulanger decided to contest the elections and his Flemish supporters revolted against him for presenting them as 'French'. 'We are Flemish and Flanders is our land' was their war cry. They saw France as an entity that merely sucked their blood.[21]

We can dispose off one possible line of argument of old historicist thought, right away. Such an argument will hold that we are today where the French were in the 1880s or the Polish in 1919. It is also easy to explain the prevalence of these notions by pointing to the 'lack of education' and 'low level of consciousness' of the people concerned and thereby argue that, 'we are actually getting there'—this is just the road all nations traverse on the way to full nationhood. Apart from ardent nationalists, such an argument will have few takers today and it need not detain us here. It is by now widely recognized that the idea that all societies must take the same route to modern nationhood and eventual emancipation through the attainment of the ideal of abstract universal citizenship, is deeply flawed and flows from a Eurocentric conception of the world. It is generally recognized nowadays, that there is no such thing as a world-historical telos, a common goal towards which all societies—or worse, the World in the singular—are moving. There is a further recognition today that different societies may have different visions of their own 'preferred futures'.[22] Clearly, this recognition is a relatively recent development in social and political theory. But the matter does not end with this recognition. That is the easier task. We need, in that case, to ask some further questions about the persistence of notions of belonging that do not need the existence of the nation-form. What if the expression of this different sense of belonging to the *des* or *vatan* were not mere remnants of a past consciousness, a relic of some other era, but constitute a different view of the world in our 'here and now'? What if we see these notions of belonging, not as something to be overcome by 'educating the illiterate masses' and instilling national consciousness in them, but as expressions of the fact that the everyday lives of common people are negotiated through a very different set of categories from the ones that the idea of nationhood accustoms us to? What are the theoretical implications of acknowledging that different 'societies' have or can have their 'own' preferred futures? What is this entity that we call 'society' which can ostensibly have a *singular will directing it towards its preferred future*? Some of these questions call for much more sustained exploration, not all of which can be undertaken within the limits of this chapter.

I should also refer here to one line of argument put forward, for, instance, by Chris Bayly, in a different context. Bayly looks at the formation of *bazaars* and the emergence of regional marketing and financial systems between 1500 and 1800 and concomitant notions of '*deshs, watans* and *nadus*' and places them squarely in the prehistory of nationalism.[23] Bayly's use of '*desh*' is incorrect here. As we saw above, the term for this other notion of belonging, is '*des*', while '*desh*' has come to mean something entirely different, i.e. the nation. He attempts to show that these local ideas of belonging were the pre-existing bases on which later nationalism was to grow. Apart from the fact that this argument is firmly located within the telos of nationhood that I have already referred to above, it will not certainly account for the persistence of these categories in the present. It will not do to simply refer to the persistence of these notions in the present as 'survivals'—for they simply beg the question. We must ask some further questions about the theoretical status of these 'survivals', especially when they continue to be critical to the lived experience of large numbers of people in the present. My argument is that the nation-form cannot really deal with the ideas of *des, vatan* or *nadu*. It is precisely by erasing the presence of these notions of belonging that the nation seeks to establish its sovereignty. I might also mention that this kind of nationalist teleology is seriously problematized even by Britian's recent history with the Scots and the Welsh reasserting their own distinct identities—or more recently the fears of the break-up of Belgium.[24] These developments indicate, at the very least that nationalism may not really be the last station on the road to abstract universal citizenship.

The central problem of what I am referring to as the 'paradigm of nationhood' is that of aggregating what have been till then so many different social, cultural and geographical entities into a single entity of the nation. It must weld together all these different entities—let us call them 'localities'—with different pasts and different presents, into one big modern Nation. As Eugen Weber has suggested in his study of the French nation, at least in this respect, the process of nation-formation functions in quite the same way as colonialism. *The claims of the Nation's sovereignty can become real and tangible only to the extent that the pasts of the localities are either erased or reproduced within a narrative of the Nation's history.* History, as the new 'science' becomes the weapon of the nation in its fight to produce a common past and thereby posit a common destiny, against the claims of the locality. The profound insight that, in a sense, *colonization/colonialism constitutes the paradigmatic form that is the basis of all nation-formation* is crucial here. For the Nation to emerge, then, its sovereignty over its 'own' territory is established through the marking out of the territory (and people), in the first place (which is in effect, simultaneously, a demarcation of its external sovereignty), and through their assimilation into a new national culture.

This historical possibility, however, is closed for anti-colonial nationalisms, which began taking shape in the course of their fight for liberation from colonial rule, and thus had to hammer out an agreement with different kinds of political aspirations that began emerging alongside them. This process was undoubtedly complex and multilayered but nationalisms, so long as they remain such (caught within the imaginary of the nation-state with a single culture), can never give up the ambition of eventually erasing all difference. That is where minority cultures become problematic. That is also where the attempts by nationalism to give itself an ancient and glorious past, creates more problems than it can solve, for not all communities can ever share that particular past.

There are enough instances in India's own history, especially in the colonial context, which indicate the desire of oppressed cultures to seek their liberation by aligning with the colonizing power. I have argued elsewhere that Dalit and lower caste assertions in late colonial India represent one important current that seeks to constantly disrupt the binary of colonialism/nationalism in the course of charting out its own path of liberation. It is well known that Dalit and 'lower caste' ideologues and intellectuals have always seen colonialism as the liberator of the Dalits. I have also discussed the phenomenon of the 'opportunism of minority cultures', with respect to Muslim identity in India, elsewhere, and shall not go into it here.[25] In the remainder of this chapter, I explore the notion of transversal politics and transversal alliances and what they might mean in terms of thinking afresh the concept of power, as also the different ways of dealing with it.

## Transversal Alliances: The Global Conjuncture

Deleuze, Guattari and Foucault occasionally use the term transversal politics to refer to specific struggles but none of them really define the term. Nira Yuval-Davis has also used the category 'transversal politics' in a somewhat different sense to refer to the construction of a dialogic space across difference (between women from different cultures) that can help overcome the universality/particularity dichotomy. To Foucault, transversal struggles are not limited to any one country; they are transnational. Moreover, such struggles do not necessarily limit themselves to either horizontal or vertical alliances or solidarities. All these senses of 'transversal' however, still gesture very much to alliances or solidarities between different kinds of oppressed sections. I will use this term in order to refer to a wide range of struggles and modes of political intervention, which have emerged or become visible, over last couple of decades, including some that could fall under the category of global civil society activism, which are forced to negotiate their way within a complex web of power. There is a high degree of complexity here as it is often difficult, if not impossible, to permanently fix a hierarchy of evils; these struggles are thus often forced to seek alliances, even if momentarily, that may seem quite opportunist, if not downright dangerous.

In recent times, in India, we have seen the furious controversy that raged, for instance, over the decision of some Dalit organizations to raise the issue of caste oppression/discrimination in the United Nations Conference on Race and Other Related Forms of Discrimination, held in Durban in 2001. Both the fact that Dalit groups decided to raise the issue as well as the fact that almost all shades of nationalist opinion came out in open opposition, using the well-worn nationalist argument that this is our 'internal matter' and should not therefore be raised in international forums, underlined the extent of division between two kinds of positions. The stridency of opposition to this move of the Dalit groups, despite the fact that a UN conference does not have quite the same status as a colonizing power, revealed how resistant the dominant and powerful nationalist interests are to any move to take matters out of the purview of the nation-state's jurisdiction—never mind the fact that the nation-state itself has hardly shown any interest in dealing squarely with questions of continuing caste-based discrimination.

In the last two decades, the question of raising 'internal matters' in international forums has come up quite often and sometimes in ways more problematic than raising them at UN conferences. The question of human rights violations by the Indian state in the north-east, especially Nagaland, could not find a sympathetic ear inside the country till the matter was raised through forums like the Amnesty International. Another question that acquired the character of a serious controversy among activist groups was the attempt to lobby international support for the struggle against the displacement of the Narmada tribals led by the Narmada Bachao Andolan (NBA), especially the deposition by some supporters before the United States Congress. And yet, it is also undeniable that the only time the NBA campaign achieved some measure of success was when, as a consequence of international lobbying, the World Bank was forced to suspend financial support for the Sardar Sarovar dam. Inside the 'nation', this struggle around one of the most hotly debated public issues has routinely invited the epithet 'anti-national' by most mainstream political parties.

Once again, more recently, when the anti-Muslim pogroms in Gujarat were going on in 2002, some anti-communal activists had taken recourse to international campaigns and lobbying, including deposing before the US Congressional Committee on Religious Freedom. It was because of these and the subsequent campaign undertaken by Indian and South Asian groups in the US, that the Chief Minister of Gujarat, Narendra Modi was denied a visa to the United States.

As against these instances of struggle, let me take up one that actually lost the opportunity to fight a determined battle because its imagination continued to be hegemonized by the 'imaginary of the nation-state'. This is the instance of the Indian side of debate on the social clause. It is worth remembering that the first labour legislations in India were enacted as a result of the 'trade wars' between the nascent indigenous industry and the textile barons of England. As Bipan Chandra shows in his study of economic nationalism in India, 'first impulse towards legislative action to mitigate the harshness of the evils of capitalist industrialism in India came from England, whose philanthropists and textile manufacturers joined hands to demand statutory protection for the health of the women and children employed in Indian factories'.[26]

We know that as the final negotiations to the Uruguay Round on the General Agreement of Tariffs and Trade (GATT) came to an end, on the eve of the signing of the accord, the metropolitan countries produced their trump card: trade could genuinely be free, they argued, only when all conditions were equal. But Third World entrepreneurs have an unfair advantage because they employ cheap and over-exploited labour and child labour and have the benefit of practically non-existent environmental regulations. They thus proposed the inclusion of a clause in the international trade treaty that would link trade to certain universal labour, human rights and environmental standards. This was the proposed 'social clause' that included all those universal norms that are emblazoned on the banner of 'global modernity'.

The Indian government—and most Third World governments—protested mildly and with considerable hesitation.[27] In January 1995, the Fifth Conference of the Labour Ministers of Non-Aligned and Other Developing Countries, held in New Delhi, adopted a declaration that expressed 'deep concern about the serious post-Marrakesh efforts at seeking to establish linkage between international trade and enforcement of labour standards through the imposition of the social clause'.[28] While the government was hesitant to take a very tough stand on what was ostensibly a measure against the Indian industrialists' anti-labour policies, ironically, it was the trade unions which came out in total defence of the national capitalists. All the major trade unions gave their unstinting support to the government in the name of anti-imperialism. The CPI(M) weekly put it clearly: '*the social clause is a singular issue on which there is unanimity not only among the trade unions and employers, but also on support to the government for wanting to reject the US move*'.[29] The position of the trade unions amounted to an unconditional declaration of support to the government, leaving no bargaining possibility whatsoever.

Expectedly, the dissenting voices came from the margins, where conditions were much more difficult. So for instance, Srilatha Swaminadhan of the Rajasthan Kisan Sangathan argued that the fight over the social clause was between two sets of exploiters wanting a larger slice of the pie at the expense of the toiling people of the world and that if the Indian workers wanted to improve their lot they should use this opportunity; they should '*fight and insist on* the linkage of the social clause with multilateral trade agreements'.[30] Sujata Gothoskar of the Workers' Solidarity Centre, Mumbai, did see problems in the institution of the social clause, its monitoring, its use or misuse but underlined the need for evolving an independent worker-oriented position.[31] Thomas Kocherry of the National Fishworkers' Forum, expressed his ambivalence: 'On the one hand, it is clear that the real motivations of the developed countries are dubious, on the other hand, the failure of our government in protecting workers makes one wonder whether it is an opportunity to be exploited.'[32]

I may also mention here that the Indian case represents a higher degree of hegemony of the organized, public sector working class organizations over the trade union movement and they enjoy relatively better living and working conditions. In many other Third World countries, the situation is such that even the mainstream trade unions find it difficult to take such a straightforward nationalist position. For instance, take the case of the Malaysian Trade Union Congress. In March 1994, it announced in anticipation, that '*it supports a GATT social clause*' according to the International Metalworkers Federation. The MTUC statement went on to argue that 'if the world's companies can have common global rules, then so too, can the world's workers'.[33] According to the International Metalworkers Federation, the MTUC statement was only one more position in a chain of similar stances adopted by trade union leaders in Singapore, Pakistan, Bangladesh, Uganda, Ghana, Chile, Argentina and Venezuela.[34] Even more interesting and symptomatic of the difficult conditions of struggle in the Third World, is the instance of the Peruvian government threatening union leaders with life imprisonment, branding their action of deposing before the United States Trade Representative (USTR), as 'treason against the state'. Three union leaders including

Teodulo Hernandez, the Secretary General of the Confederacion General de Trabajadores del Peru (CGTP) and representatives of Center for Labour Counsel (CEDAL) and Coordinadora de Centrales Sindicales del Peru, had earlier met representatives of the USTR to give their perspective on their government's response to a complaint before the US Generalized System of Preferences sub-committee. They had argued that Peru 'failed to qualify for the programme, which provides duty-free access to the US market because it is not affording workers the rights of association and collective bargaining'.[35]

From the above description then, it is evident that wherever the conditions of survival and struggle were more difficult, even mainstream trade unions adopted a position of welcoming, in a manner of speaking, the imposition of universal norms by the Western countries. At the very least, their position amounted to a tactical support, utilizing the conflict between two capitals or between their nation-states and Western governments, to extract a better bargain for the workers. In India, where the trade unions are dominated by fairly comfortable public sector workers, who in any case receive more than prescribed minimum wages and enjoy trade union rights, the trade unions' investment in nationalism was much greater. More importantly, from our point of view, unlike the other instances discussed above, these *are* struggles within political society that in a sense, even function on the logic of political society—extended on a global scale. Let us recall Chatterjee's own argument: one of the crucial aspects of the logic of political society is that it does not have recourse to the language of rights but makes its claims on the state by utilizing the opportunities afforded by the electoral-democratic system, striking alliances with or seeking the support of political parties and their leaders or groups within civil society that are willing to take up their cause. The logic of struggle within political society is such that sections of such groups in struggle might ally with one arm of the state against the other.

## Flight, Escape, Play

A closer look at these movements and struggles will show that they operate without the luxury of the Manichean imaginary of a world divided into two camps—with all the oppressors on one side and all the oppressed on the other. If it is true that an 'overdetermination of contradictions' that would lead to the fusion of a vast range of forces into a ruptural unity, is but a rare occurrence in history; if it is true as Gramsci observed, that the history of the subaltern classes is always episodic, being always subject to the disorganizing activity of the ruling classes, then we must begin to see such struggles in a different light.

These struggles respond to a world that is messy; where the oppressor could be on any side of the Left/Right divide. Hence, the proliferation of what Laclau and Mouffe have called 'democratic struggles'.[36] Most of the movements discussed above are also self-consciously 'anti-imperialist' and opposed to the domination of Western powers. This is certainly true of the NBA and many of the anti-communal groups in India; it is also true of most of the mainstream trade unions from different parts of the world that have either supported the social clause, or sought to utilize the opportunity presented by this threat from the Western governments. Further, some of these are movements that do not think in terms of the 'capture of state power'—for many of them have rejected such a state-centric politics. In fact, for some of them in India, the approach to state itself has changed. In a manner of speaking, many contemporary struggles operate under the unstated assumption *that there is no 'outside' to power*—either of the state or of Empire.

If that be the case, these movements then would appear to be telling us, that all struggle is about operating in the interstices of power. The old marxist debate about 'entryism' for example (whether to enter bourgeois institutions like the parliament) are thus irrelevant here. Their struggle is 'everywhere'. They thus seek to 'infect' and 'contaminate' power itself.[37] This might seem quite far-fetched for we are quite used to seeing power itself as corrupting. Who then can corrupt or contaminate power? Such a notion of power, I believe, is still lodged in the nineteenth century notion of power as sovereignty, as a thing located at a particular node of the social body. It is something that one possesses. As opposed to this, the unarticulated notion of power that underlies many of the new kinds of political practices that I have gestured towards, is a notion that is of a capillary or network form. If we are always-already constituted as subjects by power and we are always in its web then the question is not one of entering or exiting an imaginary space—outside of which one may choose to remain pure and uncontaminated. Rather, the question then is, of identifying the relations of power that one is inserted into and evolving responses adequate to that context. In these kinds of contexts, the domain of political action is constituted by counter-strategies that play off one kind of power against another, without permanently committing to one side as though it were a battle between Good and Evil. We might need then, to see these kinds of movements and struggles as practices (and subjectivities) that emerge with the collapse of many of the modernist conceptual boundaries that had defined our world so far. Paradigmatic of such boundaries was, of course the territorial borders of the nation-state. But there are certainly others that I have discussed above such as those between say the Left and the Right, which scarcely exhaust the entire conceptual political space of the contemporary any more.

## NOTES

1. For a perspective on this issue, see Zizek, 'NATO, The Left Hand of God', 1999, http://www.lacan.com/zizek-nato.htm, downloaded on 22 January 2008.
2. Michael Hardt and Antonio Negri, *Empire*, Cambridge, Massachusetts and London: Harvard University Press, 2001, p. xi.
3. Ibid., p. xii.
4. Ibid., p. 9, emphasis added.
5. Ibid., p. 15.
6. Arjun Appadurai, 'Patriotism and Its Futures', *Public Culture*, vol. 5, no. 3, Spring 1993, pp. 411-29.
7. Ibid., p. 411.
8. Ibid., p. 418.
9. Ibid., p. 420.
10. See discussion in Jurgen Habermas, *The Postnational Constellation—Political Essays*, London: Polity Press, 2001, p. 107. Also see, Daniele Archibugi, David Held and Martin Kohler, *Re-imagining Political Community—Studies on Cosmopolitan Democracy*, London: Polity Press, 1998. This idea of 'world citizenship' is of course a far more legalistic one than the romantic, neo-Deleuzian one referred to earlier.
11. Partha Chatterjee, 'Beyond the Nation? Or Within' in *Civil Society and Democracy—A Reader*, ed. Carolyn M. Elliott, New Delhi: OUP, p. 143.
12. Ibid., p. 143.
13. Ibid., p. 143.
14. Habermas, op. cit., p. 123.

15. Nivedita Menon, *Recovering Subversion—Feminist Politics Beyond the Law*, Delhi: Permanent Black and Urbana and Chicago: University of Illinois Press, 2004, pp. 225-8.

16. See Nivedita Menon, 'Surviving Gujarat 2002', *Economic and Political Weekly*, vol. xxvii, no. 27, 2002, pp. 2676-8.

17. 'Bindravan' was Zubeida's way of pronouncing Vrindavan, the land of the birth of Lord Krishna and an area, which for that reason is considered a pilgrimage site.

18. The Urdu word '*vatan*' is actually the exact counterpart of the '*des*' of the spoken Hindi language.

19. Ernest Renan, 'What is a Nation?', in *Becoming National—A Reader*, ed. Geoff Eley and Ronald Grigor Suny New York and Oxford: OUP, 1996, pp. 42–55.

20. Miroslav Hroch, 'From National Movement to the Fully-Formed Nation: The Nation-Building Process in Europe', Eley and Sunny, ibid., pp. 60-77.

21. Eugen Weber, *Peasants Into Frenchmen*, California: Stanford University Press, 1999, p. 100.

22. I have borrowed this term from Javeed Alam, *India: Living with Modernity*, Delhi: OUP, 1990.

23. C.A. Bayly, *Origins of Nationality in South Asia—Patriotism and Ethical Government in the Making of Modern India*, Delhi: OUP, 1998, p. 20.

24. See for instance, Robert Weilaard, 'Belgium Downplays Break-up Concerns', 2007 http://ap.google.com/article/ALeqM5giuTgSuY0w-QpxD2CWsu3uP8gk8g D8S4HP380, downloaded on 9 October 2007.

25. For both, see Aditya Nigam, *The Insurrection of Little Selves: The Crisis of Secular-Nationalism in India*, New Delhi: OUP, 2006.

26. Bipan Chandra, *The Rise and Growth of Economic Nationalism in India*, New Delhi: People's Publishing House, 1966, p. 327.

27. *Social Clause in Multilateral Trade Agreements (A Dossier on Social Clause)*, New Delhi: Centre for Education and Communication, p. 163. All documents quoted in relation to the social clause debate, unless otherwise stated, are from this dossier published by the CEC (henceforth, CEC Dossier).

28. Ibid., p. 161.

29. *People's Democracy*, 4 December 1994, New Delhi. That this unanimity was a fiction existing only in the imagination of the Left, is evident from the positions adopted by the government and industry.

30. Srilata Swaminadhan, 'Towards International Solidarity', *People's Democracy*, New Delhi, 4 December 1994, pp. 57-8.

31. Sujata Gothoskar, 'The Social Clause—Whose Interest is it Serving', in J. John and Anuradha Chenoy (Eds), *Labour, Environment and Globalization*, New Delhi: Centre for Education and Communication, 1996, pp.59-65.

32. Ibid., p.162. Thomas Kocherry has since taken a position in opposition to the social clause. However, the fact that it did present a dilemma in the initial stages, before the overall position of the trade unions hegemonized this space, is important.

33. 'Asian Unions Join Call for Social Clause' *Workers' Rights News*, issue no. 9, Spring 1994, p. 6.

34. Ibid., p. 6.

35. 'Testimony at USTR Draws Attacks on Peruvian Labour Representatives', *Workers' Rights News*, issue no. 9, Spring 1994, p. 3.

36. Ernesto Laclau and Chantal Mouffe differentiate between what they call 'popular struggles', which are based on the idea of two camps (the oppressors and the oppressed), and 'democratic struggles', which are based on the proliferation of antagonisms of different kinds—none of which, by implication can be treated as less important.

37. I borrow this expression from Linden Farrer, 'World Forum Movement: Abandon or Contaminate', http://www.nadir.org/nadir/initiativ/agp/free/wsf/worldforum.htm (accessed on 4 September 2007).

# 5

# NAXALBARI, NARMADA, NANDIGRAM
## The Crisis of High-Modernism

### Modernist Politics and Social Movements

In his important work, *Seeing Like a State*, James Scott identifies 'high-modernism' as an ideology that is best conceived as a strong, muscular (and we might add, masculine) version of 'the self-confidence about scientific and technical progress, the expansion of production' and 'the mastery of nature (including human nature)'. Above all, Scott suggests, this ideology is based on a faith in 'the rational design of social order commensurate with the scientific understanding of natural laws' (Scott 1998: 4). In a chapter devoted to Lenin's idea of the revolutionary party, Scott makes an interesting comparison between Le Corbusier's idea of the modernist city and Lenin's idea of revolution as the product of a vision that entrusted their respective objectives to 'the professionalism and scientific insight of a trained cadre, with full power to see the plan through' (ibid.: 147). Scott assigns special importance to Lenin's formulation in *What Is to Be Done*, that the vanguard party must be made up of *professional* revolutionaries: those who are experienced, full-time, trained revolutionaries, which Lenin repeatedly contrasts to the workers' organization which can, at best only generate 'trade union consciousness'(ibid.: 152). We know that Lenin's insistence on the 'professional' aspect—which he repeatedly contrasted to amateurism—was not simply a matter of exigency; he saw to it that this logic of high-modernism was extended undiluted to the running of factories, where he threw his lot with the bureaucratic idea of one-man management. His deep distrust of spontaneity—at least theoretically speaking—found its expression in repeatedly entrusting all important roles to a small elite of trusted and trained professional cadre.[1]

The communist movement in India, largely an offspring of the leninist, indeed stalinist Communist International, is constituted through this high-modernism. Even the small Left wing groups across the country have, by and large drawn their poetry from the high-modernist ideology identified with this leninist-stalinist orthodoxy. Here we are not interested in high-modernism and its crisis in general in India, but mainly in its manifestations on the Left.

However, it might not be out of place to situate this crisis within a larger crisis of political high-modernism, the history of which goes back to the late 1960s. It was in the 1980s that the real crisis of secular-nationalism, the official ideology of high-modernism in India, burst out into the open (Nigam 2006). Political theorist Sudipta Kaviraj remarks that the entire climate had changed so radically by then that the new players who emerged on the scene, rustic and untrained in the ways of Western modernity, could only have been bemused at the political differences between the Left and the Right. To them these would have appeared, Kaviraj suggests, as 'insubstantial differences within a modernist bloc of privilege'. Kaviraj thus marked the emergence of a whole new breed of politicians who, if one were to take Jameson's description of the postmodern, represented the end of the era of the avant-gardes.

Frederic Jameson, we might recall, identifies the advent of postmodernity with the 'staging of aesthetic populism' in the domain of architecture, given that high-modernism is identified 'with the destruction of the fabric of the traditional city and its older neighbourhood culture (by way of the radical disjunction of the new Utopian high-modernist building from its surrounding context) . . . .' (Jameson 1992: 2).

We could see a parallel here in the domain of party politics and representation as well, where the decline of the Nehruvian 'avant-gardes', drawn largely from the Westernized, English-speaking elite, is heralded by the emergence of the new 'popular-vernacular' elite in the persons of a Laloo Prasad Yadav or a Mayawati.

However, it is in the realm of Development that the 'radical disjunction between the new Utopian high-modernism' and its surrounding context is registered in all its starkness, resulting in the relentless violence of the state on its largely rural population. The space in which high-modernism meets its first crises in India is not the urban but in fact the rural where it wreaks havoc with the local spaces and the forms of life inhabiting them. To the extent that the 'rural' represents the 'non-modern', in the context of the postcolony, the 'postmodern' takes into its fold this so-called 'non-modern'.

In our context, this moment in politics is also expressed in the decline of 'modernist class politics' and the emergence of social movements. The decline of one and the emergence of the other, however, do not come in temporal succession: they exist on stage at the same time, often locked in conflict and sometimes working in tandem. The relationship between the two is, in either case, quite fraught. One expression of this simultaneous 'working together' and fighting it out, came into public view around a controversy that erupted around the organizing of the World Social Forum in Mumbai in January 2004.

In the run-up to the fourth World Social Forum (WSF 2004) a debate suddenly broke out in Left circles in India. It took the form of an attack on the very idea of the WSF by a section of the far Left, initiated by one of the most dogmatic and sectarian Left outfits, the People's War Group (PWG) of the Communist Party of India (Marxist-Leninist).[2] The initiators of the attack were not content with merely issuing pamphlets and writing critiques; they went further and decided to organize a parallel event on the same dates, just across the road from the WSF. This parallel event was called Mumbai Resistance 2004 (MR 2004), which was in turn attacked by another equally sectarian naxalite group which held a third event by the name of Peoples' Resistance.

It is well-known that the WSF includes a vast array of forces who share, to whatever extent, an opposition to the current corporate globalization. Beyond this they have their own 'worldviews' and agendas and their own fairly strong critiques of each other. Many of them are also unhappy with the way in which the WSF idea has developed in practice, with big NGOs and big stars being seen to take over the platforms of the WSF. Among these groups are those who have been most active in the Seattle and post-Seattle mass struggles. Nonetheless, most of these groups have remained part of the WSF, even while making often very sharp critiques of the process. With MR 2004, however the situation was different. The MR actually split the incipient movement in India even before it had got off the ground. The divisions now go much deeper and even affected citizen's groups, which had been working together locally with a number of smaller Left groups and social movements on a number of urgent issues. Apart from the PWG, a number of other groups of the naxalites also joined the MR; what is more, the MR managed to also involve some respected individuals and some of the Indian social movement groups. This became possible because, in the first place, many who consented to associate with the MR, did so out of a sense of general solidarity in those troubled times, not realizing that this move amounted to an attempt to split a fledgling movement.[3] Many such people eventually decided to register their presence in both forums. But equally importantly, this became possible because some of the concerns that the MR focused on are actually questions that have been disturbing many independent Left wing individuals and people associated with social movements. Important among these is the question of funding, its impact on social and political struggles/movements and the very central role played by many funded NGOs in influencing the emerging direction and structure of the WSF.

This is undoubtedly an issue that calls for more a serious debate than has been possible so far. However, that is beyond the purview of this chapter. For the moment, I wish to briefly focus on the substantive 'ideological' critique of the WSF as presented by the MR, and follow it up with a broad map of social movements which are all-too-often collapsed into that catch-all category—the 'NGO'.

What exactly was it that moved the organizers of the MR to come out so strongly against the very idea of the WSF? After all, like most Old Left formations elsewhere in the world (and in India), they too could have seen in the WSF an opportunity to reach out to a larger audience for themselves. Given that for the last two decades the Left wing critique of corporate globalization had come to be seen as passé and very few people had any patience left for their affirmations of faith in some abstract theology of marxism-leninism, this should have been a golden opportunity. The easy answer to this, of course, is that their sectarianism did not allow them to take this opportunity. But this sectarian outburst also gives us a peep into the inner world of the authoritarian, vanguardist Old Left and the way in which it views movements and struggles that arise independently of them.

The central line of argument of the MR attack was directed at the WSF's declared intention to be a forum for 'reflective thinking and democratic debate', rather than a forum of action: MR declared that what was required was resistance to globalization, not 'mere' reflective thinking and debate. And resistance required clarity; it required a clear-cut critique of globalization and a blueprint for the future. This could not be done with the diffuse and amorphous character of a forum like the WSF.[4]

What also rattled the drafters of the MR critique was the fact that the WSF charter of principles explicitly declared its commitment to non-violent means. In fact, the WSF position was not a position of blanket 'opposition' to violence but one that stated its preference saying that it would seek to promote linkages and alliances that would 'increase the capacity for non-violent social resistance to the process of dehumanization the world is undergoing and to the violence used by the State'. Wedded as the PWG and its close allies were to a nihilistic cult of violence, they chose to read this statement as a 'ban' on all violence. This is not the place to go into a full-fledged discussion of violence but to my knowledge, the WSF position is very close to the one espoused by even the most uncompromising armed struggles and revolutions of the twentieth century. None of them ever made a cult of violence (before they came to power) and they formally held on to the position that violence was being foisted upon them. It may not be out of place to mention here that the Russian revolution effected a capture of power without a single life being lost or that communists in China and Vietnam, during the revolution often willingly courted defeat than take civilian lives. The PWG and the Maoists, having made a cult of violence per se, found this part of the WSF charter unpalatable.

However, this part aside, there were other aspects of their authoritarian politics that moved them against the WSF. Thus their document says: 'MR 2004 is a part of the process of building a strong and worldwide anti-imperialist movement *with a clear and unambiguous focus*. It seeks to unite those struggling organizations *that are genuinely opposed* to imperialist globalization and wars of aggression.'[5] And further: 'MR 2004 stands for a concretely defined alternative socio-economic structure [unlike the amorphous "another world is possible" of the WSF] built on a basis of self-reliance, moving towards a genuine socialist order.'[6]

The point about 'meaningless debates' and the 'amorphousness' of the WSF idea are thus repeatedly underlined. Thus the document avers, 'This [self-reliant socialism] *can* be achieved through struggle, *not endless and often not so meaningful debates*.'[7]

It is interesting that the position of the major mainstream parliamentary communist parties, which were actually playing an important role in the WSF process, was practically identical with that of the MR.[8]

Take for instance, CPI(M) Polit Bureau member Sitaram Yechury's defence of the party's relationship to the WSF. Yechury accepted that the WSF initiative had behind it the tremendous force of the 'anti-globalization' movements that have come to the fore since Seattle 1999; nevertheless, he was at pains to explain to his Left-wing critics why his party should be in there with 'foreign-funded NGOs'. He responded at two levels and both are important from the point of view of uncovering the mindset of the authoritarian vanguardist Left. At one level, he cites Mao Tse-tung back at his Maoist critics. This is the quote from Mao's famous 1927 report on the peasant movement in Hunan, where Mao anticipates the storm that is about to come and says that 'every revolutionary party and comrade' will have to choose—and there are but three choices: 'To march at their head and lead them? To trail behind them, gesticulating and criticizing? Or to stand in their way and oppose them?' The CPI(M), he says is quite clear about the option it wants to choose. Even though he knew that it is impolitic to actually say so in so many words, it was quite clear his party chose the first option. While joining the movement, he says, his party will 'oppose the efforts to obfuscate the only alternative to imperialist globalization being socialism [*sic*]'.[9]

The second, 'theoretical' level of Yechury's response is more interesting. He likens the 'NGO-sponsored anti-globalization movement' to a 'safety-valve in a pressure cooker'.[10] In Yechury's perception, the term 'NGO-sponsored movement' includes all kinds of social movements about which the traditional Left has little idea, assuming that they are all part of a larger 'anti-Left' universe. It is Yechury's argument that this safety valve nevertheless needs an 'ideological construct' to back it and this is provided by the basic position articulated by these movements. I quote: 'Shorn of its high-flowing terminology . . . the ideological positions of the NGOs "peoples" movements' [*sic*] can be summarized in the following: the alternative to globalization can come only when we achieve peoples' control over world's resources.' Yechury then goes on to explicate what this ideological position of the 'NGOs peoples' movements' 'really' means: 'This means that the movement against globalization must oppose both the corporate control over resources and the State control over resources. By opposing corporate control they seek to present themselves as being opposed to capitalism. By opposing State control, they seek to present themselves as opposed to the experience of the socialist countries and *therefore to socialism itself*.'[11] There is no need to labour the point here as Yechury's statements are self-explanatory: anyone who is opposed to the historical experience of the socialist countries, also stands opposed to socialism itself. In any case, any attempt to chart out a third course, distinct from both corporate and State control, is mere pretense ('seek to represent themselves') and woolly-headedness. If the MR found the WSF too amorphous, Yechury also finds it too nebulous: 'It is this nebulous concept of people's control that they advocate which essentially dilutes the effective opposition to globalization and the projection of the socialist alternative.'

Between the MR and the CPI(M) then, we have the perfect articulation of the authoritarian Old Left positions that will decree, even today, what or who is or is not 'opposed to socialism' (whatever socialism might mean).

There is just no space, even after the collapse of socialism, in the world of the Old Left, *to begin to think of alternative possibilities*. The mere opposition to 'state ownership' of property is seen to be a nebulous idea. Perhaps Yechury and his party might consider even cooperative forms of ownership, now being experimented with in different parts of the world, too as 'dilution of the socialist alternative'.

Also worth noticing in Yechury's statements is the complete conflation of the terms NGOs, social movements and people's movements—all of which are, in his understanding, an off-shoot of foreign funding. Here, the MR position at least seems to recognize that everything is not simply an outcome of foreign-funding but might have larger theoretical-intellectual coordinates as well. Their position therefore attempts to argue against the WSF by outlining what I think are the most important issues at stake. Take for instance, the companion document that was circulated by the MR, brought out by an outfit that styles itself as the 'Research Unit on Political Economy'(RUPE), where the emergence of all 'non-class' movements such as those we are considering, are attributed to the influence of 'postmodernism' and dismissed. Consider the following: 'Postmodernism places *all struggles on par with class* as just another social category jostling with gender, ethnicity, nationality and so on . . . .'[12] This pamphlet goes on to critique postmodernism for 'ruling out the possibility of united action by various social sections on the basis of *common objective interests* . . . '. and merely talking about 'varying *coalitions/alliances*'.[13] Here we cannot enter into a discussion of 'postmodernism' but we should nevertheless point out that the document lumps together as 'postmodernism', one hundred years of internal critique of marxism, on grounds of gender and race-blindness, for example. Nonetheless, the MR document recognizes a real difference of perspective with the WSF here that is important. We need to mark the epochal shift that has taken place and to recognize the most significant difference registered here. While the old model was predicated upon the idea of a certain unity behind a 'blueprint' or a 'programme' expressed in the body of the vanguard, the logic of the new movements is that these are built upon an implicit equality between different constituents: there is no vanguard and no *commonly defined programme* based on '*common objective interests*', to which all must submit before becoming a part of the movement. The logic is one of horizontal coalitions and networks, rather than top-down organizations. This is why this idea appears so threatening for self-styled vanguards; that is why they feel threatened and destabilized by the very idea that 'all struggles' could be 'treated at par with class'.

Since there is such a widespread conflation of these different terms—social movements, NGOs and people's movements, a brief discussion might be useful here, in order to clarify the sense in which I use these terms.

## The Non-party Terrain

I shall use the term/s 'non-party political formations' or non-party political movements' to refer to a specific set of movements and struggles that have emerged in the 1980s and 1990s but whose genealogy can be traced back to the mass movements of the late 1960s and the first half of the 1970s.

In its broadest possible sense, the term *non-party domain* could be used to include anything and every political expression that is outside the formal structure of party-politics, including what political science of an earlier era would have called 'interest groups', 'pressure groups' and 'lobbies'. Such interest groups and lobbies would include organizations like manufacturers' or industry associations like the Federation of Indian Chambers of Commerce and Industry (FICCI) or the Confederation of Indian Industries (CII) at the all India level or their numerous less powerful and 'lower order' versions that operate as traders and manufacturers associations, *vyapar sanghas* or *udyog bharatis* in different parts of the country. These are associations that function, unlike say the trade unions of workers, behind the scenes, away from public gaze and their forms of intervention too have been, by and large, lobbying in the corridors of power. This is particularly true of the more powerful ones like the FICCI and the CII. The smaller, city based organizations of industrialists or market-based associations of traders, have of late, occasionally had to take recourse to more public, trade union methods of protest and action as for instance the recent strikes on the issue of the value-added tax (in the case of traders) and more militant actions including demonstrations by the small manufacturers associations in Delhi against the Supreme Court orders to close down or relocate polluting industries, or the sealing of commercial units more recently.[14]

However, by and large, these are organizations which function not on the principle of publicity and campaign—in other words of transparency—but rather, on the logic of clandestine manipulations of the levers of power, far away from public gaze. Unlike them trade unions, on the other hand, function on the logic of public campaigns and protests and at least to that extent need to provide justifications for their cause before a larger public.[15] In a sense, this difference between the two is a consequence of the relative powerlessness of the workers and thus the need to appeal to a larger public, as opposed to the relatively thicker connections with power in the case of the industrialists/manufacturers and traders. In this sense, it seems to make more sense to differentiate between the two different kinds of associations or organizations and not club them together in some general category called 'interest groups' or to subsume all of them under the rubric of the non-party political sector.

One of the reasons for discussing the two kinds of associations at some length, therefore, is also to enable us to identify more clearly the object of our investigation. That is to say, I am suggesting that organizations such as the FICCI or CII do not form part of the category of the non-party political domain. At the moment, I am interested in looking at the ways in which this domain impacts upon structures and processes of democracy and thus in radicalizing it. At best, organizations like the CII or FICCI can function as negative instances of the non-public and hence fundamentally anti-democratic—or at the very least, non-democratic—character of such organizations. The point that I am trying to make is that the criterion of publicity or 'publicness' is, in a sense, central to the identification of the kind of movements that we will be concerned with under the rubric of non-party politics.

A point of clarification regarding the criterion of publicity or transparency, however, is in order. I am certainly not suggesting that all the movements and groups that we can group as social movements *are* fully transparent to public gaze insofar as their internal structure and functioning are concerned. That is unfortunately not the case. The crucial point, however, is that their very location as organizations or movements of the relatively powerless and underprivileged makes them appeal to a public sense of justice and fairness and to that extent, they have to justify themselves to this larger public. In that sense, *potentially* they are always open to public scrutiny and answerable to questions not only with regard to their policies but also with regard to their methods and organizational forms. So for example, in the case of the Mazdoor Kisan Shakti Sangathan (MKSS), Aruna Roy and Nikhil Dey state that as their campaign for the 'right to information' gathered strength, one immediate backlash was that 'MLAs and ministers began to abuse the Sangathan and express open hostility towards its activists' and 'a counter demand for information about the Sangathan, its expenses and sources of funds was raised' (Roy and Dey 2004). For the MKSS however, this led to the exercise of preparing comprehensible accounts for the people, 'which increased its credibility and neutralized the whispering campaigns inevitably used to undermine such agitations' (ibid.). A similar thing happened with the Narmada Bachao Andolan recently when it was accused of receiving foreign funds and it had to open itself to public scrutiny—and needless to say, came out clean, as in the case with MKSS.[16]

I shall therefore, use the term/s 'non-party political movements' or 'non-party-political formations', to refer to organizations or movements that are also alternatively called 'grassroots movements', 'new social movements' or simply 'social movements', and 'movement groups'.

Another set of organizations and formations that are quite often conflated with such social movements and are seen as critical parts of this 'non-party political domain'—or more fashionably, 'civil society organizations'—is the wide range of funded institutions called NGOs (non-governmental organizations), which present a specially complicated case, for on the one hand, unlike social movements that are answerable to their constituency and to their public, *most such NGOs consider themselves primarily accountable to their respective funders*. Many of these large NGOs are plush with funds, their functionaries maintain fairly high standards of living and have swamped a large part of the voluntary activism of the earlier period. Yet, there are also funded NGOs which have been carrying out very significant work in different arenas and have maintained a fair degree of public accountability in their practice. From the standpoint of the functioning and vibrancy of India's democracy, these need to be considered more carefully.

Developing on a distinction made by Ernesto Laclau and Chantal Mouffe, I will refer to these new struggles as *democratic struggles*, as distinct from *popular struggles* (Laclau and Mouffe 1985: 131). As we have noted earlier, Laclau and Mouffe propose the category 'democratic struggles' to refer to those struggles that are based on a *proliferation of new conflicts or antagonisms* and thus the emergence of newer and newer points of resistance to relations of domination. As opposed to these, 'popular struggles', they suggest, are struggles that are broadly based on the imagination of the division of society into two antagonistic camps—those of the oppressor and the oppressed and thus, occur only in specific conjunctures.

Democratic struggles have the effect of radicalizing democracy by introducing newer concerns and continuously subjecting its practices to interrogation. Analytically, we also need to distinguish between two distinct kinds of democratic struggles. This is the distinction between the *social movements* and *citizens initiatives*. The main distinction here is that we reserve the term 'social movements' for movements based on some kind of mass mobilization; citizens' initiatives, on the other hand, refer to specific kinds of groups based by and large, within *urban civil society*, which concern themselves with specific issues.[17] As will be evident, this awkward and necessarily tentative distinction is being made here to distinguish between struggles involving mass mobilization as for example, in the case of the Chipko Andolan, the Narmada Bachao Andolan (NBA), Ekta Parishad or the Mazdoor Kisan Shakti Sanghathan (MKSS), on the one hand and the more recent citizens' actions, primarily based in metropolises like Delhi, Kolkata or Mumbai, which are more in the nature of loose and relatively diffuse networks of individual citizens.[18]

## Democratic Struggles

By and large, what I am referring to as democratic struggles have also been referred to as 'new social movements'. The term 'new social movements' 'groups together a series of highly diverse struggles: urban, ecological, anti-authoritarian, anti-institutional, feminist, antiracist, ethnic, regional or that of sexual minorities' (Laclau and Mouffe: 159). I use the term 'social movements' and/or 'new social movements', in a very descriptive sense, to refer to those struggles and movements, distinct from citizens' actions groups, that have emerged and acquired immense significance in the 1980s. However, while using the category of NSMs it should be borne in mind that the attempt to define what is 'new' about them can lead to more obfuscation rather than provide analytical clarity. In a sense, the category of new social movements seems to have a very specific reference in the Western experience after May 1968, where the situation in this respect is much clearer. For, May 1968 and the emergence of the New Left did announce the end, at least for the time being, of the old kind of class-based politics and the eruption of a whole new range of assertions from anti-race struggles and feminism to ecological struggles and the peace movement, or the movements of alternative sexualities like the gays and lesbians. To that extent, it was possible to describe the 'newness' of these movements with reference to the old class-based politics which they, in a manner of speaking, superseded. In our context, the newness—as well as the decline of modernist politics—is to be identified not so much with the decline of class politics as with the crisis of the party system and of representative politics. It is not so much identified with the decline of class politics for the simple reason that class politics never had the overarching salience in India as it did in the West more generally.

To be sure, there certainly has been a debate of sorts in India too, on the criteria that make some movements part of the phenomena of 'new social movements' and others not. By and large there is agreement among scholars that the newness of the 'NSMs' has to do with the fact that they effect a break, in some significant way, with the old kinds of political mobilization, especially those based on class, and with old frameworks of representation based on the institution of the political party (Guha 1989; Omvedt 1993). This, in fact, emerged as a significant point of departure and was recognized even by other scholars like Rajni Kothari, D L Sheth and Harsh Sethi, who were among the earliest to theorize the emergence of these new kinds of movements. However, Kothari, Sheth and Sethi have, by and large, avoided using the category of NSMs to identify these movements. Their preferred term has been 'non-party political formations' or 'non-party political process', which was meant to emphasize the fact that their emergence had something to do with the *crisis of the party system* itself, rather than of class-based mobilization (Kothari 1984, 1988; Sheth and Sethi 1991; Sethi 1993a, 1993b). On the other hand, there are some broadly 'class-based' movements with a very significant mass following, like the farmers'/peasants' movements—if one could see the entire peasantry as a class—of the 1980s (led by Sharad Joshi, Mahendra Singh Tikait, Nanjundasamy) which scholars like Gail Omvedt prefer to count among the Indian NSMs (Omvedt 1993). In Omvedt's reading the farmers/peasants i.e. small commodity producers, struggling against the State and the capitalist market are strictly speaking not a class.[19]

I will then, include all kinds of non-traditional, radical initiatives that arise outside the framework of institutionalized politics within this rubric of democratic struggles, which we will further sub-divide between social movements and citizens' actions. In that sense, our reference point is the one identified by Kothari, Sheth, Sethi and others, namely, the decline of institutional, party-based politics. Citizens' actions have been discussed at greater length elsewhere and will just be referred to briefly here.[20]

It is not within the scope of the present chapter to enter into an elaborate discussion of the proposition that there has been a decline in institutional and party politics. This assertion seems to fly in the face of all empirical evidence of the increased participation rate in elections over this same period but let me suggest that this empirical evidence of increased participation need not necessarily suggest a heightened legitimacy of the electoral or the institutional political system. Rather we need to recognize that the contemporary Indian voter relates to the electoral and party process as an active player who has learnt to 'play' the electoral system as s/he has learnt to play, for reasons of survival, many other mechanisms of the state. This 'play' may not indicate 'legitimacy' of institutional politics so much as its entrenchment as a given of everyday life. 'Tactical voting' is generally more noticed among the minority community voters but it seems, this might be a more pervasive, paradigmatic question to explore in this context. More importantly, what we might have to reckon with here is that there is no homogeneous category that goes by the name of 'the people' any more and that only very limited kinds of issues can be raised through such large electoral/democratic constructs as 'the people'. Most issues raised by the social movements precisely are sectional and cannot invoke 'the people'. This is a point we will explore as we go along.

For our purposes then, it makes more sense to consider as democratic struggles, the whole range of new kinds of assertions that have sought to find expression outside the framework of established parties and old modes of doing politics. These would include struggles and movements ranging from the long drawn out trade union struggles of the kind led by Datta Samant in the Bombay textile industry and later, in his wake, by Lalit Maken in the textile industry of Delhi—both in the early to mid-1980s—to the more sustained new forms of trade union movement, symbolized for instance, in the Chattisgarh Mukti Morcha (CMM) on the one hand, and the National Centre for Labour (NCL) and the recently formed, more ambitious, New Trade Union Initiative (NTUI) on the other. Scholars like D L Sheth have traced the genealogy of such non-party 'micro-movements' back to the great mass struggles of the 1970s like the JP-led movement. Thus, according to Sheth, 'what we recognize today as movement-groups emerged and were consolidated in spaces made available to them by the decline of mainstream institutions of representative democracy: the legislatures, elections, political parties and trade unions' (Sheth 2004: 46). In his early intervention, theorizing the non-party movement, Kothari included in his list 'movements launched by the non-traditional Left', among which he included movements like 'the Chipko, the miners' struggle in Chhattisgarh, the Ryot Coolie Sangham in Andhra Pradesh, the Satyagraha launched by the peasants movement in Kanakpura in Karnataka against the mining and export of granite, the Jharkhand Mukti Morcha' and such other struggles (Kothari 1984: 220). Also falling within the ambit of the social movements in the non-party political domain are some other very important movements like the women's movement or the struggle for caste equality.

Clearly, the range of struggles that fall under the category of democratic struggles is so large that it is impossible to draw up an exhaustive list—leave alone do justice to them in the space of one chapter. For this reason, the discussion that follows should be taken merely as a broad treatment of major trends of these movements.

In the following sections, I will briefly examine the context of emergence of these democratic struggles. Since it is not possible to detail the actual histories and experiences of these movements, I will try to simplify the discussion by analytically separating out two distinct kinds of democratic struggles in our context that I have referred to earlier, namely, (a) social movements and (b) citizens' initiatives.

In our context, the crisis of high-modernism appears through three specific moments which I designate as Naxalbari, Narmada and Nandigram respectively. These moments represent different impulses at work and may often overlap either with each other or with other currents. However, I suggest that these three have acquired a sort of symbolic charge that exceeds the specifics of the movement concerned, which I will outline in the remainder of this chapter.

## Social Movements: The Sign of Narmada

One commentator, Ponna Wignaraja, saw the emergence of the new peoples' movements in the global South as 'manifestations of a new pluralistic paradigm of development and democracy' (Wignaraja 1993: 5). While this seems to be an overstatement insofar as none of these movements really had any alternative paradigm to begin with, they certainly did embody a dissatisfaction with, if not outright rejection of, the dominant model of top-down development. As Rajni Kothari noted while surveying these movements in the first half of the 1980s, they were parts of a democratic struggle at various levels, 'at a point in history when existing institutions and the theoretical models on which they are based have run their course, when there is a search for new instruments of political action (existing ones being in a state either of complacency or of weariness and exhaustion' (Kothari 1984: 219). It is significant that this reaction to the complacency/exhaustion of the existing institutions and theories should have taken the form, not of a search for newer radical theories and institutions, but a *rejection of all existing blueprints*—a move towards the grassroots. If they explicitly rejected the model of capitalist development, which they directly encountered, the so-called alternative of 'actually existing socialism' did not also inspire much confidence, largely because of its highly authoritarian and centralized structure. What most such movements recognized either implicitly or in some cases, explicitly, was that no model of development that did not place the people at the centre of their vision, could be democratic. Participatory development and participatory democracy began to be seen as intrinsically linked. This clearly meant, as we shall see below, a *displacement of the State* from the central position that it had hitherto occupied in the imagination of radical movements. As Sheth and Sethi noted, it was the period between the late 1960s and early 1980s, marked by famines, inflation, devaluation, unemployment and the breakdown of Congress domination, that led to the emergence of militant movements on the one hand, and 'impelled fresh thinking and action on the *twin grids of development and politics*' (Sheth and Sethi 1991: 53). Rajni Kothari saw in these developments an attempt to redefine the very content of politics: 'Issues and arenas of human activity that were not so far seen as amenable of political action—peoples' health, rights over forests and community resources, even deeply personal and primordial issues as are involved in the struggles for women's rights—get defined as political and provide for arenas of struggle' (Kothari 1984: 219-20). We might add that these movements were not only redefining the meaning of politics; they were also redefining development itself. According to Sheth, 'the organizational form they evolved for themselves was not of a political party or a pressure group', it was rather that of 'a civil-associational group, leading political struggles on issues articulated to them by people themselves'. 'The key concept they worked with was *democratizing development through empowerment of the people*' (Sheth 2004: 46). In the context of globalization in the 1990s, Sheth in fact, sees the movements grappling with the twin imperatives of 're-politicizing development' and 're-inventing participatory democracy' (ibid.: 49). 'Re-politicizing development' should be seen here as also redefining it in fundamental ways, such that it would not remain 'Development' (with a capital D) in the conventional sense. This redefinition of development, it will be seen, was to eventually move towards fundamental and radical critique of Development itself.

Thus, what began with the dissatisfaction with formal institutionalized politics and the consequent search for more 'people-oriented' kinds of political structures and institutions, eventually moved towards a realization that it was not simply the authoritarian-bureaucratic nature of development that was problematic; that the very ideology of Development that was so centrally linked to the idea of a centralized power structure and the idea of the nation-state's sovereignty over its domain (the doctrine of 'eminent domain', for instance). The question of democratic and decentralized development necessarily raised questions about access to and ownership of natural resources by communities that had traditionally had easy access to them. So, as another important activist of the non-party movements, Sanjay Sangvai put it, 'confronting the state also takes the form of challenging the "eminent domain" of the state' (Sangvai 2003: 8). It was thus that one thing led to another and in a sense, all these movements 'made the road by walking'. Most of these new movements thus represented *a search* for a more just and equitable society; they had no 'blueprints to which the world must conform'.[21]

Thus it was that many of the movements, like the famous Chipko movement in the Garhwal hills, began with no *a priori* ideological agenda. It was rather a movement that originated from a local conflict in 1972. Vinod Raina puts the 'bare facts' of the movement as follows: 'there was a dispute between the local villagers and a logging contractor who had been allowed to fell trees in a forest close to the village. On that particular day, there was a meeting with the related government officials in their office away from the village and while the men were away for the meeting, the contractor's workers appeared in order to cut the trees. The women of this village called Reni, reached the forest quickly and clasped the tree trunks, thus preventing the workers from cutting them down' (Raina 2004: 4–5). This form of protest spread widely and was also picked up by the media, forcing the government to negotiate with the community. Thus, says Raina, did women begin setting up their communities in the region and articulating larger issues about eco-friendly development. I suspect however, that even this may be an overstatement and that the idea of 'eco-friendly development' was something that came in much later, with the intervention of middle class activists who could make the connection between the ecological dimensions of development and the relationship of local communities to forests.

Similarly, the formation of the Chhattisgarh Mine Shramik Sangh (CMSS) and its eventual transformation into the Chhattisgarh Mukti Morcha (CMM) in 1978, which clearly represents a new kind of trade unionism—a social movement unionism, if you please—tells us a similar story. Though its leader Shankar Guha Niyogi is generally presented as a 'naxalite' by both his detractors and supporters outside, the fact remains that his was a completely unconventional intervention in the field of working class politics. He began his political career in the late

1960s, when he joined the Bhilai Steel Plant as a worker and formed a union called the 'Blast Furnace Action Committee'. After being thrown out of the job for 'security reasons' he left Bhilai and went to work in the forests of Bastar. Learning the local tribal languages, Gondi and Halbi, he did odd jobs ranging from trading in goats to fishing while he was there. (Sail 1998: 18). When the naxalite revolt took place, he briefly joined the movement, but basically continued to work where he was and the way he was. After a brief association, he broke with the naxalite group he was associated with because he had sharp disagreements with their attitude to trade union work, which its members thought was 'economism' and 'reformism' (Singh 1977: 40-1). After the Emergency, he returned to Durg and worked in the Dani Tola mines near Dalli-Rajhara, where he began his experiments in 'trade unionism with a difference' (Sail 1998: 18). According to Rajendra Sail, he first joined the All India Trade Union Congress and later formed his independent CMSS, which was to initiate a completely novel form of union movement incorporating social reform questions within its activities. From campaigns against liquor to opening educational institutions (six primary schools, a training cum production workshop for unemployed youth) and hospitals, to fight against pollution and for the preservations of forests, this was truly a new kind of politics at work (Sail ibid.: 19). It is also worth registering here the transformation of this Left-wing, working class-based movement (Chattisgarh Mines Shramik Sangh) into a movement articulating regional aspirations of the people—peasants and tribals—and organizing itself around Chattisgarhi identity. This transformation also reflects a move away from the high ideology of the marxist Left displaying greater accommodation towards a more popular and local sentiment. In fact, Shankar Guha Niyogi's entire trajectory reveals a search, unencumbered by *a priori* ideological notions, for new forms of struggle, which also meant an implicit rejection of existing models.

Such was also the case with the now iconic Narmada Bachao Andolan, which began with a relatively minor demand of rehabilitation of those likely to be displaced by the dam. Groups came into existence in the concerned states that began discussing questions of rehabilitation in around 1986, and it was only by 1988, when construction started in full swing that the opposition to the dam too took the shape of an all out struggle. The larger question of the feasibility of large dams in general, however, was again, not the starting point of the struggle (Patkar 1999). It was only later in 1989, with the massive Harsud rally that slogans against 'destructive development' actually began to be raised. The point here is simple: what eventually emerged as a powerful critique of the development paradigm and began spelling out the outlines of an alternative kind of development, was actually born out of the conjunction of movements taking shape on the ground with newer theoretical and intellectual critiques that had started emerging by this time as a consequence of the awareness of the impending ecological disaster at a global level. Critiques of technological fetishism and the related drive towards centralization of power thus acquired a different resonance in this context.

The rise of such an awareness of the understanding of the ecological costs of development had earlier led to the emergence of what was possibly the first big movement and public debate on this issue. This was the well-known debate around the Silent Valley Project in Kerala and, interestingly, the forces arrayed on both sides were those of the Left. While the CPI(M) led state government wanted to push through the plan to dam the Kuntipuzha river in 1978-9, as part of its power generation programme, it was the popular science movement linked to the party, the Kerala Shastra Sahitya Parishad (KSSP), that took up cudgels against it, given the fact that this project would have inundated one of the richest rainforests in the country and destroyed its immense bio-diversity. The movement led to the revocation of the plan—though it seems to be on the cards once again, over two and a half decades down the line.

The period since the 1980s has seen some other kinds of non-party movements, some of which embody a very different ethos from that of the ecological struggles or the kind of non-hierarchical, non-authoritarian participative experiment conducted by the CMM. Important among them have been at least three, which have been widely written about and I shall not enter into a discussion on them here. These are the women's movement, the farmers' movement and the movement against caste oppression. The last mentioned eventually morphed into two distinct currents: the Dalit movement on the one hand, which has retained a non-party character of a cultural revolt, despite a simultaneous party-political expression in the form of the Bahujan Samaj Party, and the backward castes movement that has got completely integrated into the political mainstream as a powerful force in some states.

## The Revolt of the Fragment

Let me attempt in this section, to bring together some critical aspects/coordinates of the democratic struggles of the last two and a half decades.

It can be seen that even though these different movements have very different impulses that animate them, there are some interesting features or coordinates that mark them out as belonging to the specific moment or conjuncture of the crisis of high-modernism. Some of these aspects, it seems to me can be enumerated as follows:

1. *Decline of the metanarrative*: We have already seen from the above examples that these movements have emerged as a response to concrete situations on the ground. Most of them are single-issue campaigns or struggles and have no necessary larger—metatheoretical—language of either critique or of a blueprint for the future. Even though they do all refer to the ideas of equality and justice, these are more in that nature of what Laclau and Mouffe have called, after Tocqueville, the logic of equivalence that underlies their concept of the democratic revolution.[22]
2. *Crisis of modernist representational categories.* Even though some of the movements appear to retain the vocabulary of modernist representational politics, such as 'people', 'class' (or in some cases, even 'nation'), their practice has already replaced these by a different series where the categories are women, farmers, Dalits, displaced, Adivasis, and so on. The singularity of categories like 'people', 'nation' or 'class', that resided in their ostensibly having a *single will*, now stands replaced by a much more modest understanding of mobilization and representation.
3. *The suspicion of large, hierarchical structures.* The movements are generally deeply suspicious of the large bureaucratic structures of both the state as well as the political parties. The search therefore, for more responsive, locally sensitive forms/structures of government as well as opposition and dissent.
4. *The revolt against perennial deferral.* It is quite clear by now that most of the peoples' movements have lost faith in the Old Left wing or nationalist promise of the 'good life' in some unforeseen future for which they are supposed to bear with their 'oppressive present'. The question of the 'here and now' has become critical. If this is true of the ecological movements, it is equally so in relation to both the women's and the Dalit movements, where the impatience with waiting for some far-off future is quite apparent. Feminism was in fact, one of the earliest movements to assert that gender issues could not be put off to some appropriate future time, when class or such other issues had been taken care of; it had be taken up right

now. Something of this nature is now also being articulated by the Dalit movement. As Roy and Dey argue, at least some of these movements 'have begun to lay claim to a share of governance by theoretically owning the state, linking livelihood questions to the democratic decision-making process and demanding a responsible and accountable state' (Roy and Dey 2004: 3). What Roy and Dey are basically arguing here is not for 'owning' the *present* state as the quote above might suggest but of giving up the 'either/or framework' or the 'all or nothing' attitude so common amongst the marxists or Left wing activists, which can only posit an oppositional attitude towards, or a 'capture' of, state power (ibid.: 3). What Roy and Dey suggest here, then, is that it is only 'participation' 'in the processes of corrective action' that can become that basis of any useful politics in the present. It is this that the Right to Information movement, for instance, seeks to do by making the processes of 'governance' more transparent and accountable. It was the struggle for minimum wages and the proper implementation of the legal provisions in this regard, that led to the demand for making public the payment registers of the temporary/casual worker (the muster rolls), that eventually became the spark that ignited the movement. The success of the movement in this and other related matters, and its eventual spread to other places like Delhi in 2003-4 has helped in uncovering the corruption and pilferage of peoples' money in a way that large demonstrations before state assemblies/parliament that are content with making demands of the state, have never been able to do. There are interesting theoretical implications of this understanding articulated by Roy and Dey for a rethinking of the idea of State power which we can only flag for discussion at some other time.

5. *Constructive Work*. The position articulated by Roy and Dey is however, only one of the many forms that the refusal to defer gratification might take. The other position, articulated in practice by Shankar Guha Niyogi and his Chhattisgarh experiment, and put forward as a possible model by many people subsequently (Anil Sadgopal, Sangvai) is that of taking up constructive work as a part of radical, transformative political activity. In this instance, the state continues to be an adversary, both because of the ideological predilections of the CMM as well as because of the deep involvement of powerful industrial lobbies arrayed against the movement. Its

> practice underlines a new form that can be called 'social movement unionism' (Omvedt 1993: 236). Here 'constructive work' appears not merely as an instrumental mobilizational tool but becomes a key way of improving peoples' lives in the present. Here constructive work is no longer counterposed to political work as reformist but becomes a part of the radical political project itself. As Sangvai puts it, 'The New constructive work is potentially political and it sees itself linked with the struggle for justice and equality. Sangharsh (struggle) and Nirman (creativity) have become complementary for social change' (Sangvai 2003: 6). Sangvai also cites the instances of the oustee organizations in Bargi and Tawa and elsewhere who have been pursuing such a path. Such constructive work as mentioned earlier, could range from running educational institutions and hospitals to forming cooperatives.

In many ways, all these different forms of the rebellion against certain kinds of high modernist politics, based on the absolute authority of the technocrat/expert/bureaucrat, add up to a different kind of political vision and push towards a radicalization of Indian democracy.

In concluding this discussion, I will briefly touch upon one other aspect of these democratic struggles that both highlight certain extremely problematic areas as well as underline the limits of such movements.

## Relations with NGOs[23]

It is a point that is not sufficiently recognized that through the 1980s, the peoples' movements have grown and functioned in a complicated relationship with what are called non-governmental organizations (NGOs). The complication is that at one level, they have had a close symbiotic relationship where the NGOs often provided them vital support, in terms of infrastructure, campaigns and educational materials—often even providing them with activists, while at another, they have never been comfortable with the funding aspect. So, while the peoples' movements fought their battles in faraway rural or forest areas, with little access to the media, it was these NGOs that provided support for setting up and housing the various metropolitan 'support groups' whose task it was to approach friendly and influential people in the media, bureaucracy and academia for both advocating the cause of the movement concerned as well as seeking help in further campaigns. The more important aspect of the relationship between the movements and NGOs however, is the fact that for many of the critical questions relating to the movement, say the technical details and research regarding the environmental impact of something like the Sardar Sarovar Project, it was the latter once again that provided the basic support. In a sense, many of these NGOs functioned throughout this period as think-tanks for the movements, where in principle, theirs was a secondary position in relation to the movement, but which in due course began to appear as the voice of the movements, thus representing them.[24] It is not as if the relationship necessarily gets reversed but for many NGOs this has been the basis of the receiving continued funding. In some of the more well-known cases like the Ekta Parishad (EP) of Madhya Pradesh, for example, the close connections of the EP with many NGOs is quite well-known. Thus, even while the EP never really accepted any institutional funding (not being a registered body), it managed to work out a delicate balance with some of its activists working on lien from NGOs. This is a model that has been tried in some other instances where the grassroots level organizations and movements continue to get fair degree of support in kind from well-funded and friendly NGOs. Similar was the case with the Aman Ekta Manch, Delhi, formed in the wake of the war in Afghanistan and reactivated during the Gujarat carnages, or for example, the Sajha Manch, a non-party non-funded platform of urban groups. In both these cases, the platforms continued to function as non-registered movement groups but with critical and vital support from funded NGOs.

D L Sheth notes however, that in the late 1980s to early 1990s, the scenario underwent a significant change. On the one hand, he suggests, was the exhaustion that had set in among movement groups, after long years of being 'by and large fragmented into an almost isomorphic existence of each group fighting its own little battle'. In other words, they had 'lost their élan'. On the other, the funding scenario had become such that 'much larger quantities of funds were now made available to them by international donor agencies which had their own agenda for influencing the politics of discourse in peripheral countries' (Sheth 2004: 47). The thin line had been breached and as he puts it, 'most movement-groups had thus become routinized . . . and functioned as NGO bureaucracies' (ibid.). Many militant peoples' movements in different sectors, including the autonomous women's movement became funded NGOs. However, as Sheth notes, some movement-groups of gandhian, Left and social-democratic lineage 'stuck out and kept fighting their battles, thus, tenaciously retaining their character as movements' (ibid.).

Sheth also suggests that around the mid-1990s, things suddenly changed as movements got their act together and started coming into concerted actions and struggles against globalization. It is worth noting here, however, that in the early 1990s, it was not just the movements who were demoralized and on the back foot; the parties were more so, especially the Left parties whose world had just collapsed before their very eyes, like a house of cards. The strange thing—and this is where the element of complication comes in—is that in these days of despair the most refreshing critiques of globalization were made by NGOs and NGO leaders like Vandana Shiva and the Gene Campaign. There were others in the NGO sector, like the Delhi-based Public Interest Research Group (PIRG), who produced most of the popular literature that combined old Left critiques of the IMF/World Bank with the movements' perspective that also involved a critique of the development model. Shiva herself has been subsequently responsible for raising many critical issues like water in public debate.

A serious assessment of the work of the NGOs that deals with these issues in all their complexity still remains to be carried out.

## Naxalbari 1967-2007: Dangerous Liaisons

I have already discussed the first phase of the naxalite movement, at some length, in the previous chapter. This phase, we might recall, was one that lasted from 1967 to about 1971-2, where after it virtually fizzled out. This phase is marked by a certain shrillness of ideological rhetoric and a high degree of esoteric polemics based on the tenets of 'marxism-leninism-Mao Tse-tung thought'. The assessment of the Indian situation presented by different strands of the various naxalite groups was by and large, completely off the mark, based on a highly exaggerated reading of the 'revolutionary maturity' of the political situation. This was the phase when the movement had cast its magical spell all around among idealist youth and the call to make the 1970s the decade of liberation was taken very seriously by a large number of its followers. Thereafter the movement went into what seemed to many to be a terminal decline. The movement went through innumerable splits and gave birth to scores of little factions with virtually no effectivity. Observers in the CPI(M), the parent party even declared its death and conducted its postmortem (Dubey 1994: 2). One of the party ideologues declared the movement 'at an ideological dead-end' as late as in early 1985 (Karat 1985).

This was ironical. For, already by the time the CPI(M) leaders were conducting its postmortem, Naxalism had started re-emerging as a powerful force in different parts of the country. As one of the chroniclers of the movement puts it, by the end of the 1980s, a new upsurge of the movement was evident in at least ten districts of central Bihar, in the Telengana region of Andhra Pradesh and in the Bastar and Raipur areas of Madhya Pradesh (now in Chhattisgarh), apart from select areas in West Bengal, Tamil Nadu and Uttar Pradesh. While this upsurge remained largely underground till the mid-1980s, around March 1989, huge public demonstrations in Delhi and Patna announced that some of them were beginning to come overground (Dubey 1994: 2, 3). This was the second phase, which could be said to have its beginnings somewhere in the early 1980s. The two major groups working in different areas in this phase were the CPI(ML) Liberation and the CPI(ML) People's War. Apart from these there were a number of smaller groups with varying degrees of influence in some pockets in some states. Important among these were two outfits, namely the Central Organizing Committee (Party Unity) and the Maoist Communist Centre (MCC), which eventually merged with 'People's War' in the early years of this century to adopt the name CPI(Maoist), establishing a symbolic connection with the powerful Maoist movement in neighbouring Nepal. This could be said to be the ongoing third phase of the movement. This is not the place to track the history of the naxalite movement but it is necessary to briefly keep the broad contours in mind for the purposes of my argument.[25]

There is no doubt that the naxalite movement—in practically all its manifestations—is a movement whose inspiration comes from the high-modernism of Leninist ideology. All the key elements, namely, the vanguard party, comprising a cadre of trained professional revolutionaries, equipped with all the expertise that could ever be required by the revolution, are very much present in naxalite discourse. In fact, this is present to the point of a virtually theological insistence and the naxalite critique of the CPI(M) or the CPI is that they have abandoned these theological tenets.

Yet, there are two elements that, in fact, provided the openings within the movement of a move away from such high-modernism. First, it was the more youthful elements of the CPI(M), relatively new in the party (except for a section of the leadership), who were attracted to the naxalite idea. They had a double advantage: they were not yet steeled in the 'rigours of marxism-leninism' Comintern style, which is to say, the theology of Saint Stalin, along with all its cynical methods. Further, partly as a consequence of this, they could never get around to building the perfect stalinist party—closed, top-down and rigidly hide-bound. Thus, 'building the party' remained a dream and a desire for most of the naxalites, at least during the first phase. One of the factors that prevented the party from being formed in a hurry and eventually leading to its dissipation, when it was formed, was that most of the rebels who had left the CPI(M), had no agreement yet on what the programme for the future should be. They could not also agree with each other about important questions of practice such as the significance of individual annihilation or of mass organizations like trade unions and kisan sabhas.

In effect, therefore, the position that began to emerge was that the party should emerge through a process of uniting different groups over a period of time, rather than try to build one from above. In fact, as Ranabir Samaddar, one-time participant of the movement has noted, 'The Party CC [Central Committee] never met again after its inaugural meet; the local units were given absolute freedom to operate; military activities overtook political activities . . . .' And so he concludes, 'In a sense, the CPI(ML) was an antiparty' (cited in Omvedt 1993: 42).

Needless to say, this was a serious practical 'deviation' from the tenets of high-modernism. Lenin too had often deviated, but then those were days when the party of professional revolutionaries had not yet been put in place. This absence of a centralized party with a centralized command that had the ultimate power to decide on what is right and what is wrong, opened up spaces within the interstices of the movement that allowed different kinds of political tendencies to emerge. It is also of some importance that because the movement comprised so many small groups for long period of time, these groups had a more local character and established a much more direct relationship with local conditions than the all-India Left parties. The need for allies too forced them, often enough, despite their predilections to the contrary, to establish friendly relations with many emerging social movements.

Thus, for instance the emergence of one of the earliest feminist group, the Progressive Organization of Women in Hyderabad or the Magowa group in Maharashtra, within the broader universe of the naxalite movement, are a case in point. This was at a time when the mainstream communist parties were busy attacking feminism as a 'bourgeois' tendency, as they continue to do today. In fact, it might be more accurate to say that the diffusion of maoism through the movement led to its intellectual-political osmosis with many different currents, thus producing entirely novel forms of politics. While this is an old story, the fact is that such spaces continue to be available to those who wish to push for a deeper appreciation of gender questions within the movement. Thus, a meeting between women's groups and the CPI(Maoist) and CPI(ML) Janashakti, as late as in October 2004, was hailed by prominent women activists for the frankness with which these parties are said to have responded to the 'Open Letter to Revolutionary Parties', raising important issues of the women's movement (Vasanth Kannabiran, Volga, Kalpana Kannabiran 2004: 4874-5). The meeting was, in fact, an outcome of the initiative taken by women's groups. Despite continuing rigidities in terms of their own positions, the activists felt that the sheer range of issues that these parties had recognized gave the sense that the meeting could be the beginning of a longer ongoing dialogue.

With no high clergy of the Polit Bureau to police the traffic of ideas, this diffusion of maoism led to interesting political blends. So for example, the *Dalit Panthers Manifesto*, issued in 1973 took its direct inspiration from a combination of the prevailing Maoist ethos and language of the time on the one hand, and the Black Panther movement in the United States of America. Thus it stated: 'Due to the hideous plot of American imperialism, the Third Dalit World, that is the oppressed nations, and Dalit people are suffering' (cited in Joshi 1986: 145). In exact correspondence with this amazingly elastic notion of the 'Third Dalit World', it defined the Dalits thus: 'Members of Scheduled Castes and Tribes, neo-Buddhists, the working people, the landless and poor peasants, women and all those who are being exploited politically, economically and in the name of religion' (ibid.: 145). In tune with the spirit of the times, it asserted that 'the struggle for the emancipation of the Dalits needs a complete revolution. Partial change is impossible'.

More to the point however, is the relationship of alliance and tension that developed between the naxalite groups, especially the PWG (People's War Group) and the Dalit movement in Andhra Pradesh, especially under the initiative of the journal *Edureeta* (Swimming Against the Tide), started in 1990 by two former naxalite Dalit leaders (Gudavarthy 2005: 5412, 13). Gudavarthy details the struggle whereby it became mandatory to have Dalits and women as leaders in all the naxalite groups, as well as to 'accept the combined philosophy of Ambedkarism-marxism as the only alternative for the Indian situation' (ibid.: 5413). Undoubtedly these relationships were always fraught but they were nevertheless possible in ways that never became so in the mainstream communist parties.

As far as environmental questions go, despite the fact that they pose, theoretically, the biggest challenge to high-modernist ideology, Naxalism in its second and third phases has been deeply involved in taking them up. This is partly a result of the fact that over the years, as the mainstream Left retreated into the comforts of parliamentary politics, Naxalism (especially, though not solely, in its Maoist incarnation) moved into adivasi areas. Its main base being among the adivasi population, it has inevitably gravitated towards taking up these issues. This does not, of course, mean that the naxalites or Maoists have developed any larger understanding of environmental issues but spaces for such a possibility certainly open up. Thus, as Manoranjan Mohanty, a close sympathizer and observer of the movement notes,

> The naxalite movement is mostly active in the tribal areas spreading from Bihar to Andhra Pradesh and Maharashtra, and also covering parts of Jharkhand, Madhya Pradesh, Chhattisgarh, Orissa, Tamil Nadu and Karnataka. This spread is linked [not] only to the inaccessible hilly terrain of these regions, but a conscious decision by the naxalites to take up the issues affecting the tribal people, who are among the most exploited in society. India's development process has led to commercialization of forest resources, reducing the traditional access to forest produce. Alienation of tribal land to non-tribals has been a steady trend despite legal strictures. Mining-based industries and the construction of large dams have caused extensive displacement of the tribals, besides destroying their natural environment. A central naxalite agenda is for tribal self-determination, asserting the rights of the tribals over local resources (Mohanty 2005).

The second element that allows for the move away from high-modernism, thus, is at least partly linked to this circumstance. This 'conscious decision' to take up issues of tribal self-determination that Mohanty refers to is not entirely contingent and instrumental. It has also to do with a certain way in which maoism and through it, marxism itself, has been received in India, *as a romantic revolt against modern (and urban) life*, as something coterminus with capitalism and industrialism. Here the working class and the humdrum of its trade union activity actually holds no particular attraction and is in fact seen as the fount of all 'reformism'. The question is never theorized as such but it is not difficult to see that the idea of tribal self determination and control over local resources runs against the logic of industrial development—as recent conflicts over land acquisition clearly show. In fact, Maoist presence in struggles against land acquisition (for private corporations and special economic zones) has been quite significant over the last few years.

At another, very different level, the naxalite or Maoist relationship to the crisis of high-modernism in India has had to do with the specific nature of maoism's intellectual appeal. Right from the late 1960s and 1970s, maoism acquired a much broader set of admirers than strictly those within the naxalite movement. In the specific context of that time, it was the romantic vision of a China trying to move away from a centralized, heavy-industry based economy, insisting on placing 'people before technology', recycling waste, was one that attracted the attention of many gandhians as well. For the gandhians, the austerity practiced by the Maoist leadership of China too resonated with the gandhian ideal.

It is of some interest in this respect that the idea of 'socialism' and 'communism' itself has had a more complicated relationship with capitalism and industrialism through history. In a fascinating study, Maurice Meisner traces the history of utopian ideas of the early 'communist egalitarianism' and underlines their strongly anti-urban bias (Meisner 1982: 42-3). The modern city, seen as 'the symbol and center of capitalist industrialism', he writes, is a recurrent theme, right down from Babouvism to the utopian socialists. Given that capitalism in China was not an indigenous product but something that 'came under the aegis of foreign imperialism' and 'created all the social evils associated with early industrialism in the West', the reaction to it could only have been more hostile (Meisner: 53). Meisner goes on to argue that later, in the 1960s, Mao formulated his ideas on socialism by insisting that it was easier to achieve in China than in the West 'precisely because China was less 'poisoned' by modern capitalist forces of economic development and bourgeois ideology' (ibid.: 58). He also suggests that this anti-urban bias was shared by others like Castro, Frantz Fanon and the 'African socialism' of Julius Nyerere (ibid.: 72). Recent rearticulations of 'socialism' in Bolivia or the Chiapas region of Mexico, would suggest that this spirit of a romantic revolt against modernity continues to thrive in Left wing cultures. In a sense, Naxalism and maoism in India shared what was probably a larger suspicion of modern and industrial life—and indeed, it had the extremely fertile soil of a largely peasant and artisan culture and the still widely prevalent gandhian disposition towards modernity to provide it sustenance.

One of the important but little recognized—in the precincts of the academy at least—tendencies is the emergence in 1980 of a group called the 'Patriotic People's Science and Technology' (PPST), based mainly in Kanpur and Madras (Omvedt 1993: 142). Omvedt describes this group as 'a mixture of naxalite-influenced young intellectuals and old gandhians', who basically were also in debate of sorts with the Kerala Shastra Sahitya Parishad (KSSP) and Lok Vidnyan Sanghatana (LVS)—both clearly marxist in orientation and linked to the CPI(M) (Omvedt 1993: 142). The debate centred on the relationship between science and technology on the one hand and imperialism on the other, and the KSSP/LVS position clearly was that this was a contingent and external relationship, while the PPST wanted the explore what it believed was a more intrinsic connection. Science and technology, in other words, could not be harnessed for popular use simply by freeing it from imperialism control, in the PPST view.

In the debate on 'scientific temper', that followed the publication in 1981 of a 'Statement on Scientific Temper' by some intellectuals close to the Congress establishment, the dividing lines became much clearer. The CPI(M) inclined intellectuals criticized the 'lack of class perspective' in the document and claimed that 'all would be fine', only if 'the people' gained control of science and technology. The PPST position was articulated very sharply against such a stance by now: 'From the very moment of its forced entry into the third world, modern Western science has been far from being a liberating and revolutionary force as far as the people of the third world are concerned. It has since then been playing an increasingly greater role in the plunder and destruction of the third world economies and cultures' (cited in Omvedt 145). A section of the PPST represented by 'Sunil Sahasrabudhe and others grouped around the Hindi journal *Mazdur-Kisan Niti*,' according to Omvedt, tried to link the environmental critique (emerging from this critique of science) and the peasant/farmers movement, then on the rise, in different parts of the country.

The PPST, in the event, became one of the key intellectual components of the moment of the 1980s that we might designate as the moment of the romantic revolt. And in this, the peculiar blend of the naxalite/Maoist inspiration with some strands of gandhianism played an important part. It would not be out of place however, to underline here that while this moment had a significant impact on the future development of social movements in the country, it also contained within it the always-present possibility of a glorification or romanticization of 'ancient India'. This was a possibility that sadly came to pass with a section of the PPST eventually drifting towards the Hindu Right. However, it should be emphasized that a possibility is a possibility; there is nothing inevitable about such a drift. A critique of the modern can well be made by imagining a different future without necessarily affirming 'the past' (assuming, of course, that we *know*, in the first place what 'the past' was).

## Nandigram 2007

Nandigram, in early 2007, became a household word in West Bengal and a new addition to India's political vocabulary. Forty years ago, in 1967, it was the CPI(M)-led 14-party United Front government that was just taking over power, when 'Naxalbari' had happened. The United Front government was expectedly very short-lived. It survived just for about eight months—falling eventually 'under the weight of its own contradictions', as it were. Forty years later, it was Nandigram. Now too the CPI(M) was in power, with one difference: It had been in power for thirty long years without a break. The ghost of Naxalbari has never ceased to haunt the CPI(M), and if any proof were ever needed of this, 'Nandigram' is the proof. For used though the CPI(M) has been to pronounce the death of Naxalism every now and then, it has never ceased to see its potential presence everywhere. Once again, its state and all-India leaders eventually started seeing the omnipresent hand of Maoists, one of them even paranoically proclaiming that the 'Maoists were coming by the sea route to Nandigram'. There was little room for doubt that the 'spectre of Naxalism' was haunting communism in West Bengal.

If the CPI(M) has been unable to exorcise that ghost, then it seems the ghost of Nandigram will pursue it for much longer. For, Nandigram is not Naxalbari. So what is Nandigram?

It is difficult to write the story of a saga that still continues. One chapter is over. But many more remain to play themselves out, and certainly will, in the near future. In its basics, Nandigram was an upsurge of local peasants against a proposed government plan to acquire their land for setting up an industrial hub—along the lines of a Special Economic Zone (SEZ). SEZs as we all know now, are islands of pure autonomy of capital: no labour laws can operate there; tax laws are inapplicable; and on a whole range of matter relating to international trade, they are to be treated like a 'foreign territory' (See Menon and Nigam 2007: 65, 106). These zones are supposed to be interim measures—ideally of course, capital would like to see the entire world transformed in an SEZ.

West Bengal, under the stewardship of its new chief minister Buddhadeb Bhattacharya, plans to rapidly industrialize—else, says Bhattacharya, there will be the 'End of History' (Bhattacharya 2007). The exact manner in which all the developments in Nandigram played themselves out is quite well-known but it bears repeating that before Nandigram erupted in January 2007, one particularly bitter episode of land acquisition had already taken place in Singur, a few hours off Kolkata. Here

997 acres of land had been acquired, virtually at gun point, even though the CPI(M) claimed it had obtained prior consent from the farmers. It was also claimed that the farmers had been given a 'handsome compensation' for their land. None of these claims are substantiated and for a little less than half the land, the farmers contested the claim that their consent had been taken. However, the exact details of the matter do not interest us here.[26] For the moment, I am interested in underlining the fact that once Singur had happened and the Tata industrial house which was given the land, fenced it off under full armed police protection, amidst unprecedented violence, Nandigram had become inevitable. There had anyway been many rumours about the government acquiring huge amounts of land (to the tune of 65, 000 acres) for a number of industrial projects, including one where the chief minister had committed to an Indonesian group, against the opinion of the state assembly and sections of his own party. The final straw came with the leak of a notification issued by the Haldia Development Authority (headed by a CPI-M Member of Parliament), dated 28 December 2006. In what was until then a Left and CPI(M) stronghold, the peasants suddenly rose up in anger, attacked the local CPI(M) office, dug up roads and set up a blockade.

Nandigram's sorrows began soon after that. Thereafter in two rounds, the state's police and the party machinery moved to 'liberate' Nandigram, first in March and then finally in November—the second being a purely party-gangster operation. State CPI(M) leaders went on record declaring that they would make life hell for those who were rebelling. Killings and rapes were reported from the area in large numbers, on both occasions.[27] Finally, Nandigram was 'liberated' on the night of 5 November and the next day, a virtual bloodbath was unleashed by the 'cadres'—a hated word now in contemporary West Bengal. Of course, like all parties or groups in power, the CPI(M) too had its own, very classic rendering of the situation. It was far from accepting that the peasants and 'the people' had risen in revolt against them; in a befittingly stalinist manner, it claimed all this to be the handiwork of 'the Opposition' and 'outsiders' who were acting as part of a larger conspiracy that included the Maoists and the Trinamool Congress.

Already, when Singur had happened, it had galvanized large sections of the intellectuals and students of the state into coming out in support of the peasants and against the high-handedness of the state government. A veritable mass movement was in the offing—with students going to Singur, making films, circulating CDs, and organizing discussions around them in college and university campuses. The initial upsurge in Nandigram, in January 2007, electrified the entire atmosphere in the state. Students and intellectuals joined in demonstrations in support of the peasants. Nandigram therefore became a turning point.

The bewilderment of the CPI(M) leaders and intellectuals at this sudden turn of events is understandable, precisely because this aspect of social and political dynamic remains completely opaque to it—as to all Power. The point at which power insulates itself from all criticism, enveloped in the myth of its impenetrability and invincibility, is also the point at which it becomes most vulnerable.

Drawing on Ryszard Kapuscinski's account of the Iranian revolution, Slavoj Zizek underlines in one of his essays, that precise moment of the 'collapse of the Big Other'—the point at which the Revolution in Iran against the Shah's brutal regime began. Kapuscinski's account traces this moment back to one incident: The refusal of a lone pedestrian to obey the command of the policeman on a busy street: 'The "beginning of the end" of the Shah's regime took place at a certain Teheran crossroad, where a common citizen refused to obey a policeman's order to go away. The news spread like fire and, all of a sudden, people ceased to "believe in the Big Other".' Zizek designates this moment, following his Lacanian tastes, as that of the 'collapse of the Big Other' and adds that usually this moment can be traced to a very specific point in time. It is something that happens all of a sudden (Zizek 1993: 232-3).

The moment at which this pedestrian refused to obey the command, the symbolic chain of impenetrability of order was broken, and it suddenly became clear that commands could be disobeyed. More and more people joined in disobeying the command. Increasingly greater numbers joined in protests against order. In another context, Louis Althusser would call such a situation 'overdetermined'—a situation where a whole range of different conflicts and discontents 'merge' or 'fuse' into an explosive situation. That is what determines, according to Althusser, a revolutionary or insurrectionary situation.

Zizek provides another instance of such a specific moment that is extremely telling. In Romania, he says, the 'spell was broken' the moment when, at a mass rally, in Bucharest, convoked by Ceausescu after the demonstrations in Timisoara in order to prove that he still enjoyed popular support, the crowd started to shout at Ceausescu. The leader of course, could not believe what he was seeing and 'raised his hands in a tragicomic and bewildered display of impotent paternal love, as if wanting to embrace them all' (Zizek 1993: 234). In all such instances, it is the sheer unpredictability of the moment that is truly remarkable, according to Zizek. What had till a moment ago, 'evoked a mixture of fear and respect' 'is now experienced as a rather different mixture of ridiculous imposture and brutal, illegitimate display of force' (ibid.: 234). On the face of it, nothing has changed; yet, nothing remains as it was.

Something of this kind happened in West Bengal in the wake of Singur and Nandigram. The 'Nandigram effect', which could not have been possible without Singur but which took the logic of Singur to an insurrectionary level, made one thing clear: the CPI(M)-police-government-vested interest nexus could be broken; that it was not invincible. Almost within a few weeks of Nandigram, as Vaskar Nandy explained in a talk in Delhi University in April 2006, the Nandigram effect had pervaded the tea gardens ruled by a powerful nexus of vested interests of the CITU, police and the industrialists. The virtually invisible local revolts against this cadre-raj drove away the self-appointed leaders breaking these nexuses irreparably.

It was also a sign of the unprecedented nature of the situation that for the first time in the last thirty years of CPI(M) rule, middle class students, intellectuals and cultural activists responded spontaneously to the call of Nandigram. It was a replay of what the state had once witnessed in the period of the Left's ascendancy as a radical force: spontaneous activity that found new channels of communication not available till then. It was as a consequence of this transformation that numerous other movements and struggles began breaking out in different parts of West Bengal in the subsequent period. In a sense, the food riots that started from Birbhum and Bankura and rapidly spread to other parts of the state like Bardhaman and Murshidabad—were an extended manifestation of the 'Nandigram effect'. Not surprisingly, popular ire was no longer directed only against the police but had now turned against the CPI(M) machinery itself. All the signs of a popular uprising were evident in those happenings in the state.

Another crucial feature of an insurrectionary constellation became apparent in the situation—the machinery itself started breaking down and party members were beginning to desert the party. Some of them decided to continue to remain within but kept in constant touch with the movement. So when the CPI(M) claimed, for instance, that many of those killed in the Nandigram violence were, in fact, its members (thus 'proving' that they were the targets rather than the perpetrators), they were not exactly lying. Just till the other day, they were CPM members and even though they deserted the party and joined the struggle against land acquisition, they actually died while still 'on the rolls'.

However, as we know too well, not every insurrectionary situation leads to a regime change and between these two lie a whole range of other possibilities which are dependent on a number of other conditions. At any rate, not every insurrection even aspires to a regime change. It nevertheless changes many things in less visible, unintended, unforeseen ways.

Nandigram, however, is not Naxalbari. For, it signals the final crisis of high-modernism. No leader, no ideology, no banners can be associated with Nandigram. It is the 'real movement' of which Marx often spoke. True, various elements and political forces and parties have attempted to take over and 'represent' the movement but to no avail. It is only in CPI(M) 'folklore' that Nandigram was a Trinamool Congress-Maoist conspiracy. The fact of the matter is that like all movements from the uprising of the Russian revolution to the various popular movements in West Bengal itself (for instance, the food movement of the 1960s), this too was a spontaneous movement. Vanguards, parties, adventurers and demagogues are always waiting in the wings to 'take over' such movements. This suits both the rulers and the demagogues.[28] Nandigram defies this attempt and has managed to become a symbol and a call to arms not only against the ruling CPI(M) but also for the plan to take over agricultural lands and set up SEZs in other parts of the country.

Nandigram made the Central government halt and reformulate its SEZ policy. It made the globalization-drunk media stop and debate, and to some extent reformulate its position. Most importantly, Nandigram became the banner of struggle against SEZs and land acquisition in states like Haryana and Karnataka. It presaged a whole range of significant, often molecular struggles against planned retail chains by both Indian and foreign corporations.

Nandigram is all this and more. For the first time in the last two decades, especially since the collapse of socialism, has the power bloc sat up to consider the question of land acquisitions in a somewhat less aggressive manner. This is especially evident in some recent judicial pronouncements, since the judiciary had emerged in the past, especially in the context of the Narmada struggle as the most ruthless proponent of such high-modernism-laced corporate interests. The twenty years of peaceful struggles against big dams, it might be recalled, which were primarily struggles against land acquisition and dispossession, had only met with cynical disregard by the judiciary.

However, most significantly, while a struggle like the Narmada Bachao Andolan had been conveniently show-cased by both the ruling powers and the Left as a unique case, Nandigram has burst forth within the Left's universe with uncomfortable questions. Much as the dominant sections of the Left may try to evade it, the question of the development paradigm has now been placed on its plate as well. All the questions that the Narmada struggle had raised are going to haunt the future Left (whatever shape it may have)—as they have been concerning and troubling the non-party Left for many years.

## NOTES

1. Interestingly, the idea of one-man-management was rejected by Mao Tse-tung in China, though high-modernism continued to rule the roost, despite some 'deviations'.
2. The group has since merged with two others to form the CPI(Maoist).
3. That was when the NDA government, led by the BJP was still in power and the wounds of Gujarat carnage still fresh.
4. The MR argument here is a mere summary of their position in Mumbai Resistance (2003), *Mumbai Resistance—MR 2004.*
5. Mumbai Resistance (2003), *Mumbai Resistance—MR 2004*, p. 2, emphasis added.
6. Ibid., p. 2.
7. Ibid., p. 4, emphasis added.
8. Even though the WSF formally forbids any direct participation by political parties, the two mainstream CPs, especially the CPI(M), has through its front organizations, played a key role in the India Organizing Committee and the process in general.
9. Sitaram Yechury (2003), 'CPI(M) and the WSF', downloaded 17 June 2004, http://www.redglobe.org/modules.php?name=News&file=article&sid=1080. All citations are from this article.
10. The image is of course borrowed from Rajani Palme Dutt's history of the nationalist struggle in India where he characterized the Congress movement as a kind of safety valve.
11. Ibid., p. 3.

12. RUPE, The Economics and Politics of the World Social Forum: Lessons for the Struggle Against 'Globalization' 2003, http://www.rupe-india.org.

13. Ibid., all emphasis in original.

14. While in the first phase of dislocation in 1996/97, it was mainly workers' organizations who were protesting, in the second phase in 2000, employers made common cause with workers and joined together in big demonstrations. This has continued till very recently.

15. This would be truer of independent or non-party trade unions and, to a somewhat lesser extent also of party-affiliated ones.

16. The allegations against the NBA in fact took the form of a legal case filed by an Ahmedabad based organization called the National Council of Civil Liberties. The Supreme Court, on examination not only dismissed the case, but also ordered the petitioner organization to pay Rs 5000/- to the NBA as a symbolic cost of the expenditure incurred by the latter on the case. See report in http://www.icrindia.org/?p=164, last accessed on 24 April 2008.

17. A word about the term 'civil society' is in order here. Unlike the commonly misused sense of the term, especially in NGO jargon, my use here follows the more technical political theory usage, especially as elaborated by Partha Chatterjee in distinguishing it from what he calls political society. In this use, this civil society is the high ground of modernity in India and the domain of citizenship and rights. Its logic is governed by that of an active citizenry that exercises constant vigilance over the state and the excesses of the political class by appealing to the constitutionally guaranteed rights of citizens. As opposed to this, struggles and movements in political society often do not have the easy recourse to the language of rights and citizenship and depend on a whole range of other modes of justification and avenues of articulation provided by the electoral democratic system.

18. We have covered this ground at some length in Nivedita Menon and Aditya Nigam, *Power and Contestation: India since 1989*, London: Zed Books Ltd, 2007. See Chapter 5, 'Old Left, New Left', especially pp. 124-33.

19. Here we need not go into the marxist debate on the 'differentiation within the peasantry' that capitalism introduces and how, strictly speaking, the interests of the rural proletariat (the agricultural workers and the poor peasantry who work most of the time as wage workers on others' land) and the rich peasantry (or the rural bourgeoisie), really have no common ground. This is the conventional marxist position that Omvedt contests in her defense of these struggles as new

radical movements, while positing a 'non-class' notion of an undifferentiated peasantry pitted against the state and capital. However, it is interesting to note that Omvedt's own position then becomes a variation of the 'rural' (the undifferentiated peasantry) versus the 'urban'—which has been the staple of a lot of populist politics both in India and elsewhere. What should, however, be underlined here is that the really problematic part of this notion of the undifferentiated rural emerges, not only in relation to the issue of class but also of caste in contemporary India and the ways in which this leads to new ways of subjection of the Dalit castes by the middle/dominant castes who are also the rich and middle peasants who were getting organized under the banner of these movements.

20. See note 18 in this chapter.

21. This reference is to Marx's celebrated remark on the Paris Commune: the workers had no ideals to realize; no blueprints to which the world must conform; they merely had to set free the forces of change that had taken birth in the womb of the old society.

22. Following Alexis de Tocqueville, Laclau and Mouffe argue that the fact that the 'liberal-democratic ideology' of equality and liberty has been transformed into common sense, has 'laid the foundation for [the] progressive challenge to the hierarchical principle' (See Ernesto Laclau and Chantal Mouffe, *Hegemony and socialist strategy: Towards a Radical Democratic Politics*, London and New York: Verso, 1985, p. 160). They thus suggest that these ideas have become the 'new matrix of the social imaginary' (ibid., p. 155).

23. The discussion in this section elaborates upon some of the points made in Menon and Nigam op. cit., pp. 124-33.

24. Since these are extremely sensitive matters, it is not possible to name either the movements or the NGOs concerned; neither is it possible for the same reasons to reference the information. Most of the information in this section is therefore based on my close interaction with activists of such movements and NGOs and on some degree of involvement with some of them.

25. A brief periodization of the movement is provided in Menon and Nigam, op. cit., Chapter 5, 'Old Left, New Left'.

26. The interested reader may see the huge amount of literature and exchanges on the details of actual happenings in numerous reports, statements and discussions archived in www.kafila.org and www.sanhati.com as also in most newspapers of November-December 2006 (Singur), March 2007 and November 2007 (Nandigram).

27. To get a flavour of what was happening, see the report by Imran Ahmed Siddqui, 'Stockpile squad trail heads towards party—Phone records spill Nandigram secret', *The Telegraph*, 19 March 2007.

28. An important characteristic of spontaneous mass movements is that they force all political tendencies and organizations present in the field to define their stance—either join or oppose. In Nandigram too, this choice has been forced on all political groups. One of the groups present, the Jamait-e-Ulema-Hind (JUH) is an Islamic organization that has had a substantial presence in the area, especially among the mass of the Muslim peasantry. The fact that the peasants were linked to the JUH in no way prevented them from being politically CPI(M) and Left Front supporters. In the period following the eruption of the movement, much has been made by the CPI(M) of the JUH's presence and the supposed 'communal tinge' of the movement. In recent times, the position of the JUH with regard to the issue of the stay of Bangladeshi writer Taslima Nasreen has been very hostile and became tied up, in a complicated way, with the anti-Taslima demonstrations and mobilization in Kolkata. This is a more complex affair, involving a section of the ruling party as well and cannot be gone into here in any detail.

# 6

# HETEROTOPIAS OF DESIRE

## Carnival as Politics, Politics as Art

The crisis of modernist class politics can be understood, among other things, as the crisis also of a particular mode of doing politics: *politics as ressentiment*, politics as based on the two kinds of emotions—pain and anger. It is not difficult to see, however, that this 'pain' and 'anger', often enough is predicated on another, probably more fundamental emotion, found usually among the radical/liberal 'vanguards' of different kinds. This is the affect of piety—of some presumed duty towards the oppressed and the poor. In India this combines with the 'ascetic ideal', so characteristic and pervasive across the spectrum from gandhian to different shades of the Left. It is this affect that propels the vanguard/militants of Left wing politics to take upon themselves the role of messiahs with a considerable degree of moral righteousness. While there may be much to commend in the spirit that moves such radicals, not the least being their revolt against crass individualism and ego-centrism, it is probably undeniable that much of the present crisis of this kind of politics is closely tied to such vanguardism. It is the arrogation unto themselves of the role of interpreters of the 'true interests of the people' that eventually makes this politics most problematic.

In his classic study of Nietzsche, Gilles Deleuze observes that according to Nietzsche 'ressentiment, bad conscience and the ascetic ideal are the figures of the triumph of reactive forces and also the forms of nihilism' (Deleuze 1983: 87). As against the 'reactive' and the negative, Deleuze invokes Nietzsche's notion of the *tragic as affirmation*. The tragic, he says, 'is not to be found in this anguish or disgust, nor in the nostalgia for lost unity'; it is only to be found in the joy of multiplicity (ibid.: 17). '*The tragic* is the aesthetic form of joy, not . . . a moral solution to pain, fear or pity' (ibid., 17). The tragedy of affirmation lies also in the difficulty in affirming *everything*, including all forms of suffering. Everything or situation must find its own special means of affirmation.

With respect to the Dalit experience, the power of these emotions and affects—of the pain of suffering and oppression and the anger of resistance—has been so overwhelming that it seems virtually impossible that it could find any other recognizable language of politics. The liberal/radical intelligentsia, driven by piety, is only interested in endless stories of pain and oppression. This intelligentsia, whether gandhian, socialist, communist, or liberal, is ever suspicious however, of the forms of politics and political speech that actually emerge from the Dalit movement. By and large, this suspicion has to do with the fact that the different strands of the Dalit movement have usually espoused an often deliberately excessive language and style that is mocking and bitter. This style could also be understood as a different mode of the politics of ressentiment but it is one that targets precisely the very 'sympathetic' liberal/radical/gandhian who often seems to come threateningly close to taking over (once again!) the role of deciding what the real interests of Dalits are, in effect appropriating their voice. It is this surfeit of (often well-meaning) sympathizers that the nascent movement has to simultaneously deal with, while fighting its own deadly battles against caste discrimination and oppression.

It is in this context of the overwhelming force of ressentiment-driven politics that I wish to discuss one very interesting new strand of a different kind of politics of carnival, feast and laughter. This politics also involves an ironical reversal of the terms of discourse, of the gaze of the pious radical.

## Scene 1. English, The Dalit Goddess: The Party-Feast as Installation

On 25 October 2006, an interesting event took place. This 'event' was a small and, at one level, innocuous dinner get-together. The venue was a modest apartment in the eastern part of Delhi, across the river Yamuna, in one of the housing societies in Patparganj. The organizer and host of the party was a young and charismatic Dalit intellectual and journalist, Chandra Bhan Prasad, who has emerged, within the space of the past few years, as almost a cult figure, known for his extremely provocative and unconventional political positions.

The occasion was the birthday of Lord Macaulay—Thomas Babington Macaulay, the colonial official most instrumental in laying the foundations of English education in colonial India, whom Prasad hails as the 'Father of Indian Modernity'.[1] Macaulay's intervention, we might remember, constituted a major departure from the days of the East India Company, when the medium of instruction continued to be Sanskrit and Arabic. It is also useful to remember that the name 'Macaulayism' has since become something of a metaphorical expression for a range of colonial policies that were supposedly aimed at the destruction of indigenous language and culture and spawning a class of what were once called 'brown sahibs'. As a term of abuse, 'Macaulay's children' or *Macaulay ki santaanein* is often used by the spokespersons of the RSS and the Hindu Right, in the same breath as *Marxputra* (offsprings of Marx), to refer to what are seen by them to be an illegitimate breed of people in the postcolonial world. It is also worth keeping in mind that this assessment of Macaulay's role has been virtually unanimous across the board: from nationalist and marxist scholars to postcolonial theorists, all have at some point of time or the other referred to that famous—or infamous—statement where he stated that British rule must 'do our best to form a class who may be interpreters between us and the millions whom we govern', a class he described as 'Indian in blood and colour, but English in taste, in opinions, in morals, and in intellect.'[2]

The scene of the social party-feast has become Chandrabhan Prasad's preferred form of 'political mobilization'—if one were to use that term somewhat loosely here. For, the atmosphere is carnivalesque; its purpose is hardly 'mobilization' in the standard sense. Food and drinks laid out on one side, posters and slogans adorning the walls while a whole array of the city's intellectuals, from academics to journalists, mill around, a little bemused.

**Plate 1.** The English Goddess

A couple of years ago Prasad had already created a stir among his radical sympathizers by celebrating Macaulay's birthday with a party.[3] This time round, it could not be a mere repeat performance. The party must begin ceremoniously. If last time it had begun with the unveiling of a photograph of Macaulay, this time things became even more provocative. It was the just-enthroned 'English, the Dalit Goddess' who had to be venerated (see plate 1). A painting of the Goddess by Dalit artist Shant Swarup Baudha was unveiled.[4] The remarkable image represents, significantly, a version of the Statue of Liberty in whose outstretched hand we see a gigantic pen instead of the torch. The Goddess is perched atop a computer, which is apparently suspended in mid air, against the backdrop of a map of India. The map itself is unclear, except for the peninsular part. As your eyes move up, the map morphs into a sea of riotous colours: Northern India, the heart of the contemporary Dalit upsurge, is a throbbing sea of effects such as you might witness beneath the surface of an otherwise calm looking ocean.

As usual we have a range of celebrities—always only from the intellectual world—ranging from social scientists like Ashis Nandy, D L Sheth and Gail Omvedt to Rajendra Yadav and other luminaries of the Hindi literary world. Prasad's friends and admirers in the media are also present. The entire party is really an art installation and everybody present, a part of the installation. Celebration—either of Macaulay's birthday or of the arrival of a new Goddess—is certainly not the only purpose behind putting together these 'everyday objects' (social scientists, artistes, littérateurs and journalists), alongside abundant bottles of IMFL or 'beef cooked in rum' and 'pork stewed in gin'—the dishes clearly labelled to highlight the range of taboos being broken.[5] This is a carnivalesque mode of politics where the mise-en-scene is carefully set up. Prasad presents before the media, the anti-modernist Ashis Nandy, as a supporter of his cause—at this unabashed celebration of colonial modernity. Thus when *Indian Express* journalist Vrinda Gopinath confronts Nandy at the party, this encounter is not entirely unintended. 'I certainly do not agree with some of Bhan's theses,' said an aghast Nandy, 'but I certainly support every oppressed community or individual's right to pick up any weapon, be it political, academic or intellectual incorrectness, to fight the establishment. It's the sheer audacity of it that makes it so forceful.'[6]

Nandy, of course, has the resources to deal with such a situation, given as he himself is to a style of exaggerated and stylized modernity-baiting, but to many of Chandrabhan's earnest and pious radical friends, all this is unforgivable blasphemy. So it is to all liberals, nationalists and gandhians, none of whom understands the meaning of style and the performative—quite unlike Gandhi, one might add!

Expectedly, the very next day, when this flamboyant dinner party was reported in the press, the outcome intended by the installation artist came to pass. Television channels went berserk; so did a whole range of newspapers and agitated intellectuals, eager to give the correct and reasonable perspective on the matter. The throw of the dice had worked. Prasad, of course remained unmoved, actually relishing the storm that had been unleashed. In his numerous interviews, he did not stop at his act of enthroning English as the Dalit Goddess; he actually went further. To all those who were 'being reasonable' and suggesting that multilingualism and bilingualism should be encouraged, that Dalits should 'certainly learn English without giving up their mother-tongue', Prasad's nonchalant retort was that Indian languages were a 'linguistic evil': 'Goddess English is all about emancipation. Goddess English is a mass movement against the Caste Order, against linguistic evils such as Hindi, Marathi, Tamil, Telugu and Bangla for instance. Indian languages are more about prejudices, discrimination and hatred and less about expressions and communications.'[7]

In parenthesis, we may note that Chandrabhan Prasad's point is borne out by a recent controversy over the title song from film *Aaja Nach Le*, much awaited because it featured the return of Madhuri Dixit. The film was briefly banned in Uttar Pradesh by Mayawati's government, as the song made a casteist slur.[8] The lines went thus:

> *Bazaar mein machi hai mara maar*
> *kahe mochi bhi khud ko sonar*
> There's pandemonium in the market place
> Even a cobbler claims to be a goldsmith.

What was interesting was that neither the lyricist Piyush Mishra, a familiar figure of Delhi's Left-liberal theatre world, nor Sharmila Tagore, the chairperson of the film Censor Board realized that these terms were casteist. Both Mishra and Tagore argued that these terms were simply 'talking about two professions.[9]' This is precisely the point that Prasad is making: the extent to which caste-derived and caste-marked words still exist and are used unselfconsciously by most people is underlined in this episode. More significant is the fact that the Left-liberal lyricist could so lightly toss off a line that mocked one born an outcaste (a Dalit, in fact), for aspiring to a profession belonging to a higher caste.

To return to Prasad and the English deity: by this time the spotlight was on Prasad. His provocations had precisely the effect he desired. Now was the time to push. But the tone and tenor of the public debate is worth following. In order to give a flavour of the debate, let me refer to two significant comments and reflections, one by my colleague Ravikant, who is himself a keen participant of the Hindi language political scene, and the other by historian Shahid Amin. Both of them refer to a particular programme anchored by Karan Thapar on CNBC-TV18, presented in the form of a debate on whether Dalits have a better future adopting English, than one of the many Indian languages. In Ravikant's words:

> Some of us followed it keenly because we knew where it was coming from and also the dramatis personae—Chandrabhan Prasad (CP), Yogendra Yadav (YY) and Alok Rai (AR)—all very dear friends, and people who have been deeply engaged with the politics and practice of languages in North India. *It was a one-sided debate from the moment it started: clear victory to Chandrabhan Prasad from the word go*, first of all, because he had managed to pitchfork his provocative stance into a full scale discussion in the national press and the big media. Think about it: it has taken him just three consecutive annual Macaulay's birthday parties to friends, to bring it to the attention of a much wider number of intellectuals and a larger public. It was a victory for his own brand of Gandhigiri—that you could very much debate and advance your cause while having fun: '*chicken, mutton, daaru and daliton ki kuchh samasyayein*' [chicken, mutton, drinks and some problems of Dalits] is his style, in his own inimitable words.[10]

Ravikant also felt that the debate was one-sided for another reason: 'because CP's interlocutors did not have convincing answers to his extremist views on language and religion and the coupling of the two, which had to inevitably sneak into the discussion, considering that *en masse* Dalit conversions were fresh in media memory'. Thus, 'When Karan Thapar probed CP on why he suggested Dalits take flight from Hindi and Hinduism; was it because he hated Hinduism? CP had perhaps an obvious but pithy answer: I did not choose to hate Hinduism, Hinduism never loved me! YY and AR looked aghast and betrayed at the idea of rejecting Indian languages, for Dalits, after all, were communicatively, politically and experientially rooted in these languages, and beginning with Marathi, most of the (autobiographical) Dalit literature was written in Indian languages. They went on, the NRI example of turning away from one's language is not a healthy one: look how they have all become Hindutva supporters, etc., etc. CP, of course, rubbished this secular middle class sentimentalism by citing Ambedkar's example, that he always wrote in English and he did so knowing very well that it is not the Dalits who would read him!'

To historian, Shahid Amin, the tenor of the debate seemed to suggest that 'When faced with a transgressive idea to move radically beyond the horizon of possibility, most of us reach instinctively for our copybook notion of India.' He went on to observe:

> And very often this means throwing aside the opportunity of thinking with and through adversarial positions that emanate as challenges from the margins to our very sense of Indianness. Prasad's utopia is for future Dalit babies to arrive into this world to the sound of the English alphabet: mantras or azaan being ruled out, of necessity. This is an idea stunning in its novelty . . . . But as the debate with Chandrabhan Prasad unfolded over half-an-hour of late-night TV, no one engaged this Dalit thinker on his own terms: how would poor, uneducated Dalit parents in the villages of the north Indian cowbelt ensure that a Sesame Street version of fun alphabet-learning is beamed to the Sagri subdivision of Azamgarh District, where Chandrabhan grew up? . . . Instead, the discussion veered around such pan-Indian and patriotic concerns as: How would Dalits then distinguish between maternal and paternal uncles, for English terms are so limited in their kin and affinal reach? What would happen to religions of and in India, if all of us (Prasad was concerned solely with Dalits) spouted only English? Would not the resulting deracination harbinger fundamentalisms, as in Silicon Valley? Can English acquisition really put an end to deep-seated and long-enduring structures of caste oppression? But that was not, one felt like screaming through the picture tube, what the subversive proposal was about. For, except for the Pandits and Maulvis, no one lives by language alone. The Dalit-English proposal is an unexpected challenge to the mainstream view of patriotism-in-an-Indian language, preferably a north-Indian language. And now that an American accent is de rigeur for luxury-item our TVs, whither linguistic patriotism?[11]

The debate is remarkable because Chandra Bhan Prasad's interlocutors are not hostile to the Dalit cause; on the contrary they are passionate believers in Dalit emancipation. And what is more, unlike the marxist Left, they do not believe that while the cause is important, Dalits can only achieve success under the leadership of some supposedly revolutionary vanguard. Indeed, both Yogendra Yadav and Alok Rai would count themselves as votaries of Dalit autonomy. Given this, what the debate demonstrates, is the extent to which a certain literality underlies our reading of politics and political stances; it underlines the utter inability to understand 'the performative', the affect, the dramaturgy that inevitably goes with all kinds of political spectacle and speech but which Prasad raises to an entirely different level.

It is important also to bear in mind that when Prasad enacts this drama of enthroning English as the Dalit Goddess, he is actually addressing a very different public, not quite the bilingual liberal but the large sector of 'vernacular' speaking public mired in the ethos of caste and caste practices. And this public is clearly made of very different stuff. Ravikant, in his comment cited above, identifies this public squarely, even while he prepares to take on Prasad's 'linguistic extremism':

> I loved this debate because I generally like it when I am rendered speechless by good political arguments or situations, when my intellectual resources simply run dry! But this particular debate tickled me more since it was a revisit, a moment of *deja vu* for me. I was caught in a similar situation with CP on the same issue of language and politics when Nivedita Menon called us together to a refresher course lecture at Delhi University, braving academic and other objections. I had been to CP's party earlier that year and was aware of his new found love for Macaulay. He had in fact circulated some pages from his (in)famous Minutes and my task, I thought, was cut out: I reread Macaulay, and disgusted as I was with his Orientalist take on Indian language literatures, I thought I would argue my case against CP or, at the very least, maintain a critical distance from his position. As it happened, he was the first speaker and he spoke intermittently, amidst widespread and loud murmurs of discontent from the audience. I knew this audience very well—they were mostly upper caste from north Bihar, most of them having passed through Delhi University Political Science exams in English medium. So in the 'Q n A' session, they launched into a virulent defense of the national languages, which basically meant Hindi in this context. So when my turn came, I had to do a mental turn around and defend CP all the way against the marauding hypocrisy of the DU lecturers! These were significant encounters for me, reminders that I could not assume permanent connect with their ways of thinking and knowing, just because I happened to spend half my life with Dalits and went to SC/ST schools. Schools from which very few of my Dalit friends made it past graduation or even 12th grade. I do not have them as common alumni friends; I do not know them anymore. All I know is that one reason they could not make it bigger in life was 'English', which comes not only with basic schooling but with whole lot of other kinds of cultural capital. So I quite undertand the compulsions of this Dalit 'betrayal', even if it goes against their hitherto preferred language of narrative creativity.

It was necessary to quote these passages at some length, largely because they sensitively cover a whole range of issues and emerge from a ruthlessly frank interrogation of the subject-position of the upper caste self. Such an exercise is conspicuous by its absence in the world of the Left-radical (who is the least self-reflexive in these matters), the liberal and the gandhian.

Ever since Chandrabhan Prasad embarked on his distinctive style of politics, he has really managed to annoy many self-proclaimed radicals. A few years ago, when Prasad had called for a Dalit bourgeoisie and Dalit capitalism, there was a similar sign of dismay, scandal and utter incomprehension among many friends—even those who have now started recognizing that 'Dalits' constitute a key component of any future radical democratic (or socialist?) transformation. What many of these friends do not recognize is that it is not enough to say that 'the Dalit question is also important': as Khairlanji or the hundreds of other earlier episodes of everyday violence against Dalits show, there is no way in which the 'Dalits' can 'also' become part of some imagined larger unity (say the peasant unity dreamt of by communists, or the so-called 'secular unity' propounded by bleeding-heart secular liberals). For, to take the standpoint of the Dalit is to take the standpoint of a minority in the village and to incur the anger of the majority. The effort to unite might be desirable from a longer term point of view, though I am not quite sure about that too. Prasad had thus also annoyed many secularists as his attack on backward caste 'secular' parties was seen by many as a way of justifying BSP's alliance with the BJP and hobnobbing with Hindutva.

The real point about Prasad's politics that earnest liberals and radicals do not get is that irrespective of the substantive aspect/s of his argument, he opens out a new way of enunciating a politics of the oppressed: anger and emotion are sublimated here into a performative excess, thus initiating a politics of irony and hyperbole. Ressentiment is not the main mode of this politics of 'betrayal' (which I would call the politics of fleeing) which began in a true sense with Dr Ambedkar's flight from Hinduism. There is one critical difference from Ambedkar though. Chandrabhan Prasad is a deviant Ambedkarite (*kujaat Ambedkarvaadi*, to twist Lohia's term): after all, 'chicken, mutton, daaru aur daliton ki kuchh samasyayein' is certainly not the mode of Ambedkar's renunciatory Buddhist politics that still remained imprisoned within the ascetic ideal. Chandra Bhan Prasad's politics, on the other hand, is a politics of carnival, of laughter and of politics as an art form.

## Theatre of the Absurd

Let me clarify here that my reading of Chandrabhan Prasad and his stances, especially his political mode and style, do not necessarily mean that I endorse his politics in entirety. In fact, I must confess that, like Ravikant and Shahid Amin, quite often his politics makes me uncomfortable—even though I have on each occasion been persuaded enough to modify my own positions in trying to confront his ('thinking with and through adversarial positions', a la Amin, as it were). Moreover, there are still large areas of his politics that, I believe are based on a somewhat deliberately partial understanding of the situation. So for instance, his adulation of 'American society' or US corporations like Microsoft and IBM for taking the diversity issue seriously, is to say the least, naïve. It refuses to recognize that these were gains of hard won struggles against racism which are once again being seriously challenged. One only has to look at the recent agitation in Michigan University and other US universities to be able to see that the so-called liberalism of white society is in a sense not very different from modern upper caste arrogance.[12] Note also that the language espoused by both the white opponents of affirmative action in US universities and the upper castes in India is that of equality: 'affirmative action is anti-equality' is the common refrain.

Similarly, I want to underline that I totally disagree with Prasad's glorification of the state (in fact, an authoritarian state, as is evident in the Bhopal Document) against what Gopal Guru calls 'twice born civil society'. Some of us, let me state for the record, had in fact presented our disagreement in this regard in a note of dissent at the Bhopal Conference itself (and Prasad was gracious enough to photocopy and get it distributed to delegates). I have also placed this on record in an article subsequently published in the *Economic and Political Weekly*.[13] As a matter of fact, in this regard, I find myself closer to Kanshi Ram's celebrated '*humein mazboot sarkar nahin, majboor sarkar chahiye*' [What we need is not a strong government but a vulnerable one] or to put it in a statement attributed to Romain Rolland: 'where order is injustice, disorder is the beginning of justice.'

I do also see the need for a Dalit-Shudra unity—but that is not necessarily because it is good for Dalits; it is simply my wish to see the Hindu Right defeated that fuels this fantasy. But I cannot help seeing Prasad's point as well, that such unity, even if it is possible, should be prevented. The point here is really not that there should never be Dalit-

Shudra (Bahujan) unity but that it can only take place on a completely renegotiated political terrain where the Shudras, especially the more powerful among them, have been forced to accept a relation of equality with the Dalits. This fundamental renegotiation is not an easy matter and involves a long drawn out and bitter battle in every village, a transformation of everyday life.

It is nonetheless important to recognize that there is no point really contesting Prasad on grounds of Truth. I think it is easy to dismiss some of the arguments made by him on the ground of 'facts' and 'truth' and yet, none of it would diminish the power of his argument. For the argument is not being made on the grounds of Truth but of an existential experience. Prasad produces an immaculately scripted theatre of the absurd, where he invites you to participate. He invites you to a debate where the mise-en-scene is already laid out; where he has already turned the tables in a carnivalesque manner, producing a mocking laughter off-stage. He invites you to a party to celebrate the birthday of Lord Macaulay, whom he christens the 'Father of Indian Modernity'. He invites you to a party to unveil the portrait of a new goddess—the Goddess of English. He invites you to a party to celebrate Dalit capitalism where he claims that the winds of globalization are 'de-freezing us', removing the layers of ice that Hindu domination had imprisoned us under. He celebrates modernity in all its grotesque forms as well—for he knows where it hits—not only when it comes to *ponga pundit* Hindus but also to refined, modern ones—and he knows that it hits really hard.

The entire scenario is often deliberately crude, and appears grotesque to refined aesthetic middle class tastes. Earnest upper caste and upper class radicals and liberals who have ever only learned the language of Truth and Falsehood, cannot see the mode of cultural resistance that this theatre of the absurd embodies.

It is necessary, in my opinion, to see Prasad's mode and style of politics and speech both *in continuation with and as a radical break from* earlier modes of Dalit cultural politics. The element of hyperbole or excess does not simply emerge out of nowhere. In earlier (but also many contemporary) Dalit writings, there is an overpowering element of what might appear as 'unreasonable' and 'unbalanced' anger. Yet, it is not simply anger. There is an entirely different aesthetic at work in these writings and it already overturns all the accepted conventions of speech and art. Take, for instance, the famous poem by the Dalit Panther poet, Keshav Meshram:

One day I cursed that mother-fucker God
He just laughed shamelessly
My neighbour—a born-to-pen Brahman—was shocked
He looked at me with his castor-oil face and said,
'How can you say such things to the
Source of the Indescribable,
Qualityless, Formless, Juggernaut? . . .
I cursed another good hot curse,
The university buildings shuddered and sank waist-deep.
All at once, scholars began doing research
Into what makes people angry.
They sat in their big rooms fragrant with incense,
Their bellies full of food,
And debated . . .

The deliberate attempt to shock, using the choicest expletives for 'God' is of course, one part of the story. But there is something else here, in this poem written sometime in 1978, that is worth underlining. All possibilities of debate and argument are closed. The castor-oil face Brahman can only speechify, and learned professors can simply treat you as objects to be studied (what makes you angry?) What else can happen by way of exchange here but for me to hurl another 'good hot curse'?

Here is another poem 'Jasumati, my black jasmine' by another Dalit poet Neerav Patel:[14]

Whenever you come with broom and dust-bins in the street
You cease to be the black jasmine
Grown upon the dark dung-hill
Outside the boundaries of our village
The red sun blossoms upon your face
Upon your bosom
And in your heart.
Vultures wearing sacred threads take rounds
Of Ganges and you.
When you stoop to sweep,

The black berries under your nylon blouse
Peep to the sunny embrace of the earth.
You, Jasumati, suddenly become jasmine . . .
Instantly you become a feast for the zooming vultures
 – a nasty joke
 – a quick and sudden hug
 – a slap on your heavy buttocks . . .
 You moan and become mother—
 Mother of a bastard.
 They button up their trousers and take a plunge in the ganges . . .
 And the kid is thankless too,
 Like his father.
 Drinks your milk and
 pisses upon you.
 You stink
 And become untouchable and outcaste . . .

Setting aside for the moment the objectifying male gaze, this poem sets out what become significant tropes of beauty in Dalit literature, not the least being the beauty of blackness. The description of the black jasmine 'grown upon the dark dung-hill/outside the boundaries of our village', recalls other dominant imageries of romantic poetry: the hills, often outside the city, which would normally recall a colourful landscape of wilderness. Here everything that is associated with such imagery becomes 'black', colourless. Appearing on the street with broom and dust-bins, the red sun lighting up the body of the beloved, bespeaks of a different life, unfamiliar to us, so much so that simply speaking about it can make it sound unaesthetic. Yet, there is a distinctly different aesthetic at work in these lines, where bitterness and abuse merge with love and sadness to produce an almost incomprehensible emotion. This becomes especially so when the beloved herself is presented as the abused or, as beloved-because-multiply-abused (her son too being abusive of her, like his father).

What is unmistakable about both the poems, as with many other Dalit writings, however, is that they are addressed *only* to a Dalit public—a public (and this is the crucial point) that did not exist prior to these writings. It did not exist *as Dalit, as a political subjectivity* that was to soon make its appearance on the cultural-political horizon in different parts of India. This literature should therefore be seen as the expression of emergent Dalit subjectivity. And we should clearly distinguish it from the sloganeering that had marked some of the literature and poetry that emerged in the late 1960s and 1970s, in different Indian languages, under the impact of the naxalite movement. For there it was an ideologically driven, somewhat contrived bitterness that was expressed by an otherwise elite upper caste youth that bore no experience of subalternity.

That was in the late 1970s and 1980s. The Dalit Panthers lived deep in vernacular society and its literature. Unlike Chandra Bhan Prasad, they did not advocate flight from the vernacular; they transformed the very language they spoke, as indeed the non-Brahmin movement had transformed Brahminical Tamil. They took a part of their inspiration from marxism and maosim—much like the young Chandra Bhan Prasad, Udit Raj (at that time Ram Raj), and many others. Ideologies failed them. Parties failed them and the secularists failed them. The Dalits have none but themselves to depend on and hence the insistence that only Dalits can speak for Dalits.

Bitterness and Anger were the main mode of Dalit politics of yore—but as Ravikant rightly points out, appreciation of Dalit literature and writings calls for an entirely different order of aesthetic tools. Much the same can be said of its politics—it is about an existential truth no doubt but not, emphatically, about 'Truth'. It requires different tools—in fact, precisely aesthetic tools—for its appreciation, as the difference between real life and fiction, between performance and politics exists no more in this theatre. From then to now—from the voiceless days of state sponsored reservations to now, the moment of the breakdown of upper caste/class hegemony, the brave new world of globalization and a newfound voice, anger and bitterness have given way to a resounding laughter. One might say, even a condescending laughter which seems to say good-bye to the nation and its custodians: I did not choose to hate Hinduism, says Chandra Bhan nonchalantly; it was Hinduism that never loved me. So fare thee well. This is the logic of cultural resistance at work, in the form of fleeing.

For those who still want to read Chandra Bhan Prasad literally, let me just say that he is perfectly well aware that he really gets his main audiences not from *The Pioneer* that very few people read; it is the lakhs of Telugu readers of a *Vaartha* or those of *Rashtriya Sahara* that make him what he is—a pain in the neck for many.

Let us however, leave Chandra Bhan Prasad and move to another scene from this absurd drama. Let us enter this scene through a quick look at media representations of Mayawati, the powerful Dalit woman chief minister of Uttar Pradesh and leader of the Bahujan Samaj Party (BSP) that has led the political upsurge of Dalits in northern India in recent decades.

## Scene 2. The 'Opulent Leader of the Outcastes'

'*For the Oppressed, Covered in Diamonds*—govt plays host at Mayawati birthday bash'—ran the headline in a front page story of a leading English daily in India a couple of years ago.[15]

The report continued:

'Uttar Pradesh chief minister Mayawati today celebrated her 48th birthday in style at a grand function on the La Martiniere grounds here, brushing aside accusations of using the occasion to "mint" money.' The report went on to say that the 'Lucknow bash began with Mayawati, dressed in a pink salwar suit, cutting the cake and distributing colour TVs—sponsored by Bharat Petroleum—to women heads of 47 Ambedkar villages.' It did not forget to add that '*she wore a diamond necklace, diamond-studded earrings and bracelets that had diamond coating over gold*'. Another news website ran a report which went something like this: 'Mayawati, who was laden with diamond jewellery, celebrated her 47th birthday in such style that it would have put many tycoons to shame.'[16] Further: 'A 51 kg cake, 100,000 laddoos, 60 quintals of marigold flowers and 5000 bouquets were among the few highlights of the day.' The report also said that the 40 x 60 feet stage was reminiscent of the Hindi blockbuster film *Mughal-e-Azam*. Apparently, the architect of the stage, Janardhan (a BSP activist himself) confirmed this: 'Yes, we have tried to copy the sets shown in a sequence from the legendary film when heroine Madhubala dances . . . .'[17]

Now consider this story in *The New York Times*, which appeared a few months later. 'An Opulent and Pugnacious Champion of India's Outcasts' ran the headline. It began: 'She arrived by helicopter and spoke for an hour and a half beneath an air-conditioned canopy.'[18] The correspondent Amy Waldman, had obviously been quick to pick up on what was probably the most discussed thing about Mayawati among middle class Indians—her 'opulence' and ostentatious display of wealth. Waldman's report goes on: 'Her critics charge that she is cut-throat and corrupt in the pursuit of power, and that she lavishes more money on ostentatious displays of status than on serving the poor she claims to represent.' As evidence she cites Ram Sharan Das, the president of Samajwadi Party, which is her main rival in the state as saying that 'if a woman claims to be the champion of the Dalits after wearing a 30-million rupee necklace, there can't be any bigger lie than that'. Waldman concludes: *'Draped with diamonds, she contrasted sharply with the understated homespun style that most politicians deliberately adopt'* (see Plate 2).

**Plate 2.** Mayawati. Image courtesy: The Tribune, http://www.tribuneindia.com/2003/20030316/spectrum/index.htm

I have just cited from three news reports at random above but these could be said to represent the more general sense of disquiet, in fact, *agitation*, felt by the 'sophisticated' and 'cultured' middle class public, an agitation that routinely finds expression in the ways in which Mayawati is talked about and reported in the media.

The contrast of Mayawati's style with what Waldman calls 'the understated homespun style' adopted by the political class in India, could not be sharper. As is well-known, since the advent of Gandhi on the political scene in the early 1920s, there has been a strong emphasis on spinning and wearing *khadi*—a coarse homespun cloth, usually white in colour. Gandhi, as is well known, returned from his sojourn from England and South Africa, shed his western attire and donned the loincloth—effecting a shift to a different semiotic register, as he sought to take on the task of welding together the nation that was waiting to be born. This shift was undertaken as an act of affiliation with the large and poverty-stricken masses of Indians. In doing this and in evolving the code of dressing in homespun, coarse *khadi*, Gandhi was also establishing a connection with the idea of *swadeshi*, which followed the partition of Bengal in 1905 and provided the ammunition for the major nationalist struggle for reunification. 'Swadeshi', which literally means 'of one's own country', was the idea that became a point of mass mobilization against British-manufactured cloth. The struggle of Indian nationalism was closely meshed in this period with the struggle against the domination of cloth from the textile manufacturers of Manchester and Lancashire. It was in this context that nationalist singers like Mukunda Das of that time sang:

*ma-er deoya mota kapor mathaye tule ne re bhai*

*deen dukhini ma-ar je mo-der, er beshi aar shaddhyo naain*

treat this coarse cloth given by our mother with respect, dear brother,

for this is all that this poor and forlorn mother of ours can afford.

In a recent essay Dipesh Chakrabarty has suggested that if the most common uniform for the politician has been, from before the time of independence, white *khadi*, it has something to do with its symbolism 'as intended in official/nationalist discourse': the white *khadi*, he says, 'stands for the Hindu idea of purity (lack of blemish, pollution), its coarseness symbolizes an identification both with simplicity and poverty'.[19] Citing from a study by Susan Bean, Chakrabarty asserts that Gandhi's own gloss on *khadi* (in 1921) mobilized all of these meanings with an added one: 'I consider the renunciation [of foreign cloth] to be also necessary as a sign of mourning, and a bare head and a bare body is such a sign in my part of the country.'[20]

For the nationalists, the matter then came to acquire a highly emotive charge where the poverty of the large masses of Indian people came to be represented in the poverty and helplessness of 'Mother India' and wearing the mill-spun cloth from Britain represented sacrilege—feeding into the drain of national wealth into the coffers of the British exploiters. There is, of course, a seeming irony in this, insofar as Dr B R Ambedkar, the representative of the Dalits, the poorest and most oppressed section of the Indian society, whom all Dalits will swear by (and who was Gandhi's contemporary), always preferred his Western style suit to *khadi*. Ambedkar has now emerged in Dalit consciousness, not merely as one of the great political leaders of the community but has also been iconized as a godly father-figure. Neither in Dalit iconizations of Ambedkar nor in official representations of him as a national leader does he figure anywhere in anything but a western suit and with a book—the constitution of India, whose drafting committee he headed—under his arm (See Plate 3).

**Plate 3.** Statue of B R Ambedkar with the Constitution of India, under his arm.

Image courtesy: http://rajyasabha.nic.in/photo/princets/p8.html

**Plate 4.** A cinematic representation of Dr Ambedkar in a Kannada film poster.

This image (See Plate 4) of Ambedkar's stands in sharp contrast to those of other leaders of the nationalist struggle like Gandhi in his loincloth, Nehru in an *achkan* and *chooridar* or Maulana Azad in a *sherwani* or *achkan*. Kancha Ilaiah, for instance, invokes this Westernized image of Ambedkar in order to underline that the ordinary Dalit—or Dalit culture in general—does not place any special value on any indigenist notion of 'authenticity'. So he asserts that 'Unlike Gandhi and Nehru, Ambedkar wore a suit throughout his life without facing any problems from his community' whereas 'Gandhi had to struggle a lot to de-Westernize himself.'[21]

Lest we begin to think that this representation is uniformly and uncritically extolled in the same way by all Dalits, let me also state that there is actually an element of the tragic here that might also point to one of the deeper conflicts within the movement. Let me therefore cite a slightly long passage from Anand Teltumbde, a leading intellectual who represents the Left wing of the movement:

> The first attempt to iconize Ambedkar, and considerably successfully so, as the later times proved, is apparent in this early *post-Ambedkar* episode. That was the icon of the saheb—the epitaph [*sic*] used for an Englishman but later used as an honorific for natives who were educated, westernized and placed in bureaucratic authority. It denoted someone far above the masses, one who was endowed with authority and power. It was the icon of the saviour. It projected the leader as the saviour incarnate who would liberate them from their bondage and lead them to prosperity. All that the masses had to do was to stand solidly behind him . . . . This particular icon distanced the Dalit leadership from the masses in every way, in terms of physical attributes like appearance, clothes, language and life-style. It promoted blind and servile notions. The leaders were to be treated as their quasi-monarch (a la *Bhim Raja*).[22]

Teltumbde goes on to argue that this 'sahib' syndrome, to the extent that it represented middle class aspirations, 'helped petty bourgeois-ize the entire Dalit movement'. These reflections by Teltumbde are important for us, not simply because they present an important critical counter position from within the movement, but also because in making this critique they actually point to what is the dominant tendency at least among the emerging elite/middle class sections of the movement. In Teltumbde's view, after Ambedkar's death, the leadership of the movement fell into the hands of Dadasaheb Gaikwad, a close associate and 'trusted lieutenant' of Ambedkar since the days of the famous Mahad struggle. Gaikwad led, according to him, a militant struggle for land in Maharshtra, involving large masses of Dalits. But, says Teltumbde, 'while the movement caught the fancy of the Dalit masses, the rest of the Dalit leadership thought otherwise'. Gaikwad, says Teltumbde, was 'a rustic in the common man's Dhoti-Kurta attire, and not embellished with university degrees'. He was thus 'unacceptable to these people'. Teltumbde criticizes this section of the Dalit leadership, who claimed they 'fitted into the Ambedkarian mould' (as they conceived it) better than Gaikwad because, as he puts it 'this mould was based on middle class cultural norms that Ambedkar displayed in his attire and general demeanour'.[23] However, Teltumbde reads in Ambedkar's own self-presentation 'a counter to Gandhi's belaboured austerity' and 'a representation of modernity as against Gandhi's anti-modern views'.[24] In Teltumbde's reading this specific contextual countermove by Ambedkar, when generalized into an overall valorization of the Westernized image by the post-Ambedkar leadership is deeply problematic and has conveyed a wrong impression about the movement, and even fostered self-defeating tendencies within it—for instance those that led to the rejection of Gaikwad.

Modernity is certainly an issue here and the conflation of the 'modern' with the 'Western' is quite widespread among all classes through the late nineteenth and twentieth centuries. At one level, this is what Teltumbde is trying to disaggregate by bringing in the rustic counter figure of Gaikwad in his *dhoti-kurta*—a perfect counter, one could imagine, to Gandhi. Gandhi's investment of a very specific meaning in the act of wearing *khadi*—the dual signification of Hindu idea of purity and the existence of British rule as something to be mourned, give us some further clues as to why this move is shunned by Dalits like Mayawati even today. In the Hindu idea of purity, Dalit existence is the embodiment of pollution itself. They are Untouchable precisely because they exist to undertake all the polluting work of upper caste society so that the upper caste may retain their 'purity'. Further, to the Dalits, foreign rule appears as the harbinger of liberation and is therefore to be celebrated, not mourned. Mayawati's 'ostentatiousness' and her sartorial preferences can in fact be read as her symbolic countermove which mocks at Gandhi's attempt at 'representing poverty' and mourning through the semiotic transformation of his own body. If Gandhi the *baniya* (a trader caste) had to display the poverty and suffering he never actually lived, here was Mayawati, a representative of the really poor and oppressed, by her very appearance ridiculing that attempt much like Ambedkar's Western suit did (See Plate 5). It is tempting therefore to read the Dalit rejection of the Brahminical idea of renunciation and purity being allegorically performed here on the stage of *Mughal-e-Azam*, recalling Madhubala in the role of Anarkali, the defiant slave-girl dancing for her love and mocking the power of Akbar, the Great Mughal Emperor.

**Plate 5.** In this picture, we see three statues behind Mayawati, the father-figure of Ambedkar a few steps behind, with Mayawati and Kanshi Ram—the man who single-handedly built the BSP, the party that brought Mayawati to power. Notice that Kanshi Ram too is represented wearing trousers and shirt and not the usual attire of the 'political man' in India.

At this level, at least as a first approximation, it is possible to see why there might be such a reaction to the renunciatory moves of the nationalists. What of course made matters worse, right from the days of the nationalist struggle, was Gandhi's defence of the caste system—what is known as *varnashrama dharma*. He had after all declared openly on numerous occasions that he was only against the practice of untouchability; the hierarchy of the caste order was not something Gandhi wanted to disturb. Mayawati, unlike Ambedkar, is an entirely homespun Dalit—without the benefit of the latter's education in the US and his deliberately more modulated and cultivated speech and appearance. Mayawati arises from a different world—at once much more ruthless and degrading. Her style is therefore marked by a certain performative excess: the apparent crudity and aggressiveness of her language that appears galling to her critics. This performative excess, we have noted, is not a peculiar characteristic of Mayawati's personal style alone; it is something that is evident in much of Dalit speech and literature as well as in other forms of writing. That however, is not our immediate concern, but for the present, let me just note that if this is what arouses the strongest feelings of hatred among the upper castes or the twice-born (*dwijas*), it is precisely what endears her to her people and provides them inspiration. Even the reports mentioned above that describe Mayawati in such negative ways, concede that it was an impressive turnout at the rally and that people 'had started pouring in from the morning, braving dense fog and bone-chilling winds'.[25] One of them also mentions many ballads sung in praise of Mayawati during the programme.[26]

Waldman's report for instance cites one of the BSP supporters as saying that 'she and her party have empowered the poor people'. More significantly, it also cites one of the many admiring young Dalit women, Nirmala, who says: 'Mayawati gives inspiration that anything can be achieved.' I want to underline the word 'anything' here and will return to it in a moment, for I believe that this 'anything' is not just anything—it also refers to something very specific. Nirmala's is not an isolated instance. The overpowering impact that the image of Mayawati—confidently and aggressively dealing with upper caste men—can have on young women like Nirmala, is yet to be fathomed. Waldman probably sensed that something more is going on here when she noted in her report that '*In putting on an imperial show of power, she has touched something deep.*' In order to try to unravel this 'something deep', let me take the help of a fictional representation of Dalit life and for the moment, leave Mayawati's story here.

## Scene 3. The 'Dystopian' Space of the *Paracheri*

Let me try to understand some of the questions above with the help of a Dalit short story. This story 'Reet' (Custom) is by an important Hindi writer and journalist, Mohandas Naimishray.[27] The story is set in a village called Kisanpura and begins with what could be one of the most familiar descriptions of the spatial layout of a Dalit settlement:

'On the north of Kisanpura village, at some distance from the village, a colony of Mehtars with some makeshift houses of Chamars, right next to them.[28] The atmosphere permeated with a stench and alongside, the gurgling sound of earthen *hookahs*. Piles of garbage spread out here and there and innumerable diseases 'swimming around' in the pool of dirty water that has collected nearby. Some pigs rolling around in the muck. Half-naked children playing in the open space, their space—but cut off from the rest of the village. Completely isolated, like an island in the sea.'

As Naimishray puts it, an invisible *savarna rekha* (literally, a line of casteness), divides the village. Everything—the temple, the well, the pond, even the land—is marked by this line of difference. Inhabited on the one side by those who have the language of rights and power and on the other by those who have but duties.

This is the spatial layout of what is called the *paracheri* in Tamil—meaning the living area of the pariahs (Dalits), situated on the outskirts of the village. I will use this Tamil term to refer generally to Dalit settlements.[29] The pariahs/Dalits do not strictly speaking belong to the caste order—the *chaturvarna* of the four *varnas*. They are the fifth, often therefore referred to as the *panchamas* or the outcastes. Hence their living space is relegated to the outer limits of the village—the access to which is also different in most cases. As is well known, traditionally the pariahs are not allowed to walk the roads used by the upper castes; they cannot drink water from the village wells nor worship in the temples.

The story goes on: Despite this chain of duty—or maybe *because* of it—every year people from this hellish part of the village escape to the city, in search of a heaven. Who knows whether they ever find it . . . ? Some time ago, yet another such man disappeared from this hell. His name was Bulaki. His wife Phulo pined and cried for him day and night, for years. She was going on sixteen when Bulaki married her and brought her home. She came dressed in colourful clothes from top to bottom, hands and feet coloured with henna. She also wore a little jewellery that tinkled with each step she took. They had to cross two villages on the way and, at one point had to announce who they were: 'the sweepers of Kisanpura, my lord'. Her father had repeatedly warned her not to wear anything that made a sound and could thus attract attention. Had he not taught her over and over again the difference between the high and the lowly? Didn't she know? All these things were forbidden for members of their caste.

Phulo did not listen. The old man's eyes darkened with fear as he bid his newly wed daughter farewell and prayed for her well-being. When Phulo left, she had only one regret: her man had not come to her on horseback because people of their caste were not allowed to sit on horses. On a couple of occasions in the past, the upper caste people of the village had set their colony on fire because one of their grooms had dared to come on horseback.

The pigsty had been emptied and cleaned up for her to spend her ceremonial first night with her husband. There she waited and waited but Bulaki never came. However, some other men did, who forcibly took her away to the landlord's house where he clawed and consumed her all night. Slowly it dawned on Phulo that this was not accidental. This was the custom.

But her man, her Bulaki never returned—even after that disastrous night was over. Not for the next five years. And in all that while she never left the pigsty. She stayed there, thinking of her husband. People were convinced that she had gone mad. And then suddenly, one night, she heard his voice. He was calling out her name. She thought she was dreaming. The shouts became louder and louder. She got up and looked out. There was Bulaki—on horseback. What is more, he had grown a moustache—which too was forbidden for 'them'—and to top it all, he was carrying a double barrelled gun. She went up to him and jumped on to the horse. For the first time, five years after their marriage, he held her and said, 'Come, Phulo, we will not live here any more' and they sped away. As they came out of the village, he pulled in the reins and the horse stopped. Behind them arose a great furore. Phulo looked back—the sky above the upper caste village was red with flames. And as he sped off once again, Bulaki told Phulo, 'No landlord will play with the respect of any woman of the village any more.'

The story is in many ways typical. However, I do not want to use it to simply narrate another instance of the everyday violence and oppression that marks Dalit life even today, nor of resistance to it. Rather, I want to use it to reflect on the figure and trope of the '*paracheri*' as a particular kind of space and through it, delineate certain lines of *desire*.

The hellishness of the dystopic space of the *paracheri* is, of course, underlined by the series of prohibitions that its inhabitants have to observe. And certainly, the most obnoxious of these prohibitions have to do with the denial of access to even clean drinking water from the wells, so that often these inhabitants have to drink the same dirty water that animals drink from the open ponds. But all this is too well-known by now and appears even in non-Dalit fiction, as in the stories of Premchand for instance. But it is not only acts which involve the movement of untouchables into common spaces—thus carrying the threat of polluting the upper castes—that are prohibited for them. The 'untouchability' of their caste is marked on their bodies; their very appearance is strictly policed—what they may wear, how they may look, is the target of violent control. Marking the bodies as untouchable is also not always enough; in many parts of the country, the untouchable was till very recently, required to announce his/her appearance from a distance so that the upper caste may escape the polluting shadow of this impure body.

The *paracheri* is a dystopic, but certainly not an imaginary space. It is a 'real place'—located at the periphery of the village or the town. It is an exclusive space that is meant to house people who are to undertake what orthodox Brahminical/Hindu society considers polluting activities, so that 'purity' may rigorously be maintained within the precincts of caste society.

It is useful in attempting to understand this space, to recall Foucault's reflections on a whole range of 'other spaces' that he calls heterotopias. In the first place, heterotopias, says Foucault, are real places, as opposed to utopias, which are 'sites with no real place'.[30] As is well-known, this essay 'Of Other Spaces' was excavated from some old lecture notes prepared by Foucault in 1967 and was incorporated in 1984, into an exhibition in Berlin and was published in English in *Diacritics* in 1986.[31] Foucault never really prepared them for publication and they therefore do not have the character of a finished work. Precisely for that reason however, they provide an opportunity to work on this extremely suggestive idea.

Foucault talks especially of two types of heterotopias. The first, in primitive societies, a particular form that he calls '*crisis heterotopias*'—which are privileged, or sacred or forbidden places, reserved for individuals, who in the context of those particular societies, are considered to be in a state of crisis: adolescents, menstruating women, pregnant women, the elderly, etc. These, says Foucault, are now disappearing in contemporary Western societies and are being replaced by the second type, those he calls '*heterotopias of deviation*'. These are places for those whose behaviour is considered to be deviant in relation to the norm and would include rest homes, psychiatric hospitals and prisons. There are two other kinds of spaces that Foucault discusses, although in passing, namely, the heterotopias of 'illusion' and those of 'compensation'—those that either expose all other lived spaces as equally illusory or those that approximate some idea of perfection. Exemplifying the latter, says Foucault, were the early Jesuit colonies established in South America, 'marvelous, absolutely regulated colonies in which human perfection was effectively achieved'. As an instance of the heterotopias of 'illusion', he mentions in passing, 'those famous brothels' about which we are given no further elaboration. The range of spaces that Foucault identifies under the rubric of heterotopias then, are still in some way related to some unstated notion of 'utopia', propelled by a desire for some kind of 'normalcy' or perfection—either by segregating the deviant or the crisis-ridden on the one hand, or by replicating some idea of perfection in some other place—presumably uncontaminated by history (as in the case of the Jesuit colonies).

One of the features of heterotopias enunciated by Foucault is that they are 'linked to slices in time' or what he also refers to as 'heterochronies'. Here he presents three kinds of heterotopias: first, those that embody a sort of absolute break with their traditional time, as for instance the cemetery. Second, those that embody 'indefinitely accumulating time', for instance the museum and the library. Thirdly, 'those linked . . . to time in its flowing, transitory, precarious aspect, to time in the mode of the festival.'

Given the immense diversity of the kinds of spaces that Foucault seeks to cover by deploying this term, it is somewhat intriguing that spaces like those produced by apartheid in South Africa, Jim Crow laws in the American South or the concentration camp do not figure in Foucault's list. And yet, if the psychiatric hospital and the prison constitute heterotopias of one kind (segregating those whose behaviour is considered deviant), surely it would not be stretching Foucault's sense of the term too much, if we were to include within it these other spaces—including in our case, the *paracheri*.

Edward Soja, in a fascinating discussion of bell hooks' writings, points to the idea of marginality in her spatial narratives of exclusion and struggle. Says bell hooks:

> As black Americans living in a small Kentucky town, the railroad tracks were a daily reminder of our marginality. Across those tracks were paved streets, stores we could not enter, restaurants we could not eat in, and people we could not look directly in the face. Across the tracks was a world we could work in as maids, as janitors, as prostitutes, as long as it was in a service capacity. We could enter that world but we could not live there . . .
>
> There were laws to ensure our return...[32]

The description of the Kentucky settlement by bell hooks here is similar to that of the *paracheri*—with one important difference. The *paracheri* is a non-modern space whose boundaries are maintained and enforced through religious notions of purity and pollution, while in the American South or under apartheid these spaces were carved out and protected by modern law.

Unlike Foucault's heterotopias, however, none of these spaces segregates populations that are either crisis ridden or deviant. All these are spaces that are reserved for those who are simply marked as *different*—in order to produce a *certain kind of normality* within the main body of society. Perhaps these could be designated simply as *heterotopias of difference*. The *paracheri* is an exclusive space that is meant to house people who are to undertake what orthodox Brahminical/Hindu society considers polluting activities, so that 'purity' may rigorously be maintained within the precincts of caste society.

By the middle of the nineteenth century, however, major transformations begin to take place as new, modern colonial institutions come into existence. The space of the city gets rapidly transformed into a secular modern space, thrown open, in principle to everybody, irrespective of caste or class. The prohibitions of the village and the *paracheri* are not quite possible to enforce in the city—the space also of anonymity, where the untouchable can now 'pass', as it were. No longer is it possible to identify the untouchable body by simply looking at it, as Surajpal Chauhan recalls in his autobiography. There he describes how he and his wife had asked a zamindar for some water on a visit to the village during the summer vacation. The zamindar agreed, but when he discovered Chauhan's caste identity, he became enraged and began insulting them—'The Bhangis and sons of Bhangis and Chamars *wear new clothes in the cities and no one can tell whether he is a Bhangi* or not.'

'Wear new clothes' . . . that was what Phulo had wanted in our story above—and not even everyday, but to mark that very special day of her wedding. Wear new clothes and jewellery and dress up as a bride. But Phulo lived in the *paracheri*, unlike Surajpal Chauhan, who has found a place for himself in the city. However, the inhabitants of Phulo's *paracheri* too have now heard of this other place—an utopia, at least for those who still remain here. It is a place that beckons and every now and then some inhabitants, usually males to begin with, 'disappear' in search of that heaven. That is where Bulaki also disappears. When he returns after five years, we can see him sporting a moustache, with a gun and on horseback. That was after all, one regret that Phulo had continued to have—that her groom did not come on horseback. Coming back from the city, he fulfilled that desire—the city which had transformed Bulaki from the helpless Mehtar who could do nothing but run away, abandoning his wife to the wolves on the very first night, into this confident man. This is the story of Bulaki's becoming-Dalit—becoming-Dalit in the city.

It is also interesting to recall that in his prefatory comments to his reflections on heterotopias, written in the context of mid to late twentieth century Europe, Foucault suggests that 'contemporary space is perhaps still not desanctified'; that many distinctions such as those between private and public space are 'still nurtured by the hidden presence of the sacred'.[33] It is this 'hidden presence of the sacred' that in the context of our exploration of the becoming-subject of the Dalit assumes a certain critical import. If the *paracheri* was the place of virtual confinement of the untouchable castes almost till the middle of the nineteenth century, it is its peculiar transfiguration into an imaginative space in the modern age that possibly underlies and provides the clue to many of the puzzles of contemporary India.

As modernity begins to reconstitute the spatial configuration of Indian society, carving out new and secularized public spaces in urban areas, the *paracheri* and all the lines of casteness that define it undergo a peculiar transformation: it becomes an imaginary boundary that a caste Hindu begins to carry with him or her—a boundary that is now dislocated from actual physical space. The *paracheri* as an imaginary space pervades the entire space of the nation. The hidden presence of the caste line structures every space that a caste Hindu walks into. Invisible to the secularized caste Hindu, it is a line that is always visible to the 'untouchable' for s/he must always be careful not to transgress. Even the space of modern institutions and public spaces, where entry, at least in theory is open to all, is structured by this invisible line. The molecular structure of the village is ceaselessly reproduced in the very institutions and spaces of modern society. This is the tale that is endlessly repeated in all Dalit autobiographies and accounts. This invisible line of separation is what Ambedkar too had experienced, even in interactions with his upper caste subordinates, after he came back to India with a doctorate from Columbia University and joined as an official in the princely state of Baroda (whose Maharaja had sponsored Ambedkar's study in the US). This is what Omprakash Valmiki experiences repeatedly in apparently secular public spaces like those of the train, in his interactions with co-passengers.[34]

It is in this space—the space of the dislocated and transfigured *paracheri*—that Mayawati confronts the mutated upper caste, 'cultured' city dweller, with her '30-million rupee diamond studded necklace'. It is in this space that young Nirmala sees her—from her own very real *paracheri*—and tells Amy Waldman that Mayawati gives her the confidence that 'anything' can be done. For Mayawati to appear thus is an act of defiance—and an act of becoming Dalit. And Waldman is right in discerning that 'in this imperial display of power', 'Mayawati has touched something deep'.

## Heterotopia II: The Paracheri is Everywhere

We can now return to our second scene—that of the public rally in the La Martiniere College grounds, Lucknow to celebrate Mayawati's birthday. As we return to that scene, let us remind ourselves of the third kind of heterotopia/heterochrony that Foucault talks about—'linked to time in its flowing, transitory, precarious aspect, to time in the mode of the festival'.

The stage, we may recall, mimics the sets of *Mughal-e-Azam*. Apart from the 51 kg cake and 100,000 laddoos, there are 60 quintals of marigold flowers and 5000 bouquets, decorating the venue. The occasion is certainly Mayawati's birthday but it is being observed as *swabhiman divas* (self-respect day).[35] Arches are set up in different parts of the city, on the roads leading to the venue.[36] Songs and ballads are being performed by various groups of folk artistes and balladeers. According to one of the reports, one of the balladeers sings '*ek hi tamanna, apne hathon ab Lal Quile par jhanda phehrao*' (we have only one wish, that you unfurl the flag at the Red Fort), and in the words of the report 'sums up the feelings of her supporters who want to see her on the centre-stage of national politics.'[37] The event, covered by the *New York Times* correspondent a few months later, also presented 'an imperial show of power'. Waldman, the correspondent remarks that many Dalits who came to this imperial show of power 'had the thin frames and fraying finery of the rural poor'. 'But for a day they owned Lucknow, once defined by the extravagance of the Muslim nawabs.'[38] 'The city had shut down because of the rally . . . there were blue flags (the party flag) and blue elephants (the party symbol) and blue graffiti warning "anti-Dalits" not to tangle with Ms Mayawati, whose image was everywhere.'[39] Waldman continues: 'Rural Dalits marveled at the grand memorial she has built to Dr Ambedkar on 28 acres (of land) here.' She quotes a former police chief, Sri Ram Arun, a Dalit himself, as saying that 'These are the places where downtrodden people can come and say, "this is our symbol".'[40]

The space of a BSP rally is clearly a space of celebration, of festival, abounding in symbols. But more than that it marks the invasion of public space by the people of the *paracheri*—those who have lived in confinement for centuries. And this aspect of 'invasion' is as much present in a political rally organized by the BSP as it is in the huge public celebrations of Ambedkar's birth anniversary—popularly known as Ambedkar Jayanti.[41] To get a sense of the significance of this immense semiotic transformation of the meaning of space, one need only look at the way this event has become another mode and theatre of the fashioning of the Self. Owen Lynch's studies of the Ambedkar Jayanti celebrations in Agra (a district of the state of Uttar Pradesh) over the years are revealing in this respect. Ambedkar Jayanti celebrations began in Agra in 1957, initiated mainly by some Jatav youth of a Dalit locality called the Kaji Para.[42] Initially it was 'almost exclusively *of* and *for* Jatavs'.[43] Increasingly other Dalit *jatis*, started joining the celebrations. It was celebrated 'as a day of rest, feasting, games, political speeches and other festivities, culminating in a seven-hour parade which marches from Kaji Para, past the Jama Masjid, through several upper caste localities and Hing ki Mandi market up to the Collectorate and back again.' Sarah Beth compares this to the Chuharmal mela held in Dalit localities in certain parts of Bihar, where there was no participation of other non-Dalit caste groups.[44] However, more than participation by others, what is relevant from our point of view is that it did not involve any transgression, held as it was within the locality. I have suggested earlier that in the modern era the *paracheri* became an invisible imagined line of casteness that went everywhere the upper caste/s went and lived. It is in that context that we must see the Dalit parade entering upper caste localities and practically taking over the streets for the entire day. So, Lynch says, 'the parade was bitterly contested and participation in it was often dangerous . . . . In reaction from the roofs of upper caste homes in those neighbourhoods, stones and insults were apt to be thrown at the statue [of Ambedkar].'[45] In this connection, Beth narrates the conflict around the event in 1978: 'on the night of 14 April 1978 [Ambedkar's birthday], the parade for the Ambedkar *mela* made its way through the streets of Agra as it had done every year. However, when bricks and stones were thrown at the parade, the Jatavs retaliated and in the ensuing violence, a house and several small shops were damaged. The next day the upper castes marched to the police station shouting slogans such as 'change the parade route', 'Death to Ambedkar'. In response, members of the Jatav community staged a peaceful protest and again marched through the streets of the upper caste localities . . . . Again stones were thrown on the marchers and the police made a lathi charge to dispel the protest.' The conflict continued till 3 May when the army was called in to end the violence. Thereafter, the state and national governments stepped in and many imprisoned Jatav leaders were released and 14 April was declared a public holiday in Uttar Pradesh.[46]

Two kinds of spatial practices are registered here in these descriptions. One, there is the attempt to take over public spaces like the area around the Parliament and the India Gate in Delhi—the part studied by Sarah Beth, in her study of the Ambedkar *mela* (fair) in Delhi. Here the congregation is at a central place where people from different parts of the city and neighbouring states converge and transform the area into a veritable fair-ground. This is also the kind that marks the BSP rally. The other is that of the Ambedkar Jayanti procession/parade that originates from the Kaji Para and moves into the localities and streets of the upper castes. Note that these are technically public spaces and anybody should be able to enter them. In the normal, everyday flow of life, many Dalits do enter these spaces as these are no longer possible to guard on the strength of the upper caste population alone. Urban anonymity provides the individual Dalit the possibility of entering these spaces. Yet, for the Dalit parade to enter it, marked very clearly as a procession of Dalits, can create nothing short of a crisis for the upper caste inhabitants of these localities.[47]

These are the spaces—marked by the flow of time in its transitory, precarious aspect, in the mode of the festival—that I suspect, are the spaces of carnivalesque freedom. I would also include here the space of the party-as-installation carefully crafted as a space of carnivalesque reversal as another heterotopia. These heterotopias of the festival or the carnival, involving a moment of a semiotic transfiguration of space, occupy a place of significant importance in the anti-utopian politics of the contemporary Dalit movement.

## NOTES

1. Macaulay was Secretary to the Board of Control from 1832 until 1833. After the passing of the Government of India Act 1833, he was appointed as the first Law Member of the Governor-General's Council. He came to India in 1834 and served on the Supreme Council of India between 1834 and 1838.

2. The statement, part of his 'celebrated' minutes, goes on to say: '*To that class we may leave it to refine the vernacular dialects of the country*, to enrich those dialects with terms of science borrowed from the Western nomenclature, and to render them by degrees fit vehicles for conveying knowledge to the great mass of the population' (emphasis added).

3. The invitation to the party was unlike invitations, a pamphlet of sorts that dealt with the representation of Macaulay as a reactionary pillar of the colonial empire—a representation that has become so much part of our common sense that practically everybody, ranging from nationalists to marxists and postcolonialist scholars, has only re-stated that common sense in their writings. The picture that this invitation letter presents is one of an enlightened liberal who has been almost single-handedly responsible for opening out the world of modern education for the Dalits.

4. The picture of the painting here is courtesy Shashwati's blog: http://blog.shashwati.com/2006/11/04/goddess-english-ii/

5. IMFL stands for 'Indian Made Foreign Liquor'—an official government description of such alcoholic drinks.

6. Vrinda Gopinath 'Happy Birthday Lord Macaulay, thank you for "Dalit empowerment"', *Indian Express*, 2006, http://www.indianexpress.com/story/15423.html downloaded on 30 November 2007.

7. In an email communication to Shaswati's Blog: http://blog.shashwati.com/2006/11/04/goddess-english-ii/

8. The film makers promptly agreed to delete the lines and the ban was withdrawn in a day.

9. 'Aaja Nachle almost trips—on a caste line', *Indian Express*, front page, 2 December 2007.

10. This intervention of Ravikant's as well as a significant part of the debate can be accessed at www.kafila.org

11. See Shahid Amin, 'The Tenable Patriot', *The Hindu*, 3 December 2006, http://www.hinduonnet.com/thehindu/thscrip/print.pl?file=2006120300040100.htm&date=2006/12/03/&prd=mag&, last accessed on 27 April 2008.

12. See for instance, CNN report 'Bake sales used to protest affirmative action', 24 December 2003, http://www.cnn.com/2003/US/West/12/24/affirmative.bake.sale.ap/, accessed 27 April 2008, or Heather Mac Donald, 'Elites to Anti-Affirmative Action Voters: Drop Dead', *City Journal*, Winter 2007, http://www.city-journal.org/html/17_1_prop209.html, accessed 27 April 2008.

13. Aditya Nigam, 'In Search of a Bourgeoisie', *Economic and Political Weekly*, vol. 37, no. 13, 30 March 2002.

14. Both Meshram and Patel's poems have been taken from the English translation in Barbara Joshi, *Untouchable! Voice of the Dalit Liberation Movement*, New Delhi: Selectbook Service Syndicte, and London: Zed Books Ltd, 1986.

15. Yogesh Vajpeyi, 'For the oppressed, covered in diamonds—govt plays host at Mayawati birthday bash', *The Telegraph*, 16 January 2003, front page.

16. Sharat Pradhan, 'Mayawati spends crores to fulfill her birthday dream', 15 January 2003, http://www.rediffmail.com/news/2003/jan/15up.htm

17. Ibid.

18. Amy Waldman, 'An Opulent and Pugnacious Champion of India's Outcasts', *The New York Times on the web*, 4 May 2003.

19. Dipesh Chakrabarty, 'Clothing the Political Man: A Reading of the Use of Khadi/White in Indian Public Life', *Postcolonial Studies*, vol. 4, no. 1, 2001, pp. 27-38.

20. Ibid., pp. 27-8.

21. Kancha Ilaiah, 'Cultural Globalization', *The Hindu*, 22 February 2003. http://www.thehindu.com/2003/02/22/stories/2003022200621000.htm

22. Anand Teltumbde, 'Ambedkar' in and for The Post-Ambedkar Dalit Movement, Pune: Usha Wagh/Sugawa Prakashan, 1997. http://www.angelfire.com/ak/ambedkar/BRanand1.htm#post-ambedkar

23. Ibid.

24. Ibid. In fact, Teltumbde then goes on to launch a scathing attack on these middle class Dalit leaders, who he said could only 'project themselves as better clones of Ambedkar', who wore their shirts and trousers, were 'suited and booted [a deliberately sarcastic and funny Indian way of referring to such a mimetic taste], had university degrees and could command better sophistry than Gaikwad'. Gaikwad and his ilk could only be activists and not leaders, in this view, says Teltumbde.

25. Vajpeyi, op. cit.

26. Pradhan, op. cit.

27. Mohandas Naimishray, *Awazein*, Collection of short stories, Delhi: Samata Prakashan, 1998, pp. 105-10.

28. Mehtars are a caste of sweepers and the Chamars are leather-workers. However, the words 'sweepers' and 'leather-workers' are deceptively benign. The Mehtars have been traditionally forced to carry night soil and do the most demeaning of jobs for the village, while the Chamars scavenge dead animals under filthy and degrading conditions.

29. The settlements are generally known by different names in different areas—often even within the same linguistic region. I have therefore chosen this term as a more general one.

30. Michel Foucault (1967), 'Of Other Spaces—Heterotopias', 1967 p. 2. http://foucault.info/heteroTopia/foucault.heteroTopia.en.html, downloaded on 15 March 2006. All references here are to this text.

31. For further details see Edward W. Soja, *Thirdspace—Journeys to Los Angeles and Other Real-and-Imagined Places*, Oxford and Boston: Blackwell Publishing, 2004, p. 154.

32. Ibid., pp. 99-100.

33. Michel Foucault op. cit.

34. See his autobiography, Om Prakash Valmiki, *Joothan: A Dalit's Life*, tr. Arun Prabha Mukherjee, Kolkata : Samya, 2003.

35. Pradhan, op. cit.

36. Vajpeyi, op. cit.

37. Ibid.

38. Waldman, op. cit.

39. Ibid.

40. Ibid.

41. For a study of Ambedkar Jayanti celebrations, see Sarah Beth, 'Taking to the Streets: Dalit *Mela* and the Public Performance of Dalit Cultural Identity', *Contemporary South Asia*, vol. 14, no. 4, December 2005, pp. 397–410.

42. Jatav's are one of the many caste groups (*jatis*) that constitute the Dalits. All references to Lynch's study are cited from Beth, ibid.

43. Ibid., p. 4.

44. Ibid., p. 4.

45. Ibid. p.6. I am not sure though that the stones were hurled at Ambedkar's statues alone and not on the processionists.

46. Ibid., pp. 6-7.

47. My colleague Bhagwati Prasad informs me that now it is virtually mandatory for all Dalit wedding processions in Agra to carry a portrait of Ambedkar and Buddha along. This way of marking a wedding procession as Dalit, with the groom mounted on horseback and the procession indulging in every possible prohibition, bespeaks of a sea-change in the power matrix of contemporary Uttar Pradesh.

# 7

# THE NON-CONTEMPORANEITY OF M N ROY[1]

## Radical Democracy and the Party-Form

*What tends to disappear in the political world that is shaping up, and perhaps in a new age of democracy, is the domination of this form of organization called the party, the party-state relation, which finally will have lasted, strictly speaking, only two centuries . . . a period to which belong as well certain determined types of parliamentary and liberal democracy, constitutional monarchies, Nazi, fascist or Soviet totalitarianisms. Not one of these regimes was possible without what can be called the axiomatics of the party.*

—Jacques Derrida[2]

## Introduction

On the morrow of Independence, Mahatma Gandhi emerged as a tragic figure—all but abandoned by his followers, who were all set to take power and become the guardians of the new nation-state. Gandhi, in sharp contrast was at his utopian best, arguing that the Congress should disband and transform itself into an organization for the service of the common people. The continuous strain in Gandhi's thought, which considered politics as a necessary evil that had to be engaged in for the sake of freedom from colonial rule, now came to the fore. Gandhi's gesture was an attempt to underline his disavowal of power, which he had always seen as suspect. At around the same time, another figure, a sworn enemy of all that Gandhi seemed to represent, also came to the conclusion that politics as such was mainly concerned with power and was therefore, an evil and decided, against the wishes of his party comrades to disband his party. This figure was M N Roy and the party concerned, the Radical Democratic Party that he had led for its brief life of eight years. This is about the only time that Roy succeeded where Gandhi failed, for while the Indian National Congress ignored the Mahatma, Roy almost forced his followers to accept his position. Of course, this was possible largely because the RDP was really a small sect of Roy's personal followers who did not really 'represent' any social force within society at large.

In this period Roy came to believe that 'spiritual liberation is the condition for social and political liberation' and in the inseparability of means and ends. He began to increasingly argue that good ends could not be secured by bad means and scholars have noted that in both these respects, his position came quite close to Gandhi's, even if in contrast to Gandhi, Roy believed this spiritual liberation could only be grounded on secular rationalist ethics.[3]

Gandhi and Roy actually present a study in contrast. For, Gandhi, despite his disavowal of power, was always in the thick of power and politics leading the nationalist struggle, while Roy, fired by the 'will to power', almost always operated on the margins of mainstream politics. In a sense, it was Gandhi's magical hold over popular imagination that probably puzzled Roy the most. It was what he called the 'Gandhist cult' that occupied Roy to a considerable degree and as Shiviah notes, in the days of the Radical Democratic Party he saw this cult as the chief obstacle to the democratic revolution in India. The masses, Roy believed, 'have been accustomed to the language of Gandhism' and hence 'do not easily respond to any other language'.[4] Roy's reading of Gandhi and 'Gandhism' was quite one-sided and hopelessly off the mark, abstracted as it was from all social and political context. In fact, as Sudipta Kaviraj has astutely noted, Roy's critique of Gandhi followed a peculiar trajectory, starting from the more complex appreciations of his early communist days to the more simplistic and one-sided ones of his later writings.[5] As Kaviraj points out, in his earlier marxist assessment, he acknowledged Gandhi's role in breaking 'the class insularity of the Congress' and making it 'truly representative of the national aspirations of all classes of Indians'. He even considered non-cooperation 'much more dangerous than an armed uprising, which can always be met face to face and put down'.[6] This shift in Roy's assessment is all the more interesting for it was precisely in the period that Roy moved closer to Gandhi in his disavowal of power and his insistence on morality and ethics in politics that he became more intolerant of Gandhi—whom he even termed 'fascist' quite often, in this period.

But Roy was not responding merely to the Gandhian puzzle. As I will argue later, in his later period, Roy retreated almost entirely from the world of real politics and was pre-occupied with a contemplation of 'world-historical' questions. In this period, he was theoretically more preoccupied by the appalling experience of the rise of fascism of the very recent past. He lived in the twentieth century but was increasingly deeply troubled by his times. He had begun to see the twentieth century as a disastrous one that saw the unprecedented rise of totalitarian regimes of both the Right and the Left. Somewhere in between, he felt, the great aspirations for human freedom that the European Enlightenment had aroused had got smothered. The 'sovereign individual' lay buried deep under the edifice of these regimes. To recover this sovereign individual from the clutches of totalitarian ideologies became, eventually, his life's mission.

It is important to remember that Roy, who has been often severely criticized for his high rationalist predilections and what Sudipta Kaviraj has called his 'heteronomous radicalism', actually began his journey as a staunch 'cultural nationalist'. Drawn into the terrorist movement in Bengal at an early age, Roy was influenced, according to his own account, by Bankimchandra's *Ananda Math*.[7] Shiviah has suggested that the terrorist nationalist group of Bengal with which Roy worked, had through the influence of Pramatha Mitra, imbibed much from both Vivekananda and the mystic nationalism of Aurobindo Ghosh. In the course of his nationalist career, he was sent on a mission to collect a cache of arms for revolutionary activities, from Germany and landed up in the event, travelling through Java, Japan and the United States to Mexico. It was during his stay in the US, where he met Evelyn Trent (who became his first wife), that he encountered different currents of socialist and anarchist radicals. Yet socialist radicalism did not come easily to him. Even though he was persuaded by their concern for the oppressed, by his own admission, 'as Indians, we vehemently opposed Marxist materialism with our spiritual genius'.[8] It would be quite a while before he would become a convinced universalist rationalist and atheist. It was while in Mexico that he underwent a major transformation and through his contact with Mikhail Borodin, came in contact with the Comintern. It was Borodin, Roy acknowledged later, who introduced him to the 'intricacies of Hegelian Dialectics as the key to marxism' and it was through this introduction to European philosophy and culture that his 'lingering faith in the special genius of India faded'.

He became active in Mexican politics and having played a central role in transforming the Mexican Socialist Party into the first communist party outside Russia, was invited to attend the Second Congress of the Communist International. That was when, as we know, he entered into his famous debate with Lenin on the 'National and Colonial Question.'

Let us also register here a point of some importance, made by Shiviah, regarding the nature of Roy's disagreement with Lenin. It was Aurobindo Ghosh who had argued against the 'moderate' leadership of the Congress of his time, that 'the proletariat is the real key to the situation' and that 'our first and holiest duty is the elevation and enlightenment of the proletariat'.[9] This reference to the *sarbahara* (proletariat) and *samyabad* (communism) was of course not peculiar to Aurobindo. Vivekananda himself had spoken and written about them. Aurobindo, however, invoked the proletariat in his critique of the moderate leadership whom he ridiculed for their 'policy of prayers, petitions and protests'. In Roy's debate with Lenin, Shiviah detects a trace of this critique of the bourgeois leadership of the Congress: 'To the nationalist Roy the "moderate" attitude of the bourgeoisie was suspect to the Marxist Roy, it was even more so.'[10]

Another article of faith that Roy presumably retained from Aurobindo's trenchant critique of the moderates—and which gelled perfectly with his new marxist beliefs—was the idea that 'a subject nation does not prepare itself by gradual progress for liberty' but 'opens by liberty its way to rapid progress'. In other words, political freedom and capture of state power were the precondition for progress and social transformation. Eventually not only did Roy abandon this idea; he also became the most inveterate critic of both his earlier creeds, namely, nationalism and communism. It was his new belief, what he described as Radical Humanism or New Humanism, that prompted him to dissolve the RDP and proclaim that a philosophical revolution or an Indian Renaissance would have to be the precondition of true human freedom—a freedom that would be predicated upon the sovereign, autonomous individual.

It is in the period of his transition from marxism to New Humanism that Roy begins to think most productively about radicalizing democracy and offers one of the most interesting critiques of representation as such. However, once he disbands his party and moves fully on to the terrain of the new philosophy his concerns increasingly shift towards an elaboration of this philosophy, away from the world of real politics. In this period, which I shall briefly return to, later in this chapter, Roy's retreat into the world of philosophical contemplation signals, in fact, a highly problematic regression into eighteenth century European philosophy. Nonetheless, this should not in any way, detract from a proper assessment of the normative value of his critique of democracy and representation, for, however wrong-headed his philosophical positions might be, he was at some level pointing to a real crisis.

In this chapter, I will not be concerned with a comprehensive assessment of Roy or his legacy; nor will I try to discuss his entire *oeuvre*. My concern will rather be with a limited part of his work and writings, which relate to his critique of parliamentary/representative democracy, and attempt to relate it to some wider discussions on the subject in political theory. In the final section, I will offer a critique of what today appears to be Roy's naïve faith in Reason and Progress, upon which he based much of his critiques of representation.

## The Crisis of Representative Democracy

The key question that Roy was grappling with, once he was convinced that soviet-style communism was not the way to 'real freedom', was the problem of radicalizing democracy itself. He agreed with Lincoln's famous aphorism that democracy was rule 'of the people, by the people and for the people'. However, in the actual practice of democracies, the best that one could get, he argued, was government *for* the people. The problem as he saw it was that 'the people' had been swamped by another entity of modern polities, namely *the masses*. It was with the emergence of 'the masses', so easily amenable to nationalist, fascist or other totalitarian mobilizations, that the entity called the 'people' had dissolved. He held all modern political ideologies and thought responsible for this eclipse of 'the people' by 'the masses', for in his view, the people could only be composed of 'sovereign' individuals. Modern thought had denigrated the individual and come to 'characterize freedom of the individual as a fictitious abstraction, an illusion'.[11] And freedom, according to Roy, was a property of the individual alone; it was not compatible with any 'collective ego'.

All totalitarian mobilizations, whether of the Right or of the Left, Roy believed, were based on the some idea of a 'collective ego' that demanded the surrender of individual autonomy to collective interests. He believed that it was such collectivist ideas that privileged some larger collective entity over the individual that resulted in 'the mental attitude' which 'completely disregards considerations of ethics, of morality in social behaviour', presumably because they could always refer back to those 'larger interests' to justify any amoral act. This was also what led to the continuous privileging of ends over means.[12]

At another level, Roy saw a profound contradiction at the heart of the democratic project, arising from the privileging of the state over the individual. But more importantly, he held two concepts, which were coeval with democracy, as responsible for the degeneration of democracy: in the political field, he held *parliamentarism* and in the economic, *laissez faire* to be squarely responsible, for, both of them, in their own way, gave unbridled power to a small minority to exploit the majority.[13] In his words: 'Although the problem of reconciling the apparent contradiction of man and the State has occupied political thought ever since antiquity, the eclipse of the individual at the cost of growing emphasis on the State, first under theocracy, later in monarchies and yet later in parliamentary democracies, not to mention modern dictatorships, is one of the outstanding features of history.'[14] While the eclipse of the individual under other forms of government was understandable, it was simply not, with respect to democracy. His critique of *laissez faire*, of course, draws directly from marxism and important though it be, is not directly relevant for our purposes here. What is interesting from our present point of view is his claim that while 'parliamentary democracy formally recognized the sovereignty of the individual', *in practice*, 'it deprived all but a privileged few of the effective use of that sovereignty'.[15] A word here about the use of the term 'in practice' in this statement. From the detailed examination of the problems of contemporary democratic theory and practice that Roy undertakes, it is clear that he is not referring here to the cruder sense of 'practice' as opposed to the theory of democracy—which he would somehow exonerate. A reading of his speeches and articles where he elaborates his critique is enough to show that it is democratic theory itself that he finds wanting in this regard. In other words, there is an implicit distinction here between the idea of democracy and the actual *theoretical practice* of elaboration of that idea as a workable one in modern polities.

Now, how did this state of affairs come about? Roy examines the history of parliamentary democracy at one level and democratic theory at another, in order to find his answer. His conclusions are startling: delegation and representation are the very negation of democracy. 'The delegation of power to elected representatives is the legal sanction of parliamentary democratic governments. Constitutional pandits declare that this is democracy itself; but in reality *it is a negation of democracy, based on the contempt for the demos*.'[16] This in itself is not very novel for we can already hear the voice of Jean-Jacques Rousseau here: sovereignty is inalienable, untransferable and indivisible. Sovereignty cannot be represented as it lies in the General Will and this Will does not admit of any representation. Now if this were all that Roy were arguing then he would merely be echoing Rousseau, whose critiques of representation in the name of 'direct democracy', as Lucio Colletti among others, has reminded us, provided the bases for generations of radical critiques of bourgeois democracy including Lenin's. But the point is that this is precisely what Roy is not saying, for as we have seen, he has already identified any form of the 'collective ego' as an enemy of the sovereign individual—and to him the General Will is the Collective Ego *par excellence*. Roy *does* want to speak in the name of direct democracy but he will not yield any quarter to any theoretical stance that will allow any new oligarchy to assume power in the name of some larger collectivity, be it nation or class. It is at this stage that Roy begins to identify that organism of modern society that has gradually, over the last century, *usurped the sovereignty of the people*: the political party. In an article entitled 'Democracy and Party-Politics' published in 1951, where he surveys the developments in the party system in Britain, he explicitly says as much and compares this situation with the early days of parliamentary democracy where the electors directly elected the representatives whom they knew. Individual merit alone counted, for, the representative represented none but those who elected him. With the emergence of political parties, the entire situation had changed. Thenceforth the elected representatives were answerable to the party they belonged to. In parliament, the representative is responsible, not to the people who elected him 'but to the party machinery which has ensured his election by supplying money and the brass-band'.[17] On another occasion he wrote that 'it is through the instrumentality of political parties that power is concentrated in the hands of minorities . . . .'[18] We might recall here our discussion of the crisis of the party-form in the 'Introduction' and the emergence of new forms over the past couple of decades, to be able to see how prescient Roy's critique of the party-form was.

This identification of the political party as the main organism responsible for the decline of democracy goes hand in hand, for Roy, with another equally important recognition that we have already mentioned. The rise of the 'masses' or what Hannah Arendt, in her studies of totalitarianism, has called the 'mass man'. With the emergence of this 'mass', says Roy, 'on the one hand, we have the mass of people and on the other, we have parties. The individual man and his judgement, his discretion and will are nowhere in the picture.' Parties now appeal, not to the reasoning of the individual but to 'the sentiments of the masses'. 'The purpose of election propaganda is to create a state of mass hysteria.'[19] But it is not enough, in Roy's reading, to simply say that the parties mislead 'the people' when they mobilize them. It is equally important to explain why the people follow certain parties or leaders? And here he sees a fundamental problem with parliamentary democracy and 'its philosophy', namely Liberalism, in that they see individuals as scattered, atomized beings. This notion of the atomized individual parallels, in Roy's view, the emergence of the phenomenon of 'the mass'. The helpless, atomized individual produced by modern society begins to seek security in the mass, giving rise to the tendency to identify themselves with others who are equally helpless, in some collectivity such as the nation or the class.[20] Roy seems to be drawing here on the work of theorists like Erich Fromm, since he mentions 'works' that have described this 'mass mentality' as 'the *fear of freedom*' though he does not explicitly refer either to Fromm or to other more conservative theorists of 'mass society'. This view, as we know today, runs counter to the dominant strands of liberal and rationalist/secular thought that assumed, somewhat naively, that modernity would usher in the rational, autonomous and disengaged subject by progressively dissolving all community bonds. That the very processes of modernity would—or could—bring forth a kind of disembedded agent who was fundamentally 'afraid' of 'his' autonomy or freedom and sought the comfort of a new figure of authority was something that this Enlightenment inherited view found difficult to deal with.

Roy concedes that in modern polities, with large populations spread over vast areas, it is utopian to expect that everybody can individually participate in administration and decision-making. He acknowledges therefore, that it was out of this contingency that 'a system was devised by which people constitutionally delegated their authority to a smaller group of people which ruled the country as custodians of the sovereign people and its power'.[21] He traces the problems of contemporary democracies, often wrongly, to Rousseau's notion of the General Will, which he seems to suggest, lies at the heart of the principle of delegation and representation. In fact, much as Roy might like to deny it, his own critique of representation seems to draw precisely on Rousseau's claim that 'the moment a people gives itself representatives, it is no longer free; it no longer exists'.[22] He also concurs with a particular tradition of liberal scholarship that sees in Rousseau's 'metaphysical conception of the General Will' a 'moral sanction for dictatorship'.[23] There is, it seems to me, a conflation, here of the liberal, representative idea with the more expressivist democratic strains of Rousseau's notion of the General Will but that does not directly concern us here. For the moment, let us return to Roy's critique of representation as such.

The problem that presented itself before Roy was the same that Carl Schmitt had in the 1920s and 1930s noticed: the rise of mass democracy—even if their concerns were diametrically opposed to each other. The most serious crisis of representative democracy in Europe, which formed the backdrop of the frightful rise of fascism had to do with this phenomenon. Schmitt's scathing critique of liberal parliamentary democracy, let us recall, had to do with liberalism's belief that democracy was about free and fair exchange of ideas, of deliberation and what Habermas calls rational-critical discourse. Schmitt, who celebrated the rise of mass democracy was convinced that the point where liberalism had got it all wrong was in its refusal to recognize that politics was fundamentally about 'friend-enemy relations' where opinions were formed, not on the basis of the correctness or the force of logic of an idea but by interests. Passion and interests were what motivated people to act. Here Schmitt, that inveterate enemy of liberalism, pointed to the one major elision of all liberal thought: the institution of the political party. What Derrida has called the 'axiomatics of the party', in the epigraph to this chapter, has remained a blind spot for liberal political theory. Let us remind ourselves also that the late nineteenth century had seen the rise of huge, bureaucratic, mass political parties throughout Europe and it was these, that had engaged the attention of a scholar like Robert Michels when he propounded his famous 'iron law of oligarchy'—which incidentally, was based on the study of the German Social Democratic Party. If it was Michels' argument that large bureaucratic organizations inevitably led to concentration of power within them, in the party oligarchy, that was not a problem that worried Schmitt. To him, on the contrary, the political party *was* the instrument of modern mass politics—of propaganda and mass mobilization. Unlike Roy, two decades later, Schmitt was concerned primarily with the question of sovereignty and the ways in which the 'will of the people' is constituted. In his critique of liberal democracy, Schmitt touches the raw nerve of modern democratic politics when he points to the hiatus that divides the enlightened elite and the 'masses'. 'It often happens' he argues, 'that democrats are in a minority. It also happens that they decide on the basis of a supposedly democratic principle in favour of women's suffrage and then they have the experience that the majority of women do not vote democratically.'[24] Schmitt then goes on to mount his attack on the 'programme of people's education' or the belief that the people can express their 'true will' only when they are properly educated. He then goes on to suggest that this 'educational theory' is really a form of dictatorship, insofar as it 'suspends democracy in the name of true democracy that is still to be created'.[25] If that be the case, says Schmitt, then it follows that democracy is not quite incompatible with dictatorship. It is then basically a question of *who controls the means with which the will of the people is to be constructed*. Among these 'means', Schmitt identifies military and political force, propaganda, control of public opinion through the press, party organizations, assemblies, popular education and schools. In short, in a breathtaking assertion of realism, Schmitt turns the classical problem of democratic political theory on its head: '*Only political power, which should come from the people's will, can form the people's will in the first place*.'[26] This is Schmitt's wager that democratic theory has yet to come to terms with.

As we have seen, this hiatus between the enlightened 'democrats' and the 'backward' people, was something that Roy, like a good Enlightenment-inspired humanist recognized very candidly. However, he did not think in terms of education through the state but through an intellectual and philosophical revolution. His role for the short-lived RDP and later the Radical Humanist movement, was one that would lay the basis for a philosophical revolution that would liberate the people from their 'enslaved' ways of thinking. Roy would have agreed with Schmitt that, as things were, it was political power that really formed the people's will, but while the latter took that situation as a given, it was precisely what Roy wanted to challenge and change. He believed that this situation could be transformed and the more he thought about this problem the more convinced he was, that what had really changed the terrain of democracy was the institution of the political party. It was this that had become the instrument of the rule of an oligarchy in the name of the people. Schmitt too saw the party as that key instrument which had transformed the terrain of liberal democracy. Parties now faced each other as organized groups representing interests and relying on a propaganda apparatus for mobilizing the masses through an appeal to their interests and passions.[27]

It may not be out of place to mention here that the two factors that Habermas considered to be responsible for the decline of the public sphere were the rise of the mass media and mass political parties. To Habermas too, these had fundamentally changed the character of the public sphere as public opinion was now often manipulated through these institutions to the extent that rational-critical exchange between citizens was no longer possible.[28] Clearly, the rise of mass political parties, in close conjunction with the notion of the 'masses' in one form or the other, seems to have been noticed by more than one scholar. So when Roy set out to find a way out of this complex problem of the constitution of the people's will within the democratic framework, there was no doubt in his mind that it was the party-form itself that had to be abandoned. But this can only be achieved if and when people are able to exercise their critical faculties. And this, Roy was quite clear, could not be done by asking governments to provide education because awakening people's critical faculties is a subversive task and no government would do it. All governments, he held, wanted people to 'sing patriotic songs, salute national flags and read patriotic history as compiled and edited by governments so that all people be merged into a homogeneous collectivity and forget that they are individuals'.[29] This had to be the work of an autonomous intellectual movement. It was an intellectual resurgence spurred by such a movement that alone could change the situation. And 'such an intellectual resurgence', he believed, 'will take place together with the resurrection of the individual from the grave of the mass'.[30] Then alone will democratic practice become possible in which governments by and of the people can be established.

## Outlines of a Radical Democratic Polity

Even though Roy is a passionate advocate of some kind of direct democracy, he makes it clear that the anarchist ideal of a society without the state is too utopian for his tastes. Even in his retreat from the world of politics into philosophy, he wants to spell out a *workable* ideal. He is not satisfied by offering a mere critique. He, therefore, argues for a form of party-less democracy where the relationship between the represented and the representative will be direct, unmediated by the institution of the party. He spells out his notion of radical democracy in the context of his much expected intellectual resurgence of the people, when 'the individual will rise from the grave of the mass'. It is in such an atmosphere that the possibilities of a really radical form of direct democracy will open up. It will then become possible 'to practice direct democracy *in smaller social groups*'. This proposition is of critical importance in his scheme of things 'because to make the individual self-reliant, they must be freed from the feeling of being helpless cogs in the wheels of the gigantic machines of modern States, which allow them no other function than to cast a vote once in several years'.[31] It is of critical importance, in my view, to recognize here that this vision is being spelt out by a 'high-modernist' in the period when the gigantic and the monumental forms of political and economic architecture were quite an article of faith. Ecological critiques that spoke of the 'small' as 'beautiful' had not yet emerged and it was only in incorrigible romantics that one could expect any desire to reclaim the small and the beautiful. It is probably here that we might find the crucial clue for Roy's fascination with Romanticism which keeps appearing repeatedly in his works.

To continue with his argument: Roy believed that once this precondition of an intellectual resurgence materializes, people can then 'create local democracies of their own'. Voters need not remain like scattered atoms any longer but can 'organize themselves into People's Committees and function like *local republics*'.[32] At the time of elections, then, 'they will not have to vote for anybody coming from outside' but can nominate their own candidates from among themselves. Creating such conditions then becomes, for Roy, the most important political activity. Roy even believed, naively, that this process could begin right away, by picking up a few constituencies and getting 20 or 25 people dissatisfied with the present state of affairs together, to start this experiment. It would be possible, he thought, to begin the preliminary work of 'educating' the people, and at some later stage, call local conferences in a constituency to elect delegates for a constituency-level conference, which could at the time of elections elect a candidate from among themselves to contest the elections. Such a candidate, if elected, would not be responsible to any party machinery but only and solely to his electors. In this initial stage then, 'delegation' would have to remain in some form. Eventually, 'a growing network of such organized local democracies will be the instruments through which the electorate can assert its influence from day to day and ultimately exercise a standing control over the State as a whole.'[33]

It is interesting that, despite Roy's aversion to Gandhi's 'irrational' religious communitarianism, there is some strange resemblance of this idea of a network of local republics with Gandhi's own emphasis on village communities, where the state would have a marginal role. The significant difference between his vision and Gandhi's, of course, lies in the fact that Gandhi's was a more culturally nuanced and rooted one. However, Gandhi's culturally rooted notion of village republics, as Ambedkar was to point out, was itself quite problematic from the point of view of the Dalits—which is why he characterized (the idea of) these village republics as 'sinks of localism'. But where Ambedkar's rejection of Gandhi's emphasis on tradition took him to a strong advocacy of a centralized modern state, Roy seemed to offer a way that retained the best of Gandhi's vision while aligning himself with the kind of rationalist anti-traditionalism that Ambedkar valued. Scholars have drawn attention to the close similarity of some of Roy's ideas on radical democracy with those of Jayaprakash Narayan's idea of 'partyless democracy'. D C Grover claims that Jayaprakash 'shows remarkable influence of Roy in his plea for the reconstruction of Indian polity and acknowledges it on the evolution of his political ideas.'[34] In fact, JP seems to repeat Roy's precise argument that 'present-day mass elections, manipulated by powerful, centrally controlled parties, with the aid of high finance and diabolically clever methods and super-media of communication represent far less the electorate than the forces and interests behind the parties and the propaganda machines'.[35] Others like Niranjan Dhar see a striking resemblance of Roy's idea with Rabindranath Tagore's idea of 'swadeshi samaj', even if Roy, unlike Tagore, did not draw on the 'age-old Indian tradition of the panchayeti system'.[36]

It is, of course, quite surprising—or may be not so surprising—that Roy seemed to be, all through his writings in this phase, completely unmindful of the debates and actual political developments that were taking place within Indian politics. Gandhi is probably the only personality that he occasionally refers to, usually in a highly dismissive way. Other personalities and their thought figure by their complete absence in his writings. It was as if he was merely responding to some global developments, from the standpoint of an abstract rationalism and as Kaviraj has argued, merely expecting European history to be re-enacted on the Indian stage.

However, to return to Roy's elaboration of the idea of radical democracy, we have noted that he, unlike the anarchists, recognized that the state was an indispensable institution for large and complex modern societies. He therefore found the marxist idea of its 'withering away' also too utopian and empty a concept. He visualized a situation where the state could become 'coterminous with society'. He claimed that such an idea of a future state, gave content to the marxist ideal of the state withering away, for 'when it will no longer remain an institution over and above society, it will cease to be an instrument of coercion, and *as such* it will wither away'.[37] In present conditions, the state had become an abstraction that only existed in some central place, far beyond the reach and influence of members of society. When the state becomes 'coterminous with society', the requisite decentralization of the state will have taken place and it will then become no more than a clearing house of information, an advisory and administrative machinery to coordinate and supervise policies framed directly by the people as a whole operating through local People's Committees.[38]

Roy saw the possibility of the state becoming coterminous with society in the fact that 'until a few centuries ago, the government did not interfere, for instance, in the economic life of society, beyond raising taxes'. In those times, 'the requirements of the community were met by peasants, artisans and traders'.[39] In order to posit a different kind of state in the future, he had to show that such a state was not a logical impossibility. Thus, apart from his theoretical and normative argument, he searched for historical instances to show that a different relationship between the state and society was indeed possible. He, therefore, occasionally seemed to make claims that would neither be historically sustainable in their entirety, nor justifiable in terms of his own theoretical framework. 'Individual freedom and institutional autonomy in the educational and cultural fields were particularly beyond the jurisdiction of the State. The government of Pericles did not dictate what philosophy Plato or Aristotle should teach. In those days, there was no national education. The educational institutions not only of the ancient, but even of medieval times were autonomous.'[40] He went on to suggest that this was not true only of Europe but also of the classical seats of learning in India, like Taxila and Nalanda.[41] At the moment the historical veracity of these claims is not really relevant. What is interesting is that where his theoretical predilections were such as would see nothing but the 'irrational' and the oppressive in the past, especially India's past, there are such odd moments when he seemed to see some value in premodern societies and their ways of being (for instance, the reference to the ways in which needs of 'the community' were taken care of by artisans and peasants, or the relationship of the state to society). He had a very positive assessment of classical Greek antiquity and the spirit of free inquiry in what he called the 'pagan rationalism' of those times. He, in fact, held Christianity squarely responsible for the regression into spiritual slavery of the Church. Before we proceed with his elaboration of radical democracy further, let us register that in the passage cited above there is not only a positive reference to some aspects of pre-modern societies, there is a simultaneous juxtaposition of the pre-national state with the modern nation-state, its reach into everyday lives of all sectors of society and its attempts at homogenization through national education. Michel Foucault's later theorizations of 'governmentality' provide an interesting lens through which to understand the new and modern forms of power that take form in the body of the nation-state. Roy is essentially arguing against such a state, for to him it is much darker than what the idea of 'pastoralism' in the later Foucault suggests. Roy's counterpoint to homogenization, however, is not the pre-modern community but the sovereign individual but as we shall see later on, in a much more complicated way.

Roy was aware that despite his repeated insistence to the contrary, he too would be open to being labelled as a utopian. How else could he argue, in the face of such overwhelming evidence of the 'crisis of modern civilization', that the innate rationality of 'man' would one day assert itself. At one level, his was a normative *project* which, he claimed, could only be realized when the 'modern philosopher-kings' will take charge of the world. These modern philosopher-kings would be the 'spiritually free men' of Reason, detached from any passion for power. He, therefore, posited a politics without power. His modern philosopher-kings would actually have to be people who, while detached from the passion for power, would not be confined to a contemplative life but be centrally concerned with the affairs of the world. At the same time, they had to be philosophers-in-opposition for, they could not really be true to the project defined by him if they linked themselves with any figure of authority, however benevolent and benign it might be. These 'spiritually free men', Roy believed, will function as the 'guides, friends and philosophers of the people, rather than as their would-be rulers'.

It may not be out of place to mention here, that with the collapse of the socialist world and the end of the Old Left imagination, there have been renewed attempts to think through a possible new project of radical democracy. Some of the more explicit articulations of this project have followed the extremely significant intervention of Ernesto Laclau and Chantal Mouffe, first articulated in the mid-1980s, and later continued by Mouffe. Needless to say, these articulations are lodged within a much more uncertain world than the one that Roy lived in. At least theoretically speaking, Laclau and Mouffe made their intervention in a context where the old certitudes of the Telos of History, Progress and Reason had given way. It is also relevant to note that there have been other kinds of articulations in political practice, especially from the country of Roy's political and intellectual 'rebirth', namely Mexico. The legendary revolt in 1994, in the Chiapas mountains, by the Zapatistas, is significant in two respects, in this context. First, there is a conscious effort by the Zapatistas to eschew the 'representational' mode of politics that so troubled Roy.[42] Second, despite the fact that they formed their own army (the EZLN), the Zapatistas have declared that they do not want to 'capture power'. John Holloway's recent book, *Change the World Without Taking Power*, which attempts a theoretical articulation of the Zapatista position, in fact, is a tract that picks up these concerns with representation and power, that animated Roy but in a time and context very different from Roy's own.

One can go further and suggest that much of what is often derisively called 'postmodernism' by its detractors, has been centrally preoccupied in the last few decades with precisely the two concerns mentioned above: representation and power. Jean-Francois Lyotard's well-known call to 'wage war on Totality' as that precise epistemic category, behind which lies concealed the drive towards totalitarianism, and the more generalized critiques of power and the paradigm of sovereignty made by Michel Foucault, resonate with some of the concerns that preoccupied Roy some decades in advance. It is postmodernism's critique and disavowal of the politics of 'taking power' that has in fact made the target of much marxist critiques, especially in the last two decades. Coeval with the philosophical assault of 'postmodernism' on many of the certainties that are so dear to Roy, there is however, another point of convergence: the move away from the large, monumental forms towards a greater attentiveness to the local and the everyday. Here, the philosophical critiques of modernity offered by 'postmodernism' have found important resonance with the new ecological movements that seek to reclaim the local, especially local control over natural resources, thus, throwing into question the very idea of the state's 'eminent domain'. If one were to work through the implications of Roy's own idea of a network of local republics in the present context, one suspects, the idea of such an eminent domain could not remain untouched.

It is also important to register that many of the struggles of the recent past, both in India and in the West, have sought to articulate themselves outside the framework of the party-form as such. As I have discussed in Chapter 5, in India, this phenomenon was noticed by scholars like Rajni Kothari and D L Sheth, and others intellectuals associated with the *Lokayan* initiative, as far back as the early 1980s, and characterized as the non-party political process. Many of these movements have, in fact, even had a local character, though in ways entirely different from the kind visualized by Roy. As we saw in our earlier discussion, these movements represent a search for forms of political action that go beyond the framework of representation, even if in somewhat limited ways.

In this sense, we could say with some justification, that Roy's was a visionary critique of contemporary democratic politics and the problems inherent in the representational framework. In this sense, politically, he was probably able to see far ahead of his times. And yet, in philosophical terms, Roy's move, in this period of his turn away from marxism marks a sort of regression into eighteenth century humanism. In that sense, there is a vast gulf that separates Roy's attempts to articulate a project of radical democracy from the more contemporary attempts to imagine 'another world'.

## The Return to 'Man': The Search for Foundation/s

Even if Roy is a political being, his is a philosophically oriented mind. He is, therefore, not content to merely lay out a normative framework for politics; he must ground it in a first-order Truth. His search for a philosophy that will provide the foundation of his new politics based on the 'sovereignty of the individual' therefore, leads him to a journey into the philosophical world.

Roy, as we said, began his first journey as a nationalist revolutionary political activist in a highly provincial milieu in Bengal and set out from there on an odyssey that took him around the world in different capacities. From being the founder of the first communist party outside the Soviet Union, to being the special emissary of the Comintern to China, his was a life full of adventure on what can only be called the stage of World-History. By the time he came back to India in the 1930s, his horizons had become truly world-historical. From then on, he thought almost entirely in terms of the world as a single entity, and India and the specific trajectory of Indian political history figured in his discourse almost entirely as an episode in the larger world-historical drama. That is why, for instance, when the Second World War began, and Roy and his RDP were the first to support the war, their decision was entirely guided by what he saw as the logic of world-historical developments and at no stage did the specificity of Indian politics and context figure in their assessment. The logic of World-History was to remain his sole point of reference all through his life.

Quite naturally then, once the idea of World-History as a singular entity became embedded in his thought, everything else became a corollary of this recognition. If the world is a single entity, there can at any moment, be only one historical present—and needless to say, that 'present' is elsewhere. All other societies, including Indian society became a relic of the past, struggling to catch up with that present. It was with this belief that Roy launched on his second journey, now through time—philosophical time. Once he reached the realization in his political life that marxism no longer provided the answers to the central question of 'freedom' that he was seeking an answer to, he became restless for an answer. As we have already seen, the fundamental problem that he saw with marxism was that it privileged a collective ego over the sovereign individual and he had already come to believe that it was the individual who was the subject of the freedom he was seeking. He had to urgently find an answer.

It is to seek this answer that Roy, in the period after the dissolution of the RDP, embarks on his philosophical journey through time. We may note, in parenthesis, that as he began his journey, he made some initial attempts at grappling with the Indian philosophical tradition. He recognized that in India 'the Vedic age of natural religion was followed by a period of rational enquiries, fragmentarily recorded in the Upanishads,' out of which arose different systems of philosophy. 'Hindu religion as expounded in the Vedanta and Gita was a later development.'[43] However, he notes that the sequence of these development is not very clear, 'with a good deal of overlapping and many long gaps, because Hinduism is not a revealed religion'. As D C Grover notes, Indian philosophical history too, appeared to Roy as following essentially the same trajectory 'as everywhere else'. As everywhere else, philosophy in India too, was originally materialistic; physics preceded metaphysics. It was the materialist speculations of the rebels against Vedic natural religion, contained in Vaisesika, Sankhya and Nyaya, which provided the inspiration for what Roy considered the 'greatest event' in the history of ancient India—'the Buddhist revolution'.[44] This great philosophical event, according to Roy, was finally overwhelmed by the forces of superstition and Hindu orthodoxy. That was the greatest tragedy that, in a manner of speaking, arrested Indian thought for centuries to come.[45]

These are some fragmentary indications that in the initial period of his quest Roy did make some attempt to inquire into the philosophical traditions of India. But very soon he decided that the actual history of these philosophical systems had yet to be recorded. Hence the next best thing that he could do was to concentrate his energies on Western thought, since thought everywhere, basically followed the same movement. To quote: 'In the present stage of world history, pending the composition of a universal history, the evolution of thought in the western world has to be taken as the general pattern.'[46] Thus, began his new journey and he decided to start 'more than six hundred years before the rise of Christianity' when 'there developed in Greece an intellectual life which had laid the spiritual foundation of modern civilization'.

We need to register at the outset that Roy's decision to extricate the individual from the clutches of the 'collective ego' was a political project, that is, in some sense, a pre-philosophical decision, born out of his aversion to twentieth century totalitarianisms. Even as he began his philosophical sojourn then, he already knew where he wanted to go. He had to reinstate the individual human being at the centre of his philosophy. To that end, he rushes through centuries of philosophical debates like a restless traveller picking and choosing what he wanted, in order to fashion his new politics. His main philosophical work, *Reason, Romanticism and Revolution* is a work that betrays a singular lack of engagement with major philosophical debates and their contexts and in fact puts together a vast range of positions from which he then picks and chooses according to his liking. This search for the sovereign individual and his consequent move away from Marx takes him back to the humanism of seventeenth and eighteenth century Europe. The complex debates on subjectivity that ensued since leave practically no mark, nor cause any anxiety in him. So for instance, Marx's famous assertion in the *Theses on Feuerbach* that the 'human essence is no abstraction inhering in each individual, but the ensemble of social relations' is read by him as a burial of the individual under the social. So, he claims that despite his partially valid criticism of Feuerbach, instead of improving him, Marx actually 'buried Humanism for a long time to come'. His effort to improve upon Feuerbach 'led to the burial of the individual man who was submerged in the collective being of society'.[47] He considers this 'a throwback' as 'modern political theories developed in the seventeenth century, all started from the individual.'[48]

Roy then sets about reclaiming this legacy of humanism. His problem is to find a humanist philosophy that will establish the individual as a moral being. His explorations lead him to the conclusion that 'the tradition of eighteenth century naturalist Humanism and of its development in the nineteenth century alone can inspire a philosophy that will set man free'. He calls this philosophy, now recast by him, New Humanism: 'new because it is scientific and integral; because it conceives human sovereignty not as a differentiation from the mechanistic processes of nature, but as their highest product'.[49] His problem with the 'former conception of the sovereignty of man' of both 'classical as well as romantic Humanism' is that it 'logically leads to two alternative conceptions: one is the doctrine of free will; and the other is the old Stoic faith taken over by Christianity, that man is a moral entity *because* through his soul he is in unison with the universal moral order'. While the latter is logically sound, if one grants its premises, he believes it is unable to serve as a foundation for a revolutionary social philosophy, since in the last analysis, 'man's' sovereignty here is 'derived from a greater or higher power', which essentially means that 'he' is not really sovereign. The former, that is, the doctrine of the free will, on the other hand, is perpetually caught is the riddle of deriving the *ought* from the *is*. Imperceptibly, says Roy, this conception converges towards transcendentalism.[50]

The fundamental problem of moral philosophy, he felt, was of deducing values from facts, as it was felt that there was no causal connection between ethical values and the world of science. The additional problem with the doctrine of free will was that such a conception atomizes the individual and precludes the possibility of social organization, cooperation and harmony in human relations.[51] Here we see a glimpse of the other aspect of his search. Merely to reinstate the sovereign individual through the doctrine of free will does not seem to provide a ground for understanding the moral being of the individual. This moral being cannot be, then, the self-seeking bourgeois individual but must situate herself in some 'community'.

Roy's answer to this problem is devastatingly simple. The only alternative is to ground moral philosophy down to 'the entire process of *prehuman biological evolution*'. 'An appeal to his animal ancestry will yield more satisfactory result.'[52] The mystery of man, he claims, has been solved by modern biology. This unbelievable move, is accomplished by Roy by referring back to the idea of the 'law-governed universe'—the Ontic Logos, as Charles Taylor would call it—where the biological evolution of 'man' is but the extension of the cosmic mechanism. 'Man's rationality and moral sense, which are causally connected, are the expression of cosmic harmony. Therefore, it is in the *nature of man*, as a biological organism, to be rational and moral, and as such he is capable of living with others in peace and harmony.'[53] So, with his New Humanism, we are back to the idea of the Essence of Man, with one small, though not unimportant modification that this Essence is now not distinct from the Universe or Nature. Man becomes a part of Nature. In this way, by insisting on a 'materialist monism', Roy does attempt to break free of the ontological dualism between the Subject (Man) and the Object (Nature), that grounds modern post-Cartesian epistemology, but remains caught nevertheless within the foundationalism so pervasive in his times. In actual practice, though, even the apparent dissolution of dualism does not really seem to work, caught as Roy himself remains within the representational mode, epistemologically speaking. Nowhere does Roy attempt to chart out a different epistemological position from the subject-centred ones that Heidegger called 'metaphysics' where the world is always represented to the subject from the position of the subject. At this stage, it might also be useful to refer back to Marx's sixth thesis, which Roy attempts to dismantle. Marx's point in this critique, as we know, was to interrogate precisely this notion of the Essence of Man. Thus, he began by stating that Feuerbach resolves the 'essence of religion' into the 'essence of man'. However, because Feuerbach does not recognize that the essence of man is no abstraction inhering in each individual but 'the ensemble of social relations', he is content to therefore focus his attention on the abstract individual. He cannot really explain why religious sentiment comes to hold such a sway over human beings. Unable to historicize religion, he is constrained to deal with it as a self-contained entity. Thus, in the seventh thesis, he asserts that this is why Feuerbach cannot see the 'religious sentiment' itself as a social product and the individual too, as belonging to a particular historical social form. Hence Marx's claim that 'social being determines consciousness'. One can legitimately quarrel with Marx on the precise meaning of 'social being': can it be reduced to the 'mode of production'? Or, can it be understood as some other version of the 'structure' as structuralists would later argue? Or, can it be even further recast as the discursive or linguistic constitution of the human world, a social world of practices constituted through the complex play of meanings, as poststructuralism would claim?

Whatever, be the case, in a sense, through this intervention Marx is able to displace the question of the 'essence of man' from the realms of speculative philosophy to the terrain of history and provide a way of understanding the actual so-called 'irrationality' of 'real-empirical' human beings. The fundamental question involved here, as we know is as old as humanism itself. What is this Essence of Man? Clearly 'Man' here does not refer to the real-empirical human beings, for they are precisely what Roy's project of social transformation (or the Enlightenment project) wants to change. They are the human beings who are today mired in 'irrationality' and 'tradition'. The 'Man' here then, refers to some Real Essence. The problems with such a conception are only too well-known today. In the first place, they do not really take us beyond a metaphysical notion of the Real Essence, whose 'reality' remains untouched by the 'corruptions' of the empirical-real. In the second place, such a notion of Essence of Man requires that there are at least some people who know 'its Reality', who then become the agents of Enlightenment. It is this notion that lies at the root of the pedagogic mission of 'making people aware' of their 'real nature'.

In Roy's specific construction, it is an Essence whose reality, as part of a law-governed universe, can only be derived from the laws of the Universe itself. If we were to stretch the implications of this proposition to its logical end, we would then have to assume that the human world too, is as rationally law-governed as the natural world. This is where the problem of human volition presents itself before Roy. If human society is really law-governed, can human beings really do anything to change it? He however, does not enter into the question in all its ramifications. He merely posits an idea of a determinism that subsumes 'human intelligence': 'But just as in nature, there are more than one determining factor in history. Human intelligence is one of them . . . . The logical development of ideas and the generation of new social forces take place *simultaneously*, together providing the motive force of history.'[54] He acknowledges that philosophy has its own independent logic and cannot be reduced to an expression of any 'class interest' or the interest of any other social force. Nonetheless, he must still retain a close, largely unspecified, organic connection between the 'new social forces' and 'new ideas', since without recourse to this, the attempt to subsume human intelligence in the 'law-governed-ness' of society, while retaining a sense of human volition, cannot be sustained. It might be interesting to contrast this position with say Louis Althusser's attempts in the late 1960s, to argue on the contrary, that the time of philosophy, punctuated by its own specific rhythms, is irreducible in principle to the time of politics or the time of the economy. Althusser was led, in the course of his investigations into the different levels (economy, politics, philosophy, etc.) to recognize that the relationships between these different levels were *essentially relations of dislocation*. In other words, there was no correspondence between the specific histories of these levels: 'the lonely hour of the last instance never arrives'. Where Althusser, despite his marxism, sees dislocation, Roy must hold on to relations of correspondence. It is in this context, that it becomes important for Roy to continuously assert that the will to change the world is fundamental to determinism in the social world. It is in this context too that his connection with romanticism is established. 'The passionate belief in the creativeness and freedom of man is the essence of the romantic view of life. The idea of revolution is therefore, a romantic idea.'[55] This problem of reconciling determinism with volition remains one of the key difficulties in Roy's exposition of his philosophy.

Determinism, however, is not the only problem with Roy's attempt to replace post-Cartesian dualism by monism. In the absence of an alternative account of epistemology, his method remains almost entirely lodged within the subject-centred representational framework. This, along with his recourse to the idea of the Essence of Man, leaves his philosophical position well within the humanist tradition that sought to enthrone Man as the new God.

In his comment on post-War French philosophy, especially as represented by Sartre, Derrida points out, even though the concept of history is quite pervasive, 'there is little practice of the *history of concepts*' and the history of the concept of man is never examined. 'Everything occurs as if the sign 'man' had no origin, no historical, cultural or linguistic limit.'[56] Much of that ahistorical notion of 'man', torn from all context/s is evident in the philosophy that Roy attempts to expound. And as Derrida further points out, this 'unexamined concept of "Man"', named in an allegedly neutral and undetermined way, something that was 'nothing other than the metaphysical unity of man and God, the relation of man to God, *the project of becoming God* as the project constituting human-reality'. In this new philosophical anthropology [of Sartre, for instance], he suggests, '[A] theism changes nothing in this fundamental structure' and that in this respect, humanism or anthropologism was the common ground of Christian and atheist existentialisms.[57]

We need not delve any further here on the metaphysics of Man and the profound philosophical discussions that have occurred around it. In fact, in concluding this chapter, I would like to suggest that a critique of this metaphysics (philosophical humanism or anthropologism) does not necessarily imply the end of the political task that renaissance humanism or the humanism of Roy seeks to put forward. In fact, taking the cue from Antonio Negri and Michael Hardt, we might ask what would humanism be after the philosophical 'death of Man'? The critical question here is to resist the temptation of grounding politics, that is contingency par excellence, in any foundational Truth. For, that Truth, if one were to paraphrase Gandhi, is not available to anybody; we all live with partial truths and it is the politics of Truth that often becomes the carrier of new forms of totalitarianism that was so centrally of concern to Roy.

## NOTES

1. This chapter was written in 2004, the fiftieth anniversary year of Roy's death as a separate paper for the conference 'Reconstructing Democratic Concerns in Modern India', organized by Lokniti, CSDS. I have dedicated this paper/chapter to my father, R L Nigam, a life-long Royist who might have liked to read this, even while disagreeing.

2. Jacques Derrida, *Spectres of Marx*, New York and London: Routledge, 1994, p. 102.

3. M Shiviah *New Humanism and Democratic Politics—A Study of M N Roy's Theory of the State*, Bombay: Popular Prakashan, 1977, p. 91 and D C Grover

*M N Roy: A Study of Revolution and Reason in Indian Politics*, Calcutta: The Minerva Associates, 1973, pp. 66-73.

4. Ibid., p. 166.
5. Sudipta Kaviraj, 'The Heteronomous Radicalism of M N Roy', in *Political Thought in Modern India* ed. Thomas Pantham and Kenneth L. Deutsch, New Delhi and London: Sage Publication, 1986, p. 226.
6. Ibid., pp. 226-7.
7. M N Roy, *Memoirs*, Delhi: Ajanta Publications, 1984, p. 59.
8. Ibid., p. 27.
9. Ibid., pp. 2-3.
10. Ibid., p. 10.
11. M N Roy, *Politics, Power and Parties*, Delhi: Ajanta Publications, 1981, p. 23.
12. Ibid., p. 22.
13. Ibid., pp. 19-20.
14. Ibid., p. 19.
15. Ibid., p. 19.
16. Ibid., p. 77, emphasis added.
17. Ibid., p. 53.
18. Ibid., p. 76.
19. Ibid., p. 53.
20. Ibid., p. 56.
21. Ibid., p. 51.
22. Cited in Peter Gay's 'Introduction' to Ernst Cassirer, *The Question of Jean-Jacques Rousseau*, New Haven and London: Yale University Press, 1989, p. 28.
23. Ibid., p. 51.
24. Carl Schmitt, *The Crisis of Parliamentary Democracy*, Cambridge, Massachusetts and London: The MIT Press, 1992, p. 28.
25. Ibid., p. 28.
26. Ibid., p. 29, emphasis added.

27. Ibid., p. 6.

28. Jurgen Habermas, *The Structural Transformation of the Public Sphere—An Inquiry into a Category of Bourgeois Society*, Cambridge: Polity Press, 1994. See especially, p. 204-7.

29. Roy, *Politics, Power and Parties*, p. 59.

30. Roy, ibid., p. 59.

31. Ibid., p. 59.

32. Ibid., pp. 50-60.

33. Ibid., pp. 60-1.

34. Grover op. cit., p. 70. Grover cites JP's own tract *Socialism, Sarvodaya and Democracy*, Bombay: Asia Publishing House, 1964, to substantiate his claim.

35. Ibid., p. 71.

36. Niranjan Dhar, *The Political Thought of M N Roy, 1936–1954*, Calcutta: Eureka Publishers, 1966, p. 164.

37. Ibid., p. 81.

38. Ibid., p. 84.

39. Ibid., p. 74.

40. Ibid., p. 75.

41. Ibid., p. 75.

42. The Zapatista eschewal of 'representational' politics goes much further beyond pure 'political representation' in the electoral sense. However that is a separate discussion and need not detain us here.

43. M N Roy, *Reason, Romanticism and Revolution*, Delhi: Ajanta Publications, 1989, p. 23.

44. D C Grover, *M N Roy: A Study of Revolution and Reason in Indian Politics*, Calcutta: The Minerva Associates, 1973, p. 103.

45. Ibid., p. 106.

46. Ibid., p. 23.

47. Roy, *Politics, Power and Parties*, p. 105.

48. Ibid., 106.

49. Roy, *Reason, Romanticism and Revolution*, p. 490.
50. Ibid. This part of the discussion is based largely on the chapter 'New Humanism' in this work.
51. Ibid., p. 491.
52. Ibid., p. 491.
53. Ibid., p. 492.
54. Ibid., p. 10.
55. Ibid., p. 11.
56. Jacques Derrida, *Margins of Philosophy*, Brighton: The Harvester Press, 1982, p. 116.
57. Ibid., p. 116.

# CONCLUSION
## Reflections on the Future of the Planet

I began my discussion in the 'Introduction' with the crisis of the party-form. This form has run into crisis as the old style of modern politics, based on large, abstract categories of mobilization and representation like 'class', 'people' and 'nation' seem to have increasingly less purchase on contemporary radical politics. They seem to be giving way at least on the Left to new forms that are more coalitional in nature and incorporate a range of social movements in their fold. Already in these new kinds of Left-wing formations we can see a very significant presence of ecological movements, feminists, anti-war and anti-nuclear movements—all pointing towards a decentring of political agendas. In Chapter 1, I discussed the question of identity and the question of different worlds and different languages and the problems they pose before the radical project. I have also discussed 'Time' and the significance of supposedly non-modern modes of living as significant living presences within our contemporary. This concern recurs in Chapter 2, especially through the discussion of the question of industrialization as well as of Marx's encounter with the Russian peasant communes as possible bases for a future socialist society. Chapter 5 returns to these questions in the context of social movements and crisis of high-modernism, pointing repeatedly towards smaller, local, alternative experiments—both in politics as well as in 'constructive work'. The concerns of Chapter 3 and 4, with the virtual impossibility of a 'single front' against the 'Big Enemy' and with what I have called the 'opportunism of minority cultures', point towards the need to think of alternative political forms that are radically open and locally grounded. Through a discussion of M N Roy's notion of 'radical democracy', Chapter 7 then discusses a possible form that was proposed through the experience of marxist practice itself. Here the possible links of Roy's notion of radical democracy with more recent articulations by other theorists as well as the experience of radical movements has also been explored. In a sense, all these explorations, most of them emerging from within the world of marxist practice, push us relentlessly in the direction of thinking seriously about decentred political, economic and social forms as alternatives to 'the gigantic', the 'monumental', and therefore centralizing imaginary of high-modernism that has ruled radical imagination till now. What I have not explicitly discussed but which is silently at work through these discussions, is the question of the ecological crisis.

In a manner of speaking, one of the concerns that has been at work throughout this book, is the question of the ecological crisis and what looks like the imminent doom of planet Earth. No longer is this a panic-mongering prophesy of 'eco-loonies'. It is now official. As the first decade of the twenty-first century rolls by, it is clear that our planet is living on borrowed time. Global warming, climate change, the energy crisis and most recently the unprecedented global food crisis—all this shows that we might well be heading towards self-destruction.

Of course, as I have been arguing throughout this book, nothing is really inevitable. Nor is this scenario—provided, of course, we act while there is still time. The question is, will we? And how can we? There has been a growing sense among ecologically sensitive marxists that this threat to the existence of the planet is a direct consequence of the logic of capitalist accumulation and greed. My argument in this book has, on the contrary, attempted to hint at another possibility. I have been arguing that there is really no such thing as the 'logic of capital' that acts independently of 'the state', or takes hold of the state (the bourgeois state, that is). I have been trying to suggest that it is the modern state—whether bourgeois or socialist—that produces capitalism as the only way of being modern. Let me now suggest that this role of the state—the governmentalized state, to borrow from Foucault—is directly linked to a whole range of knowledges and technologies produced by it. Its logic of governmentality frames our understanding in ways that make it impossible to think of any other way of being, as legitimate. For this logic requires that 'the state' enter the deepest recesses of society, take charge of its population and its 'welfare'—health, education, and so on; it requires that it relentlessly enumerate, calculate, fix property rights, raise taxes and revenue and such other things. The governmental activities of the state do not consist merely of one-sided functions of 'welfare'; they must continuously produce the economy as such, so that its revenues are ensured. And for this it has at its disposal a whole range of disciplines—economics, law, environmental sciences, geology, and a whole range of apparatuses to put these knowledges to work by relentlessly producing the 'good citizen' (essentially the tax-payer, the owner of bourgeois property, at least in its juridical form).

That is why, I have argued in Chapter 2, capitalist development did not take place spontaneously everywhere; that in most parts of the world it was implanted by the state, often the colonial state. Where there was no bourgeoisie, the state created one. And despite this, there are large parts of the world where this bourgeois way is not the 'most natural' way people live, even today. If any further proof is required of how the logic of modern statecraft drives this capitalist logic, one only has to look at neighbouring Nepal. This erstwhile kingdom, just through with over a decade-long Maoist insurgency, has now voted the Maoists into power in the recent elections. In what can only be understood as some kind of 'reflex action', the top Maoist leadership and chairman Prachanda himself, assured the bourgeoisie and the Federation of Nepal Chamber of Commerce and Industry, that the 'CPN-Maoist will work with the private sector to create a friendly environment for foreign investment aimed at facilitating economic development in the country.'[1] With this, Nepal joins the wide array of other Leftist regimes engaged in building capitalism—often of the most vicious and predatory kind. Part of this mindset, I have tried to suggest, is the result of conflating all private entrepreneurship, production, trade and exchange with 'capitalism' and of seeing capitalism as the 'highest development' of such local and molecular 'economies'. Under the able leadership of the Leftists, such economies will be brought under the scanner of the state, made accountable to its logic of accounting and forcibly integrated into the world market. It is this vision that makes the marxist chief minister of West Bengal see the 'End of History' in the 'fettered accumulation' of earlier times and propels him to push the economy on to the high road of 'global capitalism'.

I recall a brief argument with an economist friend, soon after the violent events in Nandigram, West Bengal. She tried to convince me that the real problem was that the West Bengal government did not give proper and adequate compensation. Otherwise, as an economic historian, she went on to assert, 'I can say that this is the historical trend all over the world. Not more than five per cent of the production in advanced economies comes from agriculture.' That this is an unquestioned article of faith in the discipline is also evident from Nobel Laureate Amartya Sen's spirited defence of industrialization (in West Bengal): 'It is not surprising that no substantial country ever has crossed the barrier of poverty without very substantial industrialization. If the need for an industrial base and the corresponding skills applies to all countries in the world (as I believe it does), it has a particularly strong relevance to Bengal . . . .' (Sen 2007). Sen identifies two groups of people who stand opposed to industrialization. The first, whom he refers to as the 'politically determined' is, of course, easily dismissed. Of the other, he says:

> The second group of opponents . . . would not want to take land away from agricultural use. There are some genuine 'physiocrats' among this group, with agriculture-fetishism and a strong belief in the unparalleled—almost mystical—merits of agriculture. Their arguments were adequately rebutted about 200 years ago, and *if life has ceased to be quite as 'nasty, brutish and short' as Thomas Hobbes found it, the contribution of industrial development to that change would be hard to overlook* (Ibid., emphasis added).

That is quite neatly put. Professor Sen is not a capitalist ideologue. He is an economist utterly committed to state intervention to end poverty. It is hardly a coincidence, therefore, that he seems not to have heard of arguments against frenetic industrialization since the physiocrats. He is oblivious of the powerful ecological arguments being made in recent decades, not to speak of Gandhi's scathing critique of industrial civilization. It is unlikely though that Professor Sen has not heard of these critiques; rather he seems to consider them to be coming from some long-extinct species, not worthy therefore of being addressed.

Let us, therefore, restate some of the issues and place them on the table once more. First, a critique of industrialization need not mean a romantic fetishization of agriculture. There are undoubtedly many romantics—Gandhi was certainly one of them—who believe in the virtues of such a life close to nature. However, that is not the only argument being made here. Not all critics of industrialization would argue that all industrialization is bad, always. Most critics would in fact underline the need for a balance such that the growth of industry is not predicated either on the decimation of agriculture or of the environment. It is not difficult to see that so long as we are caught in the race to 'excel' in terms of the standards set by the industrialized countries, we cannot even begin to think of alternatives. A delinking from what I have called the time of the global is thus a precondition for thinking afresh about different ways of being.

Apart from the well-known questions of carbon emissions, water pollution and overall destruction of the environment leading to climate change, the world is also increasingly becoming aware that Professor Sen's utopia has run against a wall. It is clear that all the polluting and destructive industries are moving out of the First World to the peripheries of Asia and Africa, not out of the spirit of world exploration but for other more complex reasons. It is no longer only cheap labour that they seek; they also want an environment they can milk dry. These they cannot get in their home countries any more, for there they are answerable to the local communities and do not enjoy the impunity that they have in Asian or African countries. Most postcolonial governments have bought into Professor Sen's Industrial Utopia as never before. Countries in these parts of the world are not only desperately playing host to industries relocating from the Western capitalist countries but have also put 'their own' capitalist class into the race.

Consider this: The Indonesian government reportedly signed a deal with China that is expected to wipe out large parts of the tropical forests—the lungs of Southeast Asia. The wood from the forest is to go into meeting the flooring and furniture needs of China's ever-expanding middle class, while the space cleared by the forests will be used to grow palm oil plantations—palm oil being an important ingredient in detergents, soaps and lipstick (Perlez 2006: A1). This same report goes on to say: 'From Indonesia to Malaysia to Myanmar, many of the once plentiful forests of Southeast Asia are already gone, stripped legally or illegally . . . .'

According to another report, at the global level, 'three million out of 18 million hectares of mangroves have been lost during the 1990s on account of facilitating settlements, tourism, industrial construction and aquaculture'.[2]

Now consider the fact that a recent research study on the impact of the deadly tsunami that hit many Asian countries in December 2004, published in the journal *Science*, found that the damage was maximum in areas where mangrove forests had been cleared. The evidence from satellite pictures suggests that this was so along the coastline of five Asian countries including India and that villages located behind mangroves suffered minimal damage.[3]

If this is the picture of a small part of the damage done to forests, which themselves constitute a miniscule part of the overall environment, the picture with regard to the current global food crisis is no less frightening. Already by November 2007, reports stated that:

> Record world prices for most staple foods have led to 18% food price inflation in China, 13% in Indonesia and Pakistan, and 10% or more in Latin America, Russia and India, according to the UN Food and Agricultural Organisation (FAO). Wheat has doubled in price, maize is nearly 50% higher than a year ago and rice is 20% more expensive, says the UN. Next week the FAO is expected to say that global food reserves are at their lowest in 25 years and that prices will remain high for years.[4]

Things have rapidly deteriorated since with violence erupting in different parts of the world and food price inflation having gone completely out of control. The world price of rice has risen by 68 per cent in the last few months (from the beginning of 2008 to April 2008).[5] It is no longer the poverty stricken states of Africa or Latin America that are facing the impact of the crisis; food is disappearing from American food stores like Wal-Mart, as well.[6]

Much is being made of the changing consumption and demand patterns in India and China, with their newly affluent middle class, in order to explain this sudden spurt in food prices. However, that may be only a small part of a longer term story. If my economic historian friend is correct and it is the mark of economic progress that agriculture should be decimated, then we are probably on the right track. The more affluent middle classes with global consumption levels there are in India and China, the less of food production there should be. For the expansion of the middle classes presumes industrialization which, in turn, is supposed to be predicated upon the increasing marginalization of agriculture. But there is also another side to the story of food shortages that explains the suddenness of the change. A press release from the National Farmers' Union of Canada (NFUC) stated as early as on 11 May 2007, 'An increasing push to divert food supplies into biofuels means that we are in the opening phase of an intensifying food shortage.'[7]

While we may want to continue to believe that the current crisis is just a passing phase or even possibly a result of some long term trend which can be fixed with technological manipulations, the writing on the wall seems pretty clear. Thus, according to a report in *The Guardian*, Lester Brown, founder of the Washington-based Worldwatch Institute think-tank, went on record saying: 'The competition for grain between the world's 800 million motorists, who want to maintain their mobility, and its 2 billion poorest people, who are simply trying to survive, is emerging as an epic issue.'[8] Brown went on to say that in 2006, 'US farmers distorted the world market for cereals by growing 14m tonnes, or 20% of the whole maize crop, for ethanol for vehicles. This took millions of hectares of land out of food production and nearly doubled the price of maize.'[9]

So that is the solution to the energy crisis. We can in fact go on piling evidence upon evidence of the sheer perversity of the 'solution' to the energy crisis that the world is faced with. The more we think of solutions to our current crises, the more perverse we seem to get. We might of course want to differ with Brown's assessment that this is necessarily a result of 'market distortion'. It is, in fact, a perfectly market determined scenario: move your investments to where there is greater and quicker profit.

I do not wish to labour the point any further. It seems to be abundantly clear that unless we act now, there appears to be no future for the planet Earth. It might be argued in a situation like this, that such decisive action is inconceivable without the state. There might even be people who would see in this situation a further justification for the 'capture of state power'. However, if my argument is correct, it matters little whether power is captured through armed struggle or the ballot, for as long as alternatives are not thought through, every new regime is destined to repeat the practices of the old. If we are serious about changing this state of affairs, we have to make attempts to build alternatives now; we have to work on them in a molecular fashion—in all the pores of society—drawing upon the innumerable forms of shared economies that exist in everyday life. Needless to say, such alternatives must be built upon an altogether different culture of a need-based economy and lifestyles.

However, the struggle against the depredations of capital takes place in extremely complex circumstances today. As our discussion in Chapter 6 shows, and any number of instances from the world of the poorest and most oppressed show, consumption is one of the important domains where the symbolic battle for equality is being fought. As newer, hitherto excluded sections enter the market, consumption practices themselves become an arena of claim-making. It is, therefore, not very easy to sell the idea of ecologically sustainable life-styles to people who are just about entering the world of the global market. A new politics of the Left, it seems, must take into account these different arena and forms of contestation and cultural resistance and attempt therefore, to spell out a mode of doing politics that moves away, decisively, from the pious and ascetic mode. It must realize, even while carrying on the struggle against capital, that all consumption, pleasure and enjoyment are not an affirmation of capitalism.

## NOTES

1. See PTI/NDTV report. http://www.ndtv.co CyberLink PowerDVD m/convergence/ndtv/story.aspx?id=NEWEN20080047722

2. 'Saving lives with mangroves', editorial, *The Hindu*, 28 December 2005.

3. Ibid.

4. 'Global food crisis looms as climate change and fuel shortages bite', report in *The Guardian*, 3 November 2007, http://www.guardian.co.uk/environment/2007/nov/03/food.climatechange

5. 'Panic as global food crisis reaches America', *The Hindu*, International section, 25 April 2008.

6. Ibid.

7. 'A Global Food Crisis is Emerging', report posted by Steve Welzer on *Green Horizon*, http://www.green-horizon.org/blog/archives/sustainability/global_food_cri.shtml

8. 'Global Food Crisis . . . ', *The Guardian*, see note 4.

9. Ibid.

# BIBLIOGRAPHY


Abers, Rebecca, 'Practicing Radical Democracy—Lessons From Brazil' http://www.orl.arch.ethz.ch/disp/pdf/147/147_5.pdf, 2001.

Alam, Javeed, *India: Living with Modernity*, Delhi: OUP, 1999.

——— 'Communist Politics in Search of Hegemony', in *Parties and Party Politics in India*, ed. Zoya Hasan, New Delhi, New York: OUP, 2002, pp. 289–316.

Al-Azmeh, Aziz, *Islams and Modernities*, London and New York: Verso, 1993.

Althusser Louis, *For Marx*, London: Allen Lane, The Penguin Press. 1969.

——— 'Ideology and Ideological State Apparatuses (Notes Towards and Investigation)', in Mapping Ideology, ed. Slavoj Zizek, London and New York: Verso, 1994, pp. 100–140.

——— *The Philosophy of Encounter: Later Writings, 1978–1987*, London and New York: Verso, 2006.

Althusser, Louis and Balibar, Etienne, *Reading Capital*, London: New Left Books, 1977.

Amin, Samir 'Social Movements in the Periphery', in *New Social Movements in the South: Empowering the People,* ed. Ponna Wignaraja, New Delhi: Vistaar Publications, 1993.

Amin, Shahid 'The Tenable Patriot', *The Hindu*, 3 December 2006, http://www.hinduonnet.com/thehindu/thscrip/print.pl?

file=20061203000401OO.htm&date=2006/12/03/&prd=mag&, last accessed on 27 April 2008.

Amsden, Alice H, 'Third World Industrialization: Global Fordism or a New Model?', *New Left Review*, 182, July–August 1990, pp. 19–25.

Anderson, Benedict, *Imagined Communities*, London and New York: Verso, 1991.

Appadurai, Arjun, 'Patriotism and Its Futures', *Public Culture*, vol. 5, no. 3, Spring 1993, pp. 411–29.

Archibugi, Daniele, David Held and Martin Kohler, *Re-imagining Political Community—Studies on Cosmopolitan Democracy*, London: Polity Press, 1998.

Baiocchi, Gainpolo, *Radicals in Power: The Workers' Party (PT) and Experiments on Urban Democracy in Brazil*, London and New York: Zed Books Ltd, 2003.

Bakshi, Rajni, *The Long Haul—The Bombay Textile Workers' Strike*, Build Documentation Centre, Bombay, 1986.

Balibar, Etienne, *Masses, Classes, Ideas: Studies in Politics and Philosophy Before and After Marx*, New York and London: Routledge, 1994.

Baruah, Sanjib *India Against Itself—Assam and the Politics of Nationality*, Delhi: OUP, 1999.

Basavapunnaiah, M, 'On Para 112 of Our Party Programme', *The Marxist*, vol. 3, no. 1, January–March, (1985) pp. 28-41.

——— 'The Statement of Policy Reviewed', *The Marxist*, vol. 3, Nos. 3–4, July–December, (1985) pp. 24–83.

Barber, Benjamin, *Jihad vs McWorld—How Globalism and Tribalism Are Reshaping the World*, New York: Ballantine Books, 1996.

Basu, Amrita (2002), 'Parliamentary Communism as a Historical Phenomenon: The CPI(M) in West Bengal', in Parties and Party Polities in India, ed. Zoya Hesan, New Delhi, New York: OUP, 2002, pp. 317–50.

Bauman, Zygmunt, *Postmodern Ethics*, Oxford and Cambridge: Blackwell, 1999.

Bayly, C A, *Origins of Nationality in South Asia—Patriotism and Ethical Government in the Making of Modern India*, Delhi: OUP, 1998.

Behar, Amitabh, 'Peoples' Social Movements: An Alternative Perspective on Forest Management in India', Draft Working Paper, Overseas Development Institute, London, 2002, http://www.odi.uk/livelihoodoptions/papers/draft%20177.pdf, downloaded 9 February 2005.

Beth, Sarah, 'Taking to the Streets: Dalit *Mela* and the Public Performance of Dalit Cultural Identity', *Contemporary South Asia*, vol. 14, no. 4, December 2005, pp. 397–410.

Bhattacharya, Buddhadeb, 'Thousands of young people want jobs . . . they will shape the country's future', *Indian Express*, 19 January 2007, p. 11.

Braudel, Fernand, *Civilization and Capitalism, 15th–18th Century, vol. II: The Wheels of Commerce*, London: Fontana Press, 1982.

Brittan, Samuel, 'Globalisation depresses western wages', http://dictionary.reference.com/browse/oxymoron, accessed on 9 November 2006.

Calhoun, Craig, *The Question of Class Struggle*, Chicago: The University of Chicago Press, 1982.

Candland, Christopher, 'New Social and New Political Unionism: Labour, Industry and the State in India and Pakistan', *Global Solidarity Dialogue*, http://www.antena.nl/~waterman/candland.html, downloaded on 18 February 2005.

Cassirer, Ernst, *The Question of Jean-Jacques Rousseau*, New Haven and London: Yale University Press, 1989.

Castaneda, Jorge G, *Utopia Unarmed—The Latin American Left After the Cold War*, New York: Vintage Books, 1993.

Castells, Manuel, *The Rise of Network Society. The Information Age: Economy, Society and Culture, vol. I*, Oxford: Blackwell Publishers, 2000.

Centre for Education and Communication [CEC], *On a Rainbow in the Sky: The Chattisgarh Mukti Morcha*, New Delhi: CEC, 1998.

——*Social Clause in Multilateral Trade Agreements (A Dossier on Social Clause)*, New Delhi: CEC, 1996.

Chakrabarty, Dipesh, 'Clothing the Political Man: A Reading of the Use of Khadi/White in Indian Public Life', *Postcolonial Studies*, vol. 4, no. 1, 2001, pp. 27–38.

Chalcraft, John T, *Radical History Review*, issue 91, Winter 2005, pp. 13–39.

Chandra, Bipan, *The Rise and Growth of Economic Nationalism in India*, New Delhi: People's Publishing House, 1966.

Chatterjee, Partha, 'Beyond the Nation? Or Within' in *Civil Society and Democracy—A Reader*, ed. Carolyn M. Elliott, OUP, 2003.

Chauhan, Surajpal, *Tiraskrit*, Delhi: Vani Prakashan, 2002.

Communist Party of India (Marxist), *People's Democracy*, vol. XVIII, no. 49 New Delhi: 4 December 1994.

Cowie, Jefferson and Joseph Heathcott (eds.), *Beyond the Ruins: The Meaning of Deindustrialization*, Ithaca and London: ILR Press (An Imprint of Cornell University Press), 2003.

Ci, Jiwei, *Dialectic of the Chinese Revolution*, Stanford California: Stanford University Press, 1994.

CNN report 'Bake sales used to protest affirmative action', 24 December 2003, http://www.cnn.com/2003/us/west/12/24/affirmative.bake.sale.ap/, accessed 27 April 2008.

Dasgupta, Rajarshi, 'Rhyming Revolution: Marxism and Culture in Colonial Bengal', *Studies in History*, no. 21, 2005, pp. 79–98.

Delhi Janwadi Adhikar Manch, *The Order That Felled the City*, Delhi: DJAM, 1997.

——*How Many Errors Does Time Have Patience For? Industrial Closures and Slum Demolitions in Delhi*, Delhi: DJAM, 2001.

Derrida, Jacques, *Of Grammatology*, tr. Gayatri Chakravorty Spivak, Baltimore and London: Johns Hopkins University Press, 1976.

——*Margins of Philosophy*, Brighton: The Harvester Press, 1982.

——— *Spectres of Marx*, New York and London: Routledge, 1994.

Dhanagre, D N 'Action Groups and Social Transformation in India', *Lokayan Bulletin*, vol. 6, no. 5, 1988, pp. 37–59.

Dhar, Niranjan, *The Political Thought of M N Roy, 1936–1954*, Calcutta: Eureka Publishers, 1966.

D'Monte, Darryl '"Green" at the Grassroots', *Seminar*, 355, March 1989, pp. 16–20.

Dobbs, Lou, *Exporting America: Why Corporate Greed Is Shipping American Jobs Overseas*, New York and Boston: Warner Business Books, 2004.

Dubey, Abhay Kumar, *Kranti ka Atma Sangharsh: Naxalvaadi Andolan ke Badalte Chehre ka Adhyayan*, Delhi: Vinay Prakashan, 1994.

Eagleton, Terry, 'Utopia and Its Opposites', in *Necessary and unnecessary Utopias, Socialist Register 2000.*

Eldridge, Philip and Nil Ratan, 'Voluntary Organizations and Popular Movements in Bihar', *Lokayan Bulletin*, vol. 6, no. 4, 1988, pp. 3-44.

Eley, Geoff and Ronald Grigor Suny, *Becoming National—A Reader*, New York and Oxford: OUP, 1996.

Esteva, Gustavo and Madhu Suri Prakash, 'Re-Routing and Re-Rooting Grassroots Initiatives: Escaping the Impasse of Sustainable Development for the Narmada', *Lokayan Bulletin*, May–August 1991, vol. 9, nos 3-4, pp. 113-25.

Fabian, Johannes, *Time and the Other—How Anthropology Makes Its Object*, New York: Columbia University Press, 1983.

Farrer, Linden 'World Forum Movement: Abandon or Contaminate', http://www.nadir.org/nadir/initiativ/agp/free/wsf/worldforum.htm.

Foucault, Michel, 'Of Other Spaces—Heterotopias', 1967, p. 2 http://foucault.info/heteroTopia/foucault.heteroTopia.en.html, downloaded on 15 March 2006.

Fox, Jonathan, 'Has Brazil Moved Toward State Capitalism?', *Latin American Perspectives*, vol. 7, no. 1, Winter 1980.

Fraser, Nancy, 'Rethinking Recognition', *New Left Review*, May–June 2000, pp. 107–19.

Gandhi, Nandita, 'The Emergence of Autonomous Women's Groups', *Lokayan Bulletin*, May–August 1991, vol. 9, nos. 3-4, 1986, pp. 113-25.

Ghosh, Anjan, 'Civil Liberties, Uncivil State', *Seminar*, 355, March 1989, pp. 34-37.

Gibson-Graham, J K, *The End of Capitalism (As We Knew It): A Feminist Critique of Political Economy*, Minneapolis and London: University of Minnesota Press, 2006.

Godbole, Girija and Vira, Bhaskar, 'Towards an Alternative Politics: People's Movements Join the Electoral Process' 2004, http://www.infochangeindia.org/features161.jsp, downloaded on 9 June 2005.

Gohain, Hiren (1980a), 'Count-Down in Assam' *EPW*, vol. XV, no. 21, 24 May 1980.

——— (1980b), 'Tangle Jargonized' *EPW*, vol. XV, no. 32, 9 Aug 1980.

Gombin, Richard, *The Radical Tradition—A Study in Modern Revolutionary Thought*, London: Methuen, 1978.

Gopinath, Vrinda, 'Happy Birthday Lord Macaulay, thank you for "Dalit empowerment"', 2006, *Indian Express*, http://www.indianexpress.com/story/15423.html downloaded on 30 November 2007.

Gothoskar, Sujata, 'The Social Clause—Whose Interest is it Serving', in J. John and Anuradha Chenoy (Eds), *Labour, Environment and Globalization*, New Delhi: Centre for Education and Communication, 1996, pp. 59–65.

Grover, D C, *M N Roy: A Study of Revolution and Reason in Indian Politics*, Calcutta: The Minerva Associates, 1973.

*The Guardian*, 'Global food crisis looms as climate change and fuel shortages bite', 3 November 2007, http://www/guardian.co.uk/environment/2007/nov/03/food.climatechange.

Gudavarthy, Ajay, 'Dalit and Naxalite Movements in AP: Solidarity or Hegemony?', *Economic and Political Weekly*, vol. XL, no. 51, 2005.

Guha, Amalendu, 'Little Nationalism Turned Chauvinist: Assam's Anti-Foreigner Upsurge, 1979-80', in *Social Movements and the State*, ed. Ghanshyam Shah, London and New Delhi: Sage Publications, 2002.

Guha, Ramchandra, 'The Problem', *Seminar*, 355, March 1989, pp. 12-15.

—— 'Chipko: Social History of an 'Environmental' Movement', in Shah (ed.), 2002.

Halarnkar, Samar, Ritu Sarin, Sucheta Dalal and George Mathew, 'Rs 11,00,00,00,00,000: The Great Indian Bank Robbery', *The Indian Express*, 1 December 2002.

Habermas, Jurgen, *The Structural Transformation of the Public Sphere—An Inquiry into a Category of Bourgeois Society*, London: Polity Press, 1994.

—— *The Postnational Constellation—Political Essays*, London: Polity Press, 2001.

Hannington, Wal, *A Short History of the Unemployed*, London: Victor Gollancz Ltd, 1938.

Hardt, Michael and Antonio Negri, *Empire*, Cambridge, Massachusetts and London: Harvard University Press, 2001.

—— *Multitude—War and Democracy in the Age of Empire*, New York: Penguin Books, 2004.

Hasan, Zoya (ed.), *Parties and Party Politics in India*, Delhi: OUP, 2002.

Hawking, Stephen, *A Brief History of Time*, New York: Bantam, 1988.

Herndon, Sheri, 'No Logo: Conversation with Naomi Klein', 28 August 2000, http://www.indymedia.org/pdf.php3?article_id=3954.

Hilton, Rodney, *The Transition from Feudalism to Capitalism*, London: Verso, 1980.

Hylton, Forrest and Sinclair Thomson, 'The Chequered Rainbow', *New Left Review*, Sept–Oct 2005, pp. 41–64 for a discussion of Bolivia.

Higgins, 'The Zapatista Uprising and the Poetics of Cultural Resistance', *Alternatives*, vol. 25, no. 3, July–Sep. 2000, pp. 359–74.

—— *Understanding the Chiapas Rebellion: Modernist Visions and the Invisible Indian*, Austin: University of Texas Press, 2004.

*The Hindu*, 'Saving lives with mangroves', editorial, 28 December 2005.

———'Panic as global food crisis reaches America', International Section, 25 April 2008.

Hitler, Adolf, *My Struggle*, London: The Paternoster Library, 1936.

Hobson, John M, *The Eastern Origins of Western Capitalism*, Cambridge: CUP, 2004.

Holloway, John, *Change the World Without Taking Power: The Meaning of Revolution Today*, London: Pluto Press 2002.

Hroch, Miroslav, 'From National Movement to the Fully-Formed Nation: The Nation-Building Process in Europe', in *Becoming National—A Reader*, ed. Geoff Eley and Ronald Grigor, Oxford: OUP, 1996, pp. 60–77.

Hui, Wang, *China's New Order: Society, Politics and Economy in Transition*, ed. Theodore Huters, Cambridge (Massachusetts) and London: Harvard University Press, 2006.

Ilaiah, Kancha, 'Cultural Globalization', *The Hindu*, 22 February 2003. http://www.thehindu.com/2003/02/22/stories/2003022200621000.htm

*Indian Express*, 'Aaja Nachle almost trips—on a caste line', 2 December 2007.

Isaac, T M Thomas and Richard W Franke *Local Democracy and Development: The Kerala People's Campaign for Decentralized Planning*, Lanham, NY and Oxford: Rowman and Littlefield Publishers, Inc. 2002.

Farrer, Linden, 'World Forum Movement: Abandon or Contaminate', 2003, http://www.nadir.org/nadir/initiativ/agp/free/wsf/worldforum.htm, (last accessed on 4 September 2007.)

Jameson, Fredric, *Postmodernism Or, the Cultural Logic of Late Capitalism*, Durham: Duke University Press, 1992.

Joshi, Barbara, *Untouchable! Voice of the Dalit Liberation Movement*, New Delhi: Selectbook Service Syndicate, and London: Zed Books Ltd, 1986.

Kagarlitsky, Boris, *The Return of Radicalism: Reshaping the Left Institutions*, Pluto Press, London: 2000.

Kamat, Sangeeta, *Development Hegemony—NGOs and the State in India*, New Delhi: OUP, 2002.

Kannabiran, Vasanth and Veena Shatrugna, 'The Relocation of Political Practice—The Stree Shakti Sangathana Experience', *Lokayan Bulletin*, vol. 4, no. 6, 1986, pp. 23–34.

Kannabiran, Vasanth; Volga; Kalpana Kannabiran, 'Women's Rights and Naxalite Groups', *Economic and Political Weekly*, vol. 39, no. 45, 2004.

Karat, Prakash, 'Naxalism Today: At an Ideological Deadend', *The Marxist*, vol. 3, no. 1, January–March 1985.

——— 'Left Front Government: Bastion of Left Democratic Forces', *The Marxist*, vol. XVIII, no.2, April–June 2002.

———, 'Double-Speak Charge: Maligning The CPI(M),' *People's Democracy*, 28 January 2007.

Katzenstein, Mary; Smitu Kothari and Uday Mehta, 'Social Movement Politics in India: Institutions, Interests and Identities', in *The Success of India's Democracy*, ed. Atul Kohli, Cambridge: CUP, 2001.

Kaviraj, Sudipta, 'The Heteronomous Radicalism of M N Roy', in *Political Thought in Modern India*, ed. Thomas Pantham and Kenneth L. Deutsch, New Delhi and London: Sage Publications, 1986.

Kishwar, Madhu and Ruth Vanita, (ed.), *In Search of Answers: Indian Women's Voices from Manushi*, London: Zed Books Ltd., 1984.

Klein, Naomi, *No Logo*, London: Flamingo, 2001.

Koselleck, Reinhart, *Futures Past: On the Semantics of Historical Time*, Cambridge, Massachusetts, and London: The MIT Press, 1985.

Kothari, Rajni 'The Non-Party Political Process', *Economic and Political Weekly*, 19 (5), 4 February 1984, pp. 216–24.

——— 'On the Non-Party Political Process: The NGOs, The State and World Capitalism', *Lokayan Bulletin*, vol. 4, no. 5, 1986 pp. 6–26.

——— *State Against Democracy: In Search of Humane Governance*', Delhi: Ajanta Publications, 1988.

Kumar, Pradeep, *The Uttarakhand Movement—Construction of a Regional Identity*, New Delhi: Kanishka Publishers, Distributors, 2000.

Kumar, Radha, *The History of Doing*, Kali For Women, New Delhi: 1993.

Lachmann, Richard, *Capitalists In Spite of Themselves: Elite Conflicts and Economic Transformations in Early Modern Europe*, Oxford and New York: OUP, 2002.

Laclau, Ernesto, *Emancipation(s)*, London & New York: Verso, 1996.

———, 'Can Immanence Explain Social Struggles?' *Diacritics*, Winter 2001, vol. 31, no. 4, pp. 3-8.

——— *On Populist Reason*, London and New York: Verso, 2005.

Laclau, Ernesto and Chantal Mouffe, *Hegemony and Socialist Strategy: Towards a Radical Democratic Politics*, London and New York: Verso, 1985.

Lakha, Salim (2002), 'Organized Labour and Militant Unionism: The Bombay Textile Workers' Strike of 1982', in *Social Movements and the State*, ed. Ghanshyam Shah, London and New Delhi: Sage Publications.

Lenin, V I, *What Is To Be Done?*, Peking: Foreign Languages Press, 1973.

——— *The Development of capitalism in Russia*, Moscow: Progress Publishers, 1899/1977.

———'The Collapse of the Second International', *Collected Works*, vol. 21, Moscow: Progress Publishers, 1977, p. 213.

*Lokayan Bulletin*, 'On Communalism, Caste and Class. Hyderabad Ekta: Dilemmas of an Anti-Communal Effort', vol. 4, no. 5, 1986, pp. 37–59.

*Lokayan Bulletin*, People's Manifesto, vol. 9, no. 2, 1991, pp. 56–628.

Limbale, Sharankumar, *Towards an Aesthetic of Dalit Literature: History, Controversies and Considerations*, Tr. Alok Mukherjee, Hyderabad: Orient Longman, 2004.

Lowy, Michael, *The Politics of Combined and Uneven Development—The Theory of Permanent Revolution*, London: Verso, 1981.

Lukacs, G, *History and Class Consciousness*, London: Merlin Press, 1971.

Mac Donald, Heather, 'Elites to Anti-Affirmative Action Voters: Drop Dead', *City Journal*, Winter 2007, http://www.city-journal.org/html/17_1_prop209.html, accessed 27 April 2008.

Mamdani, Mahmood, *Citizen and Subject: Decentralized Despotism and the Legacy of Late Colonialism*, Delhi: OUP, 1997.

Martinez, Elizabeth (Betita), 'Where was the Color in Seattle? Looking for reasons why the Great Battle was so white', 2000, in http://www.corpwatch.org/issues/wto/featured/2000/6-martinez.html

Mattick, Paul, *Anti-Bolshevik Communism*, London: Merlin Press, 1978.

Menon, Dilip, *Caste, Nationalism and Communalism in South India: Malabar 1900–1948*, Cambridge, CUP, 1994.

Menon Nivedita, 'Surviving Gujarat 2002', *Economic and Political Weekly*, vol. xxvii, no. 27, pp. 2002, 2676–78.

——— *Recovering Subversion—Feminist Politics Beyond the Law*, Delhi: Permanent Black and Urbana and Chicago: University of Illinois Press, 2004.

Menon, Nivedita and Aditya Nigam, *Power and Contestation: India Since 1989*, London: Zed Books Ltd, 2007.

Meisner, Maurice, *Marxism, Maoism and Utopianism: Eight Essays*, Wisconsin and London: University of Wisconsin Press, 1982.

Mishra, Anupam, *Rajasthan ki Rajat Boondein*, New Delhi: Gandhi Shanti Pratishthan, 1995.

Mohanty, Manoranjan, 'The Course of Naxalism', *Himal* magazine, 22 September 2005, also at http://www.countercurrents.org/india-mohanty220905.htm, downloaded on 2 December 2007.

Mueller, Susanne D, 'Retarded Capitalism in Tanzania', *Socialist Register* 1980, http://socialistregister.com/socialistregister.com/files/SR_1980_Mueller.pdf , accessed on 19 February 2007.

Mukul, ' . . . And They Get Organized', *Lokayan Bulletin*, vol. 11, no. 6, May–June 1995, pp. 52-4.

Mumbai Resistance, *Mumbai Resistance—MR 2004, 2003.*

Nagaraj, D R, *The Flaming Feet—A Study of the Dalit Movement*, Bangalore: South Forum Press and Institute for Cultural Research and Action, 1993.

Naimishray, Mohandas, *Awazein*, Collection of short stories, Delhi: Samata Prakashan, 1998, pp. 105-10.

Nayar, Kuldip and Khushwant Singh, *The Tragedy of Punjab—Operation Bluestar and After*, Delhi: Vision Books, 1984.

Nehru, Jawaharlal, *The Discovery of India*, New Delhi: Jawaharlal Nehru Memorial Fund and OUP, 1946/82.

Nigam, Aditya, 'Marxism and the Postcolonial World—Footnotes to a Long March', *Economic and Political Weekly*, vol. 34, nos. 1 and 2, 9 January 1999.

——, 'In Search of a Bourgeoisie', *Economic and Political Weekly*, vol. 37, no. 13, 30 March 30, 2002.

——, *The Insurrection of Little Selves: The Crisis of Secular-Nationalism in India*, Delhi: OUP, 2006.

O'Connor, James, *Accumulation Crisis*, Oxford and New York: Basil Blackwell, 1984.

Omvedt, Gail, *Reinventing Revolution: New Social Movements and the Socialist Tradition in India*, New York and London: ME Sharpe, 1993.

Panitch, Leo and Colin, Leys, (eds.), 'Necessary and Unnecessary Utopias', *Socialist Register 2000*, London: Merlin Press and Calcutta: KP Bagchi, 2000.

Panitch, Leo and Sam Gindin, 'Transcending Pessimism: Rekindling Socialist Imagination', *Socialist Register* 2000, pp. 3-4.

Patkar, Medha, Interview to Venu Govindu, 1999, http://www.indiatogether.org/interviews/iview-mpatkar.htm, downloaded on 3 March 2005.

———, Interview to Robert Jensen, 2005, http://www.progressivetrail.org/articles/040226Jensen.shtml, downloaded on 3 March 2005.

Pendse, Sandip, 'The Datta Samant Phenomenon—I', *Economic and Political Weekly*, vol. 26, no. 16, 18 April 1981 pp. 695-7.

——— 'The Datta Samant Phenomenon—II', *Economic and Political Weekly*, vol 26, no. 17, 25 April, 1981, pp. 745–9.

People's Union For Democratic Rights (PUDR), *Shankar Guha Niyogi and the Chattisgarh Peoples Movement*, Delhi: 1991.

———, *A Tale of Two Cities—Custodial Death and Police Firing in Ashok Vihar*, Delhi, PUDR, 1996.

Perlez, Jane, 'Forests in Southeast Asia Fall to Prosperity's Ax', *New York Times International*, 29 April 2006.

Poulantzas, Nicos, *State, Power, Socialism*, London: NLB, 1978, p. 113.

Pradhan, Sharat, 'Mayawati spends crores to fulfill her birthday dream', 15 January 2003 http://www.rediffmail.com/news/2003/jan/15up.htm

Raina, Vinod, 'Social Movements in India', 2004, http://www.alternatives.ca/print1040.html, downloaded on 9 February 2005.

Raj, Sebasti L, SJ and Arundhuti Roy Choudhury, (ed.), *Contemporary Social Movements in India: Achievements and Hurdles*, New Delhi: Indian Social Institute, 1998.

Ramkumar, Vivek, 'Beyond Democratic Rights and Electoral Reform Campaign: Challenges Facing Non Party Political Movements', 2004, http://www.freedominfo.org/case/mkss/beyond.doc, downloaded on 9 February 2005.

Ray, Raka, *Fields of Protest—Women's Movements in India*, Delhi: Kali for Women, 2000.

Renan, Ernest, 'What is a Nation?', in *Becoming National—A Reader*, ed. Geoff Eley and Ronald Grigor Suny New York and Oxford: pp. 42-55.

Rich, Bruce, 'Narmada and the Global Battle for the Biosphere', *Lokayan Bulletin*, May–August 1991, vol. 9, nos. 3–4, pp.104–12.

Rodinson, Maxime, *Marxism and the Muslim World*, New Delhi: Orient Longman Ltd, 1980.

Roy, Aruna and Nikhil Dey, 'The Redistribution of Power', *Seminar*, 31 August 2004, no. 541.

Roy, Aruna; Nikhil Dey, and Shanker Singh, 'Demanding Accountability', *Seminar*, 26 June 2001, no. 500.

Roy, M N *Politics, Power and Parties*, Delhi: Ajanta Publications, 1981.

——— *Memoirs*, Delhi: Ajanta Publications, 1984.

———, *Reason, Romanticism and Revolution*, Delhi: Ajanta Publications, 1989.

RUPE, *The Economics and Politics of the World Social Forum: Lessons for the Struggle Against 'Globalization'*, 2003, http://www.rupe-india.org.

Sader, Emir, 'Beyond Civil Society—The Left After Porto Alegre', *New Left Review*, 17, Sept.–Oct. 2002.

Sail, Rajendra, 'The Man was a Machine With a Human Heart', *On a Rainbow in the Sky: The Chattisgarh Mukti Morcha*, New Delhi: Centre for Education and Communication (CEC), 1998.

Sajha Manch, *Seminar on Integrated Policy for Urban Renewal: Land Shelter and Services for Delhi's People*, Delhi: Sajha Manch, 2001.

Sampradayikta Virodhi Andolan (*SVA*), 'On the Struggle Against Communalism', *Lokayan Bulletin*, vol. 7, no. 6, Nov.–Dec. 1989, pp. 57–60.

Sangvai, Sanjay, 'Emerging Politics of Just and Sustainable Development', 2003, http://www.aidindia.org/desh/ep.html, downloaded on 15 June 2004.

Sanyal, Kalyan, *Rethinking Capitalist Development: Primitive Accumulation, Governmentality and Postcolonial Capitalism*, London, New York, New Delhi: Routledge, 2007.

Sarkar, Sumit, 'A question marked in red', *Indian Express*, 9 January 2007, p. 11.

Sassen, Saskia, *Globalization and Its Discontents*, New York: The New Press, 1998.

Schmitt, Carl, *The Crisis of Parliamentary Democracy*, Cambridge, Massachusetts and London: The MIT Press, 1992.

Scott, James C., *Seeing Like a State: How Certain Schemes to Improve the Human Condition Have Failed*, New Haven and London: Yale University Press, 1998.

Sen, Amartya, 'The Industrial Strategy—Developments in West Bengal', *The Telegraph*, 29 December 2007.

Sethi, Harsh, 'The Citizen's Response: A Glimmer of Possibilities?', *Lokayan Bulletin*, vol. 3, no. 1, 1985, pp. 59–73.

——— (1993a), 'Survival and Democracy: Ecological Struggles in India', in *New Social Movements in the South: Empowering the People*, ed. Ponna Wignaraja, New Delhi: Vistaar Publications, 1993, pp. 121-48.

——— (1993b), 'Action Groups in the New Politics', in Wignaraja (ed.), ibid., pp. 230–255.

Shah, Ghanshyam (1988), 'Grass-Roots Mobilization in Indian Politics', in *India's Democracy: An Analysis of Changing State-Society Relations*, ed. Atul Kohli, Princeton: Princeton University Press, 1988, pp. 262-304.

——— (ed.), *Social Movements and the State*, London and New Delhi: Sage Publications, 2002.

———, *Social Movements in India—A Review of Literature*, London and New Delhi: Sage Publications, 2004.

Shanin, Teodor (ed.), *Late Marx and the Russian Road: Marx and the 'Peripheries of Capitalism'*, London, Melbourne and Henley: Routledge and Kegan Paul, 1983.

Sharan, Awadhendra, 'Governing Technology: The City in the Age of Environmental Crisis', *Sarai Reader 03—Shaping Technologies*,

Delhi/Amsterdam: Sarai-CSDS and The Waag Society for Old and New Media, 2003, pp. 16–21.

Sherover, Charles, *The Human Experience of Time: The Development of Its Philosophical Meaning*, New York: New York University Press, 1975.

Sheth, D L and Harsh Sethi, 'The NGO Sector in India: Historical Context and Current Discourse', *Voluntas*, no. 2, 1991.

Sheth, D L, 'Movements', *Seminar*, 278, October 1982.

——, 'Grassroots Stirrings and the Future of Politics', *Alternatives*, IX, 1983, pp. 1-24.

——, 'Globalization and New Politics of Micro-Movements', *Economic and Political Weekly*, 3 January 2004, vol. 39, no.1, pp. 45–58.

Sheth, P N, *Nav Nirman and Political Change in India—From Gujarat 1974 to New Delhi 1977*. Bombay: Vora & Co Publishers Pvt Ltd, 1977.

Shiviah, M, *New Humanism and Democratic Politics—A Study of M N Roy's Theory of the State*, Bombay: Popular Prakashan, 1977.

Siddqui, Imran Ahmed, 'Stockpile squad trail heads towards party—Phone records spill Nandigram secret', *The Telegraph*, 19 March 2007.

Singh, N K, 'Trade Unionism With a Difference', *Economic and Political Weekly*, 16 July 1977, Reprinted in CEC, 1998, New Delhi.

Sivaramakrishnan, G., 'S&T: Road to Utopia?', *Seminar*, 355, March 1989, pp. 29–33.

Soja, Edward W., *Thirdspace—Journeys to Los Angeles and Other Real-and-Imagined Places*, Oxford and Boston. Blackwell Publishing, 2004.

Srivastava, S S and Rajesh Tandon, (2005), 'How Large is India's Non-Profit Sector?', *Economic and Political Weekly*, 7 May 2005, vol. 40, no. 19, pp. 1948–52.

Swaminadhan, Srilata, 'Towards International Solidarity', *People's Democracy*, New Delhi, 4 December 1994, pp. 57-8.

Sweezy, Paul (1980a), 'A Critique', in Rodney Hilton (1980).

Teltumbde, Anand, *'Ambedkar' in and for The Post-Ambedkar Dalit Movement*, Pune: Usha Wagh/Sugawa Prakashan, 1997, http://www.angelfire.com/ak/ambedkar/BRanand1.htm#post-ambedkar

Tse-tung, Mao, *Selected Works*, vol. 1, Peking: Foreign Languages Press, 1977, p. 64.

Vajpeyi, Yogesh, 'For the oppressed, covered in diamonds—govt plays host at Mayawati birthday bash', *The Telegraph*, 16 January 2003 front page.

Valmiki, Om Prakash, *Joothan*, Delhi: Radhakrishna Paperbacks, 1999.

——, *Joothan: A Dalit's Life*, translated by Arun Prabha Mukherjee Kolkata: Samya, 2003.

Wada, Haruki, 'Marx and Revolutionary Russia', in *Late Marx and the Russian Road: Marx and the 'Peripheries of Capitalisin'*, ed. Teodor Shanin, London, Melbourne and Henley: Routledge and Kegan Paul, 1983.

Wainwright, Hilary, *Notes Towards a New Poltics: New Strategies for People Power*, Transnational Institute, TNI Briefng Series, no. 2002/3. See http://www.tni.org/newpol, 2002.

Waldman, Amy, 'An Opulent and Pugnacious Champion of India's Outcasts', *The New York Times on the web*, 4 May 2003.

Weber, Eugen, *Peasants Into Frenchmen*, California: Stanford University Press, 1999.

Weilaard, Robert, 'Belgium Downplays Break-up Concerns', http://ap.google.com/article/ALeqM5giuTgSuY0w-QpxD2CWsu3uP8gk8gD8S4HP380, downloaded on 9 October 2007.

Wignaraja, Ponna (ed.), *New Social Movements in the South: Empowering the People*, New Delhi: Vistaar Publications, 1993.

Welzer, Steve, 'A Global Food Crisis is Emerging', a report posted on Green Horizon, http://www.green-horizon.org/blog/archives/sustainability/global_food_cri.shtoul

*Workers' Rights News*, 'Asian Unions Join Call for Social Clause' issue no. 9, Spring 1994, p. 6.

Yagnik, Achyut and Harshad, Desai, 'The Wages of Populism: The Second Anti-Reservation Agitation', *Lokayan Bulletin*, vol. 3, no. 2, 1985, pp. 3–18.

Yechury, Sitaram, 'CPI(M) and the WSF', 2003, http://www.redglobe.org/modules.php?name=News&file=article&sid=1080, downloaded 17 June 2004.

Zizek, Slavoj, *Tarrying With the Negative: Kant, Hegel and the Critique of Ideology*, North Carolina: Duke University Press, 1993.

——— (ed.), *Mapping Ideology*, London and New York: Verso, 1994.

———, 'NATO, The Left Hand of God', 1999, http://www.lacan.com/zizek-nato.htm, downloaded on 22 January 2008.

———, 'Repeating Lenin', 2001, http://www.lacan.com/replenin.htm

———, 'Can Lenin Tell Us About Freedom Today?', 2002, E-text, http://www.lacan.com/freedom.htm

# INDEX